MY HAPPY DAYS

IN HOLLYWOOD

From HAPPY DAYS *and*

THE ODD COUPLE

to

PRETTY WOMAN *and*

THE PRINCESS DIARIES

—

Tales from a Hollywood Legend

MY
HAPPY DAYS
IN HOLLYWOOD

A Memoir

GARRY
MARSHALL

with Lori Marshall

**CROWN
ARCHETYPE**
NEW YORK

Published in the United States by Crown Archetype,
an imprint of the Crown Publishing Group,
a division of Random House, Inc., New York.
www.crownpublishing.com

Crown Archetype with colophon is a trademark of Random House, Inc.

Library of Congress Cataloging-in-Publication Data
Marshall, Garry.
   My happy days in Hollywood / Garry Marshall.—1st ed.
      p. cm.
   1. Marshall, Garry. 2. Television producers and directors—
   United States—Biography. 3. Motion picture producers and
   directors—United States—Biography. I. Title.
      PN1992.4.M37A3   2012
      791.4502'33092—dc23
      [B]   2011042598

ISBN 978-0-307-88500-5
eISBN 978-0-307-88502-9

Printed in the United States of America

Book design by Barbara Sturman
Jacket design by Laura Duffy
Jacket photograph by Reza Estakhrian/Getty Images

10 9 8 7 6 5 4 3 2 1

First Edition

*For Barbara Sue Wells
and my children and grandchildren*

CONTENTS

FOREWORD

★

by Hector Elizondo

THE FIRST TIME I met Garry Marshall I almost knocked his teeth out. The year was 1979. I had flown in from New York City to L.A. to co-star in a series for CBS, *Freebie and the Bean* with Tom Mason.

I had been working onstage since 1960; in repertory theater, off-Broadway, as well as Broadway. I had already established myself in movies and television, including starring in my own series, *Popi,* for CBS in 1975 (which was, coincidentally, knocked off the air by the wild success of *Happy Days*). But I wasn't familiar with TV producers' names yet. So, when I was invited by my pal and agent Mark Harris to play in the longest running basketball game in Hollywood—it had been ongoing every Saturday morning since The Flood—I said, of course! The game would take place on the home court of writer/producer and soon-to-be-director-extraordinaire, Garry Marshall. "Who's that?" I say. "You know," Mark said, "the guy who created *Happy Days*." "No kidding," I replied.

Somehow, the day of the game Mark failed to introduce me to Garry. I had no idea that the tall guy with the wrapped knees who was guarding me like Velcro was, in fact, our host, Garry Marshall. Now Garry has very fast hands (he's a drummer, after all) but not a very fast face: my quick, behind-the-back pass to my teammate was intercepted by Garry's mouth. My host thereby dropped to one knee, whereupon he spat into his hand to check how many teeth he had lost. They were all there. That was good. He motioned me to come over. That was bad. He looked at me with a straight face and said, "You're a terrific actor but a lousy passer. I have a project to talk to you about." It was the beginning of a beautiful friendship.

Garry and I have a lot in common: both from New York City (he from the Bronx and me from Manhattan); both kids during WW II; and both products of the great New York City public school system.

Then there were the street games, baseball, basketball, and music, music, music. Whatever differences we have are complementary.

My first movie for Garry was *Garry's* first movie. It didn't take me long to realize that he's a master of comedy and a natural mentor to budding talent. I've watched him time and again inspire young people who showed an aptitude and zeal for the work, whether it was writing, acting, or producing—and always with humor and kindness.

A brief but important moment for me as an actor was when I needed an angle on the character of Barnard Thompson, the hotel manager in *Pretty Woman*. I went to Garry. He paused for a moment and said, "Just create the guy you'd like to work for." Simple as that. No long discussion. No deep analysis. A slight suggestion and I made it my own. We've done seventeen movies together that way.

We were in sync from the start. It's very much like jazz, the music we grew up with. Or like a baseball double play; scoop, second, first, and out. Rhythm.

I have a tendency to get stuck in bemoaning the human condition. Garry pauses—and then moves on. He celebrates life. Like Fellini, he loves parades, clowns, and birthdays. Someone said that Garry doesn't shoot a movie—he throws one, like a party. It's true, and he's not beyond the occasional pie-in-the-face like he did to Matt Dillon during *The Flamingo Kid*. That loosened Matt up while giving him dessert. Since then, Matt has become a fine actor and human being.

Actresses love to work with Garry because they can trust him. What a parade of talent has flocked to him: Julia Roberts, Bette Midler, Anne Hathaway, Kate Hudson, and Julie Andrews. And then there's his big, magical raptor, the Falcon Theatre in Toluca Lake, California, named after his boyhood social group in the Bronx. It's one of Garry's dreams come true—as is his family.

My life with Garry has been a slow and steady revelation of steadfastness and passion in one's work coupled with a deep sense of responsibility to one's community. Garry—not bad for a kid from the Bronx.

Oh, and by the way, did I mention we both love ice cream and happy endings?

MY HAPPY DAYS

IN HOLLYWOOD

From the start it has been the

theatre's business to entertain people . . .

it needs no other passport than fun.

—BERTOLT BRECHT

I. THE BRONX

★

Growing Up Allergic to Everything but Stickball

MARJORIE WARD MARSHALL, my mother, was the first director I ever met.

Wearing an apron and teaching tap dancing in the basement of our Grand Concourse apartment building, she was a Bronx housewife and a tap dance teacher you didn't want to mess with. She ran a tight ship, and little girls never dawdled in putting on their tap shoes and costumes in front of Mom. She believed that dancing and performing were good for children because they gave them self-esteem and a purpose all their own.

My mother taught us that the best thing in life was to entertain people and make them laugh. The biggest sin in life was to bore people.

"Beware of the boring," she said.

"What is boring, Ma?" I asked.

"Your father," she said.

Mom was a born entertainer who thought performing was not just a hobby or even a profession but a way of living that was as essential as breathing or eating. She was a five-foot-six-inch slacks-wearing perky blonde with a dancer's body and a comedian's mouth. Mom was always "on" from her hyper-cajoling of her dance students to her late-night intensity when she would type out the songs, dance routines, and skits for her dance recital. I would be in my bed and still hear her typewriter as I went to sleep. Her typing sounded like rain. Always working, she would go to Broadway shows, steal the routines, and come back and type them up for her students to perform. I knew right from the beginning that if I could make my mom laugh, then I could make her love me.

If Mom had been born at another time in history, she could have become a stage performer or actress herself. Born in 1910, Mom just missed the feminism movement and was faced with raising three children in the Bronx during the 1940s. Her goal in life was to teach as many kids as possible—including her own children, Garry, Ronny, and Penny—to tap dance. There was Ronny, the middle child and nice daughter, and Penny, the youngest child, whom my mother seemed to crown "troublemaker" the moment she came out of the birth canal. And I, of course, was the oldest child and the one who was always sick.

Mom's students adored her because she was funny and irreverent whether she was charming your pants off or hurting your feelings. She commanded a kind of power and respect as a director that even Orson Welles and Martin Scorsese would find enviable. She could be encouraging to the students with talent, but spoke with a bite to those who didn't show potential.

"You—the pretty girl with the fat legs. You should play an instrument instead of dancing."

Or she might move someone behind the scenes altogether.

"Hey, Zelda, or whatever your name is. You have two left feet. You can pull the curtain for the show."

Traditional motherhood duties took a backseat to the curtain, the audience, and showtime. Since we were always running low on milk, Mom invented the family drink "Pepsi and milk" to make our dairy supply last longer. When she didn't have time to simmer and cook fresh tomato sauce, she told us that Campbell's tomato soup with noodles was just as Italian as spaghetti. If we were rushing to get down to the basement to make our curtain calls, she might squirt ketchup on our pasta and call it a night. My mom could make us smile, laugh, and cry all in the same hour. On my birthday one time she said, "Garry is celebrating eleven years of being round-shouldered." When my sister Penny had an overbite, she said, "When I want to open a Pepsi bottle, I do it with Penny's teeth." She taught us that to dwell on our problems was a waste of time and to make entertainment for others was supreme.

This did little to impress my dad. My father, Anthony W. Marshall, was a good-looking suit- and tie-wearing art director and advertising executive who invented his middle name, Wallace, because he thought it made him sound more distinguished. Born Anthony Masciarelli, he looked like a character from the television show *Mad Men*. He liked to wear suits, carry a monogrammed briefcase, and drink martinis in hotel bars. We rarely saw him drink at home, but sometimes he would stagger in and look like he'd had a few too many someplace else. My father was not the kind of dad who would throw a ball in the street with you like the Jewish dads, Catholic dads, or even other Italian dads in our melting pot neighborhood. Throwing a ball might mess up my father's tie. He didn't talk very much but instead wrote us notes like "Sorry you had to get a tooth pulled. It's over now." When he did talk he told stories of business trips where he met men who were working on a new device called television. He traveled for business to Florida and California and brought home oranges for us. For a long time my sisters and I imagined that both states were filled with fruit instead of people. He instilled in us the idea that there was a world outside the Bronx and that we should set sail for it as soon as we were old enough.

★

I was born November 13, 1934, Garry Kent Marshall, and we lived for most of my childhood along the Grand Concourse. First opened to traffic in 1909, the Grand Concourse was modeled after the Champs-Elysées in Paris. It was four miles long and populated by Jewish and Italian families when I lived there. My apartment was in a five-story building, with empty lots on either side. We were on the first floor. It was called Argonne Manor and housed mostly Jewish families and my family. We were Italian and Christian. Most of the other Italian families lived on Villa Avenue across the street. Because I was Italian, I fit in both neighborhoods easily.

My address was 3235 Grand Concourse. My favorite number has

always been thirteen, and the numerals of my Bronx address added up to it, too. Like my father, I was given an arbitrary middle name, Kent, to give me dignity. My first name, with the rare two-*r* spelling, came from a sportswriter named Garry Schumacher. My parents didn't know him personally, but my mother liked the spelling.

My happiest moments of growing up in the Bronx were when my mom would bring home a new sports magazine from the candy store. I would jump out of bed and grab it from her. Then I'd rip the front cover right off and tape it to my bedroom wall. I would reposition myself comfortably in bed and look up at all of the athletes who floated above me like heroes and angels.

Often I would turn on the radio, lie in my bed, and listen to the Yankees baseball game. I'd dream about my hands-down favorite player, Joe DiMaggio, and the day when I might be able to have a job that I could do well, too. There were many baseball players who were just as famous but who didn't impress us, like Billy Martin and Ted Williams. To be able to make a living playing a sport you loved was what made Joe our favorite. I didn't know what job I might be destined for, but my dad told me it better be something I could do with a headache or a toothache, because the whole family agreed I was not destined for good health. As a child I was often sick, plagued by some ailment or allergy, or my ability to hang on to a perpetual sniffle or wheeze from one winter to the next. My baby book read like a list of the greatest diseases of all time. I once heard a doctor say that if we didn't move to Arizona, I might die. I packed my bags. The next day I woke up to see if anyone was packing their bags. No one was.

"Dad, when do we leave for Arizona?"

"Don't be silly," he said. "We're not going anywhere. We can't afford it."

I thought they were trying to kill me.

Despite being sick all the time, I seemed to be destined for a career in show business. My mother sent my three-year-old baby picture to a contest in the Bronx *Home News*. I won the prize for cutest kid in my age division, and received a check for fifteen dollars. This encouraged my mom to think I could go on to become a child model. I auditioned and got cast in a milk commercial. Unfortunately, I spit up all over the director, and my modeling career was short-lived.

When I was five years old my parents gave me a drum set for Christmas. My mom played the piano, and Dad played the saxophone badly. But that Christmas morning I remember we all played together and I thought it was the greatest day ever. We were a band, and I imagined us practicing and performing as a family band for years to come. Unfortunately, Dad never played the saxophone with our band again. That Christmas morning remains imprinted in my mind as one of the few times we all got along. In general my dad thought entertainment was a waste of time and did little to support my mother's dance studio or our performing aspirations.

Dad's ambivalence, however, did not stop my mother or us. One day Dad was at work and Mom had a show to put on but she didn't have a babysitter. Her mother, Margie, whom we called Nanny, used to watch my sisters and me when we were small. She was an Irish-German rail-thin brunette with a mild New England accent. As we got older, Nanny became blind and refused to go to the doctor. Without her sight it became difficult for her to mind us and us to mind her. Sometimes Penny would sneeze and then trick Nanny by saying, "It was Garry." The girls blamed me for many things because I was often too sick to put up a fight. With all of my sneezing and wheezing and pneumonia not once but twice, Nanny didn't know how to help me. I once fell down in the street and hit my head, and she said, "I'll give you a dollar if you stop bleeding." Her reluctance to go to the doctor helped make me a hypochondriac. Nanny didn't even know what to feed me because I seemed to be allergic to everything under the sun, including the sun.

I was lying in bed one day, covered in compresses and trying to feel better, when my mom came into the room.

"Get up. Let's go to the cellar. You're going to be in the show," she said.

"But Mom, I'm sick. I should stay in bed and get better," I said. I was six years old at the time, and I carried the perpetual smell of mustard plaster.

"Nonsense. Nanny can't watch you anymore and I have a show to put on. So let's go," she said, pulling the covers off my bed.

"But Mom, I'm too tired to stand up and dance," I begged.

"I know," she said, getting fresh clothes from my dresser.

"Then what am I going to do down there in the cellar?" I asked.

"Sit down."

"In the dressing room?" I asked.

"No. Onstage. You'll play the drums," she said.

"But Ma, I just started the drums. You know I'm not very good yet."

"Don't worry. You'll follow my lead on the piano," she said. "You're smart and quick. You'll learn."

✘ So we would sit onstage and she would play the piano with one hand and pat me on the back with the other. That's how I learned to keep a steady rhythm.

I became the official drummer for the Marjorie Ward Marshall School of Dance. I would perform in the basement and then travel with the troupe when they did shows in other towns and churches around New York. My mother didn't join a church based on religion. She joined whatever church had the biggest stage to dance on. Our religion was entertainment. Going to church to pray or even to read the Bible seemed secondary to delivering a great joke and making people in the congregation laugh out loud.

Ronny and Penny were reluctant performers, too, but none of us had a choice. Acting was the family pastime. However, I soon found that I liked playing the drums. Mom was right. They were a good instrument for me because they came with their own seat. From the security of my drum set, I would watch show after show of dancing, skits, and humor, and I noticed something quite amazing: Some of the skits my mother wrote got laughs and some did not. When they got a laugh I felt happy and proud for her, but when they didn't get applause I tried to figure out why. By the time I was seven years old, I was getting the hang of things. I figured out that the point was to induce them *all* to laugh, not just a few. If a skit didn't work, I would try to rewrite it for her to make it better. With tissues stuffed up my sleeves and a drumstick in each hand, I was becoming a self-taught producer right there onstage. I didn't know it then, but I was also figuring out just how I might be able to make a living while sick, seated, and nauseous.

When I wasn't playing the drums I tried to get my energy up to play baseball, basketball, or stickball. Otherwise, I spent a lot of time in my bed feeling too sick and too skinny to do much of anything. I lived in 1-H, and I made friends with a boy named Gideon Troken, a dark-haired short kid with glasses, more interested in girls than playing ball, who lived in 1-O. He was the first intellectual I ever met. He read a lot of books, went to Hebrew school, and knew how to play the piano. He even taught me to play chess. He suggested I start collecting stamps because it was something I could do from my bed that would be worldly and important. He told me that for some small countries, stamps were the biggest export and advised me that I might make some money to fall back on from stamp collecting if my life didn't turn out. In exchange, I took him around the neighborhood and introduced him to some of the guys, who befriended him instead of beating him up because he was a friend of mine. I never got beaten up because I was a wisecracking jokester. I could make a bully laugh before he delivered a punch.

I lived in a building with mostly Jewish families, but across the street was the Italian building. Since I was of Italian descent, I was able to straddle both buildings. My Jewish friends were often reluctant to go down to Villa Avenue because they were afraid of the Italian gangs. So they would all give me their money to go down to Villa Avenue by myself and buy everyone Italian ice. I would come back with dessert and no bruises. I was fine with it. I liked meeting people from all the neighborhoods. I admired their unity and camaraderie.

I was in a gang called the Falcons, but everybody beat us up so we decided to become an athletic club instead and play ball against other neighborhoods. I started the team with a kid named Melvin "never stop yapping" Yapkow. We, along with our friends Harvey Keenan, an ambitious Jewish kid with an Irish face who looked like Robert Wagner, Bernard Gwertzman, a smart writer who later worked for the *New York Times,* and streetwise Irwin "Yell" Yellowitz, a future history professor at CCNY, were the initial players. Soon after, Marty Garbus, a pensive and thoughtful fellow who worked in his dad's candy shop, joined us. Marty dreamed of being a lawyer so he could wear a suit and tie. (He went on to become a top Civil Rights lawyer.) Later we recruited John Wellington, our best athlete, who became a college administrator after playing football for Columbia, and Bobby Schwabe, the smooth, graceful basketball player who passed on last year. Gideon couldn't play ball well, so he did our bookkeeping. Once I formed the Falcons, I felt like a man rich with friends. I came up with the idea to raffle off a radio to raise money to buy us new uniforms. We had my blind grandmother choose the winning ticket. We figured we could save money on the blindfold. However, we ended up getting into trouble because we took money from people for the tickets but didn't really have a radio to auction off. I felt forever guilty that we didn't have the prize. Sometimes I still think someone is going to knock on my front door and say, "We found you. The boy who raffled off a fictitious radio."

I loved playing sports with my friends. However, I was envious of the fact that most of them could play any day of the week while I was so often stuck in bed. I could open my bedroom window and listen to my friends hitting balls in the street. Sometimes I would even take my baseball glove and throw my ball against my bedroom wall pretending I was in the street. I could even work up a sweat. When my mom came in to check on me, I would hide my glove and ball underneath the bed. She would take my temperature and after finding it high exclaim, "He's relapsed! Another fever."

To pass the time, in addition to my stamp collection, I started keeping a joke book beside my bed. I would clip cartoons and comics from magazines and newspapers and then rate them. *G* was for good, *F* was for very funny, and *E* was for excellent. A joke was not deemed excellent if it made me laugh only once. To receive an *E,* a joke had to make me laugh a second or third time days after I originally saw it. I didn't know about television reruns or residuals then, but something inside of me understood that a joke that stood the test of time was a much better joke than one that made people giggle once and was then forgotten.

When I was feeling healthy, I would walk with my friends

on Saturday afternoons to see movies at the Tuxedo Theater on Jerome Avenue under the elevator train. The running serials *The Lone Ranger, Captain Marvel,* and *Flash Gordon* were our favorites. We had an aversion to love stories and instead liked movies about the Dalton Gang and Gene Autry. Inside the Tuxedo Theater lobby there was a recruiting display run by the Boy Scouts of America. If you joined a troop and ran the display, you could get into a movie for free all week. I made Gideon volunteer with me. Unfortunately, the week we joined we were saddled with a terrible movie. It was called *Gaslight* and starred Ingrid Bergman, whose husband was trying to drive her crazy. I thought it was the worst movie I had ever seen. Nothing happened. People just talked, and there wasn't one single joke in the entire movie. We ended up seeing the movie twelve times anyway because it was free. *Gaslight* became a famous movie.

Walking home from the theater, we would reenact the scenes of cowboys and soldiers that we had seen on the big screen. We felt like kings of the Grand Concourse.

My parents were not big movie fans. My mother preferred live theater, and Dad didn't see much worth in entertainment except if it made him money. However, we did listen to the radio as a family along with Nanny and my two sisters. Nanny's husband, Willy Ward, whom I loved, lived in an apartment next door and often he would come over and listen to the radio, too. Willy was a wise, chubby, round-faced man with white hair and a Santa Claus smile. Willy and I would listen to Jack Benny and the very hip Fred Allen. I probably listened to the radio more than anything because I could do it from my bed. I thought Jack Benny was just hilarious. He was famous for being cheap, and in one episode he described how a robber came up to him and said, "Your money or your life." And then there was a long pause as Benny pondered the seemingly difficult choice. It turned out the joke was written by Milt Josefsberg who later hired me to write for Lucille Ball.

Later, when I was in high school, I met a friend named Ira Levin, who also liked to laugh. Together we would take the bus to Union City, New Jersey, to see the burlesque shows. Once Ira taught me how to get there, (I'm geographically dyslexic), I took other friends, too. My parents had no idea where we were going, but they didn't worry about us. As Ira and I sat in the audience of adults and watched the show, we found the strippers boring after a while but the burlesque comedians who performed in between them mesmerized us. We agreed we had never seen men deliver funnier jokes. Soon I started to bring along a notepad so I could write down the skits that worked and made people laugh. I wanted to remember the good ones. Sometimes I would rewrite them for us to perform back at school. Ira and I felt like pioneers, venturing into the wilds of New Jersey to bring back superior humor for our friends and fellow students of the Bronx to enjoy.

I was good at sports, and thought sports were the key to a successful life until I went to camp for the first time. Most of my friends in the Bronx were praised for their athletic ability, or for dressing well; both Calvin Klein and Ralph Lauren hailed from the Bronx. If you couldn't play sports you had to know how to throw a punch well to protect yourself. But at age thirteen I learned a new way of life when I went to Camp Greenkill, a YMCA camp in New York's Catskill Mountains. The first summer I went for two weeks and it cost my parents fourteen dollars. The next summer I wanted to stay longer, so the camp said I could be a waiter, as well as a junior counselor, which extended my stay to four weeks. Although it was a Christian camp, there were some Jewish campers there, too. When the staff heard I knew a few Yiddish words, they put me in charge of the Jewish campers. I would take them out to the woods and lead them in weekly services, which I improvised.

My best friend at Greenkill was named Pete Wagner, a cool, silent type with penetrating eyes. He was from Yonkers, and I would later base the character of Fonzie in *Happy Days* on him. Pete had the confidence, self-esteem, and "cool" quality I admired and wanted to cultivate for myself. He told me the best book you could read was *Catcher in the Rye,* and he was right.

I had a great counselor at Greenkill named Bob Jacobs, and he asked if I wanted to be in a play. I had never thought of acting before. I was a drummer. To be honest, I thought acting was for sissies. But Mr. Jacobs and Camp Greenkill opened a giant door that showed me an array of activities outside sports. I saw that people were heralded for their acting, their ability to paint and build sets, and even their writing. I tried my hand at writing original skits and was the master of ceremonies at our talent show. At night I would entertain the kids at the campfire performing silly routines. I was also the sports editor for the camp newsletter. There were so many ways I could make people laugh at Greenkill. In addition, I liked my new job as a camp waiter.

However, one night as we were walking home, I overheard some boys talking about who they were going to nominate as the captain for the color war games. Someone said, "What about Garry?" Another boy said, "He's too much of a clown." So quickly I learned how to tone down my inner clown when necessary. I saw that people who were too silly were not looked up to and applauded as leaders. You could make people laugh, but you had to have a serious, controlled, and dignified side, too.

When I came home from camp I felt like a changed person. I had discovered that a sickly kid like me could find his own niche. There was hope for me after all. That confidence helped me muster up the courage to do something that would change my life forever.

My dad hoped I would be a lawyer or a businessman. My mom would have liked me to be the next Fred Astaire. But since I had no talent or interest in either, I had to find my own path. I knew in my heart that my humor was my power and that I had to figure out a way to make money writing jokes. So I joined the newspaper at DeWitt Clinton High School. I walked right in and said, "Sign me up. I'd like to be a reporter."

It didn't matter that I didn't exactly know how to be a reporter. I knew I liked writing, and they had an opening for a sports reporter. I thought I would be great at that because I was such a sports fan. They put me right to work, and my column was called "Warmin' the Bench." Raphael Philipson was the adviser for the paper. He had absolutely no sense of humor, but he let me stick around because I showed enthusiasm for writing and sports. I also found my inspiration from two other teachers. My homeroom and English teacher was named Lou Katz, a smooth-talking mustached man. And I had a history teacher named Doc Guernsey, a balding, heavyset man and master of the frighteningly stern look, who used two canes because he had once had polio. Together Katz and Guernsey pushed me beyond my comfort zone and told me to keep writing. I remember the day I got up the courage to ask about colleges.

"I think I'm going to play it safe and apply to City College of New York, New York University, and Queens College," I said.

"Why just those?" asked Katz.

"Isn't that enough?" I asked. "How many do I need to apply to?"

"What about the Ivy League or the Big Ten?" Guernsey asked.

I knew my father would love the suggestion about the Ivy League because he had delusions of grandeur. My mother, however, would probably say, "Stay in the Bronx. You'll get sick if you leave."

However, both Katz and Guernsey thought I should aim high.

"You think I should apply to some of those?" I asked.

"Let's look at some catalogs and find you a college with a good journalism school," Katz said.

And so together my teachers, my dad, and I made a list of all the colleges that had good writing programs. My choices included Northwestern, University of Missouri, and Emory, where I thought I could play basketball. I imagined there might be a lot of cows in the Midwest, but Chicago sounded like a good town where I could get a part-time job playing drums in a nightclub. So Northwestern became my first choice.

As we looked at brochure after brochure, I realized something magical: It was entirely possible that I could go to college and learn how to become a sports reporter. Not just a high school, silly-nilly sports reporter but a grown-up-salary-earning sports reporter who wrote about the big leagues. The day I got my acceptance letter from Northwestern University, everything changed. I finally had my one-way ticket out of my bed and out of the Bronx.

2. NORTHWESTERN

★

Attending College with the Thickest
Accent Anyone Had Ever Heard

I GRADUATED HIGH SCHOOL, and while I was decid-
ing what to do next a funny thing happened. My dad noticed me.
He knew I was his son and I lived in the apartment. He would yell
a lot and whack me on the head once in a while, but he never said
very much to me. He once grunted approval about my sports column in the high school paper, but he never came to see me play ball.
The reason was that I played "amateur" sports as he called them.
I played in the Police Athletic League, the Kiwanis Club, and the
American Legion but not high school sports. But his attitude toward
me changed the day he said, "Well, let's pick a college." My father
was the only one in his family to go to college. He graduated from
New York University, and it was there that he changed his name
from Masciarelli to Marshall. So to him a name and a college with a
good name and reputation were extremely important.

I had enough credits to graduate early from high school, in January 1952, and I didn't need to go to Northwestern until September.
So my dad helped me get a job at WNYC radio station in Manhattan, where I worked from January through June. I was the station's
intern, and unfortunately for me, they did not cover sports. It was
a classical music station for serious music and opera lovers. While
the content was not to my personal taste, I did love the location. I
would take the subway to work and spend my days writing for a
show called *Sunrise Symphony*. I scripted the introductions for the disc
jockeys and also ran errands.

The longer I was there the more responsibility they gave me, including writing commercials from time to time. My sense of humor, however, was a little far-fetched for my bosses. They were working on a campaign to promote cleaning up New York City streets. I submitted, "Don't be a cheat and throw it in the street be a man and throw it in the can." But they wanted something straighter and more traditional, like "Don't be a litterbug." My favorite part of the job was lunch. I brought a sandwich from home, and I would walk around the neighborhood near Delancey Street, browsing through the different novelty shops. I would save money to buy stamps for my collection. And then in June I headed to Camp Onibar in Pennsylvania to work as a waiter and bellhop to make money to take to college.

As I headed off to Northwestern, I felt a little like a pioneer because I was the only one from my neighborhood going out of state to school. Some of the guys were going straight to work, and of those who were going to college, most were headed to City College of New York, with the exception of Marty Garbus, who was going to Columbia in prelaw. Going to a college in another state seemed special and rare to me. I figured if it didn't work out I could always come back and apply to CCNY with my friends. I wasn't afraid of failing. In my eyes, college seemed like four years in which you could experiment without anyone making a big deal about it. When you failed in college it wasn't a disaster. When you failed in life you lost your job and it could be a disaster.

The first time I ever flew on an airplane was with my dad when we traveled together to drop me off at Northwestern's Medill School of Journalism in Evanston, Illinois. We dressed in suits and ties as people did in those days when they flew and boarded the plane bound for Chicago. Because of his business trips, Dad knew his way around an airplane. My mother, sisters, and grandparents on both sides, however, had never been on an airplane before. When I left for the airport that morning in September 1952, Mom gave me one piece of advice.

"I heard there is a throw-up bag on the plane. So if you get nauseous, be sure to use that," she said. Then she hugged me goodbye.

I didn't throw up, and I remember the flight as the time I felt the closest I had ever felt to my father. He didn't talk much on the ground but was quite chatty in the air. After my teachers Lou Katz and Doc Guernsey believed in me and helped me apply to college, it seemed my dad suddenly believed in me, too. He joked that he wanted me to go to college in the Midwest so I would lose my nasal New York accent. But I knew that he thought my college admission was my ticket out of the Bronx, and he wanted that for me and secretly for himself, too. He knew there was a life beyond the Grand Concourse, and he wanted me to see and experience it firsthand. My mom had gone to a junior college for gymnasts and dancers called Savage, and she would vote for acting over academics any day. Dad, however, had the experience of a traditional four-year college. So when Dad and I boarded that plane headed for my own college experience, I felt like he was right by my side, supportive and proud.

Dad and I had done research together beforehand and decided I should join an on-campus fraternity so I could meet a strong network of people. Dad helped me write letters to some of the fraternities to introduce myself. While my dad could lack warmth in person, he had a superb gift in the area of introductory and thank-you letters. His penmanship was excellent, and he had a fine collection of embossed personalized stationery. The one thing he didn't like about me was my nickname Flip, which I carried throughout high school because I had a knack for flipping a baseball from shortstop to first base in one motion. "Don't tell the people at Northwestern that your nickname is Flip. Please tell it to them straight: My name is Garry Kent Marshall. Two r's in Garry," he instructed. Dad didn't like any funny business in a name or much in life. He was the antithesis of zany, and he wanted me to be that way, too. "Now that you are going away to college, we are spending hard-earned money on you, Son," he told me. "So don't be a wise guy."

When our plane landed in Chicago a student from the Alpha Tau Omega house was there to meet us. My dad said it was a well-connected fraternity. He used the term *well-connected* a lot. We thought the student was going to take us to my dorm, but it turned out the dorms were already full and they were in the middle of building more. So my freshman year I was assigned to live in a Quonset hut. When Dad saw the makeshift housing he was appalled. I had to admit it looked strange to me, too. I came expecting to live in ivy-covered buildings like I had heard about on a radio show about college life called *The Halls of Ivy*. My Quonset hut was not covered with any ivy. So Dad convinced the ATO brother to let me stay in their chapter house even though I was not yet a pledge.

Before Dad left he taught me some basic skills, like how to write a check and manage a small checking account. I found the lessons tedious, but I tried to pay attention as best I could because Dad said, "It's time to grow up. No more fooling around." I had never been on my own before, and everything seemed new. The one thing I was certain of was that journalism was a good choice for me. My teachers at DeWitt Clinton thought so. I came with my experience as sports editor of the *Clinton News* as well as the sports editor at my newspaper at Camp Greenkill. So it seemed like a good road to follow. My mother said, "Writing is a good profession for you because you won't break any bones." And Dad thought it was a good fit because I could write even if I was in bed with aches and pains. I knew I was not talented or strong enough to play professional baseball or basketball, but I could certainly write about them.

Dad shared with me one more piece of information before he left: "The guys from the Bronx who you grew up with aren't going to amount to very much."

"Dad, don't say that. They're great guys."

"I know, but they are never going to go to college and make something of themselves like you are," he said. "But the people you meet in college will be different."

"Different? How?"

"They are friends with a future, and you are going to want to stay in touch with these people. They will go on to do important things. They are well-connected," he said.

After Dad left I went through the rigors of fraternity rush. It was a strange series of meeting and parties that left my head spinning. In my mind, I had come to college to figure out how to make a living and how to meet girls. So joining a fraternity seemed right. The guys would take me into a room with lots of smoke and ask me to sign papers. I honestly didn't know which fraternity was the perfect right fit for me, but ATO had a mixture of athletes and academics, and I thought I could blend in well. The true turning point came when I met a heartfelt, smiling upperclassman named Jack Morossy from Cleveland. One night at a party he came over to talk to me.

"I hear you play the drums, kid," he said.

"Yes, I do," I said nervously.

"Well, if you join the frat, then you can be in our band, the ATO combo," he said.

"Really? Do you think I'd be good enough?"

"Sure. And if you're not I'll help you along," he said. "I play the bass and I'll keep you in rhythm with the music until you have our tunes down."

His method reminded me of how my mother had taught me to play the drums when I was six years old by tapping the rhythm on my back with one hand as she played the piano.

"And we're going to make money," added Jack.

"Huh?" I said.

"We're going to make money with our band. You know, play at all the sorority parties and charge money. So you'll make a dollar, too."

That statement sealed the deal. I knew I wanted to make money to buy clothing and other things. My father only paid for books. So I joined ATO and then shared a room with four other pledges. Most of the guys in the fraternity had wealthy-people names like Robert Perkins, John Gardner, William Dye, and Lee Rodgers. I wasn't used to that because in my neighborhood my friends had names like Lefty Farrell, Duke Wellington, Joe Finley Straus, the Big Ragu, Push 'Em Up Tony, and Al Jello. Most of the guys I met at Northwestern wore crisp white shirts and penny loafers. I wasn't used to that either. So I was feeling uncomfortable until I heard an accent in line while I was registering for my classes. I introduced myself to the accent.

"You from the Bronx?" I asked.

"No. New Jersey," said the student. Other people at Northwestern were from places like Nebraska, Indiana, and Illinois. So to meet a guy from a state like mine made me feel an instant connection. He didn't dress like the swells either. He dressed in wrinkled clothing like me, and was even in journalism school like me. His name turned out to be Joel Sterns, and he was from Montclair, New Jersey. Joel was a funny, heavyset kid who was an overachiever who walked around like he owned the place. He would be my first college friend and a friend for life. He later became an important lawyer, proving my dad was right. Most of my college friends did go on to have great careers.

Joel had to work to put himself through college. He got a good job at a coffee shop called the Hut. I started looking for a job for myself, but most of the good ones in town were already filled. I asked around the fraternity to see if anyone had any leads. It turned out you could work at a sorority or fraternity in the dining room. I started out as a waiter at the Kappa Delta sorority. However, I was a daydreamer, and keeping track of the orders for ninety girls was overwhelming for me. So I went to the head cook, Hattie, and asked if there were any jobs inside the kitchen, behind the scenes so to speak. That's how I become the head dishwasher at Kappa Delta. There was no mechanical dishwasher, so I had to spray, clean, and dry every plate by hand. It was a job tailor-made for me. I could wash dishes for hours and daydream as much as I wanted to.

While I was a good dishwasher, I lacked a certain amount of sophistication about other things. My freshman year the professor in Journalism 101 gave us this assignment: Go to the library, do some research, and write up a famous person's obituary. Everyone in the class was given a different famous person to write about. I was assigned Danny Kaye. I tried to go to the library but got sidetracked by a girl. So when I got back to the classroom I typed up, "Danny Kaye, who was reported dead earlier today, didn't die at all. It was a false alarm. He was sick, but he recovered." My classmates thought my answer was funny and irreverent. But my professor was not amused and gave me a C minus.

After I had been at Northwestern for two years, my sister Ronny came as a freshman. I was happy she chose to attend Northwestern.

She dressed much better than I did, joined Chi Omega sorority, and ran with a fancier crowd. Sometimes I would look out the window from my dishwashing job at KD and see her walking with her fancy friends through the sorority quad. I would call out her name and then hold up a wet dirty dish rag and wave to try to embarrass her. But we got along well, and my parents were happy to have us at the same school, too. We also could ballroom dance and made quite a good jitterbug team. It made our mother proud that we were putting our dance skills to work at college.

Academically, Northwestern opened many new doors for me. It was the first place I learned that words mattered and could lead to a real job. I knew that sportswriting was a possibility, but at college I was exposed to so many different kinds of writing. I loved Hemingway but didn't understand Faulkner. I remember reading *The Grapes of Wrath* for the first time and was fascinated that Steinbeck composed a whole scene in which the words were written to the beat of a square dance. I was amazed at the power of words. And while I knew I couldn't write as well as Steinbeck, I was convinced I could write material that made people laugh. It was my hope for the future.

In addition to Steinbeck, I read a lot of plays by Tennessee Williams and Arthur Miller (who along with Paddy Chayefsky and Neil Simon had gone to my high school, DeWitt Clinton). But my favorite book of all time proved to be Peter Wagner's recommendation, J. D. Salinger's *Catcher in the Rye*. Like Peter and many of my peers, I made a connection to Holden Caulfield because he seemed like a regular guy trying to find his place in the universe. He was a misfit like me. I felt like a fish out of water trying to make it at Northwestern. The winters were brutally cold, and I was sick all the time with asthma and allergies. But come springtime, when the snow thawed and the weather turned warm, Northwestern looked to me like the most beautiful college campus ever. Finally the *Halls of Ivy*.

Once in a while there was a teacher who truly appreciated my humor, and that was the case with Professor Nathan Leopold, a dignified history professor. He knew I loved humor and recognized that I felt confined when I had to write straight, so he would let me hand in papers written in a more creative vein. I would still get the essence of the assignment and understand the material we were studying, but instead of writing reports, I wrote dialogue and scenes. When studying Frederick the Great, I learned that he liked only tall soldiers. So I wrote a whole scene of Frederick reviewing the potential troops. "Too short, too short, too short. You're a shrimp. Go be a jester. Oh, here's tall. Go get a gun." Professor Leopold gave me a good grade, too. (I tried very hard to pass all my courses. And I just made it. My freshman year I got fifteen Cs.)

Northwestern felt like a big camp with a lot of smart campers. When I wasn't studying I was constantly on the lookout for new activities to join. Soon I started playing intramural sports on Long Field, near my fraternity. We played baseball, basketball, and touch football. I had good hands. I went to some fraternity and sorority events and played with the ATO band at many. I also dated a few girls but no one seriously. I only dated girls with cars because I didn't have one. And I wasn't very good at dating. In high school I had gone out with an olive-skinned, pretty Italian girl named Jeanie Bartalotti and taken her to our senior prom. We continued to date long distance even freshman year at college. The most serious girlfriend I had at college was a bright, curvy dancer named Cindy Peterson, to whom I gave my fraternity pin our senior year. I didn't think very much about marriage back then, only having a date to go to a formal with. Sometimes Ronny and I would double-date, and she had an endless supply of potential suitors. My mother was always encouraging Ronny to meet a nice wealthy boy from the Midwest and settle down.

Volunteering for *The Daily Northwestern* newspaper also seemed like a good activity for me. I wrote a sports column called "Sport in Short." We did not have winning sports teams. My senior year our football team was one win to eleven losses. So I wrote the humorous side of losing: "Our team was behind two touchdowns by the time the national anthem ended." I also opened each column with a quote from a Greek philosopher named Estes. I wrote about many sports controversies, including Northwestern's misfit placement in the Big Ten league. In my last column I confessed there was no Greek philosopher named Estes. I'd made him up. I tried anything to make my writing seem different and unique. While I was often praised for my humor, I was taken to task time and time again for either getting the facts wrong or not proofreading carefully enough. I was on the copy desk the day the headline meant to say BIG TEN PARTNERSHIP actually ran as BIG TEN FARTNERSHIP.

One of the most exciting things to do on campus for actors, performers, and writers was the Waa-Mu show, the annual variety show. I signed up to write skits for it and worked alongside other students such as Paula Prentiss, Richard Benjamin, and Warren Beatty. Just like my mother used to put on shows in our basement, I found my niche writing comedy for the stage in Scott Hall at Northwestern.

My senior year I heard they were looking for writers for a show called *Fashion Fair,* so I volunteered and was paired with a sophomore from Chicago named Fred Freeman. Fred was a serious-looking kid with Clark Kent glasses. He was a little more intellectual than I was, so I thought he elevated my work. For the first time I was writing with a partner and I liked it. We put more humor into the *Fashion Fair* than ever before. I remember the show was such a big hit on campus that I was depressed when the two-day event closed. I couldn't imagine how we could top ourselves after being such a success. But Fred had plans for us. He thought we could write together beyond college. I just didn't know it yet.

I worked hard all four years at Northwestern and finally made dean's list my senior year with three As and a B. I always knew I was a late bloomer when it came to school. There were some ups and downs along the way as well. My junior year my band played late at a nightclub and I slept through an economics final. I begged the professor to let me retake it. He agreed and let me take it later in his office. In those days we all smoked cigarettes, so I was smoking one as I took the makeup final. Unfortunately, I set the professor's desk on fire. He smelled smoke and came running in. "Marshall, you are done! You get a D and you are done!" he shouted. So that was the only D I ever got at Northwestern.

Going to the Medill School for four years taught me an invaluable lesson: how to write on a deadline. Sometimes we attended three-hour newswriting labs. We would sit at typewriters trying our best to write our stories and the professors would throw obstacles in our way. A typewriter would break. A siren would occur. A bell would go off. A new person would be murdered in our story assignments. I loved that class because it helped me learn to write under extreme pressure. From graduation onward I could pretty much write any place, any time. I was trained to be a reporter. It didn't really matter that I was not going to be the next great investigative reporter. It was an asset to be able to write quickly and concisely, whether it was a joke, a line, or a comedy skit. I wasn't going to stare into space and struggle with writer's block. I could put paper in the typewriter and deliver the goods. But my professors were always scolding me for putting jokes in my leads. When Eisenhower was president I wrote, "Rumors were flying around the White House like golf balls today."

My parents came out for my graduation in 1956 along with Penny. It was the first time my mother was ever on an airplane. It was a hot day, with hundreds of graduates and their families crammed into the school's Dyche Stadium. Despite the heat and the crowds it was a special day for me. I was getting my diploma, and my mom and dad and sister were there to see it. Ronny was with her fancy friends, who congratulated me, but Penny (still in high school) got bored and cranky. She climbed up to the top of the stadium and hid in the last row—always causing trouble, my mom would say. But it didn't take away from my special day. My best friend Joel Sterns and I posed in cap and gown, still with the two worst East Coast accents in school.

After graduation I filled out an application to go to graduate journalism school at Northwestern. I was accepted and sent in my down payment of fifty dollars. I thought at the time that it would be a good thing to do. School was fun, plus I was still making money with the band. I left for the summer planning to return that fall. During the summer months Fred and I wrote for a USO show called *Take a Break*. We created skits for the show, which was performed on army bases around America. They couldn't afford to pay me as a writer to travel with the show, so they paid me as a drummer who did writing on the side. We did an eight-week tour and had a wonderful time. I made friends with a young singer-dancer named Tom Kuhn, who would later play an important role in my life, and some people who would go on to become Broadway actors, such as Ken Mars *(The Producers)* and Nancy Dussault *(Do, Re, Mi)*.

During our time on the road I worried a lot about being drafted. Although the war in Korea was over, they were still drafting soldiers, and we were all on the list. Fred decided to serve in the army reserves and volunteer for two weeks a year for the next six years. Some of my other friends were exempt because they were the sole males in their households, or had a minor health problem that made them not eligible. Not me. Even with my illnesses, the army said I was in perfect shape. So, I had to make a decision for myself.

If I waited for my number to be called, I would have to serve for three years. However, if I offered to go right away, I would only have to serve two years. So that's what I did. Instead of going back to graduate school at Northwestern in the fall of 1956, I went to New York and joined the army. I lost my fifty-dollar down payment at Northwestern. My career in journalism was put on hold, and I became a soldier in the United States Army. The recruiter said I would first do basic training and then head on a boat to Korea. My mother worried, "You know how nauseous you get on boats!"

3. KOREA

★

Welcome to the United States Army,

Mr. Marshall

OVERNIGHT I WENT from being a college student to a "Fighting Machine." I had a degree in journalism that I could do nothing with because for the next two years my full-time job was for the United States of America. I was sent to Fort Dix in New Jersey for a day, and to Fort Knox for basic training. In Kentucky we spent eight weeks learning routine soldier tasks like marching in place and loading a gun. My dad had helped me fill out my application, and he wrote down that I was a television cameraman. I had done some camera work in college, but the claim was mostly fiction. But Dad said, "Don't put 'writer,' put 'television cameraman,' because television is going to be big." Dad was notorious for doing this kind of thing. Even though I wasn't a cameraman, he knew that if I stretched the truth, I would get a better assignment. He excelled at inflated résumé writing. I guess he also had confidence that I was smart enough to learn how to be a cameraman on the fly. Dad was right. That title qualified me for service in Astoria, Long Island, where I worked in a division that made army instructional films.

The films we made were about everything from how to read a map to how to detect venereal disease. I acted in one movie about dogs and ended up getting bitten by the dog. It left me with a fear of dogs for the rest of my life. The head of our unit was a lieutenant named Richard D. Zanuck, whose father was Darryl F. Zanuck, a famous producer and head of 20th Century–Fox. Richard would later become a producer and studio executive himself. In the army, however, he was a little aloof and not very friendly to enlisted men. Then, I didn't consider moviemaking a profession I was destined for. It was just a nice way to pass my time in the army.

I worked in the film department for two months. The best perk was that I could go to Broadway shows for free if I wore my dress uniform. You had to stand up for most of the show, but it was worth it. The bad news was that I had to live with my parents and Penny, which was a bit of a letdown after being so independent at college. But the time flew by as I awaited my foreign assignment. Most of my friends and I had put down that we wanted to go to Germany. But it turned out the U.S. Army was launching a series of radio and television stations in Korea, and because I'd listed myself as a cameraman, they thought I would be an asset to their broadcast division.

Before leaving I called Fred Freeman, my writing partner from Northwestern, and told him I was heading to Korea. Because he'd signed up with the army reserves, he could stay in New York and do two weeks of service each year.

"I have plans for us," Fred said when I called him.

"What kinds of plans?" I said.

"Someday we are going to move to Hollywood. But first we need to make some contacts."

"Hollywood? Freddie, are you crazy?" I said. "Who would hire us to work in Hollywood as writers?"

"Just get your stint in the army finished," he said. "And call me when you get back."

Before I shipped out I spent a week in Chicago so I could play one last job with my band. That band at the time was called the Bob Owens Trio and had gathered a lot of interest because of our front man, piano player Bob Owens. We were headlining at the Compass Room, which was a big deal for me because most of the time I was the opening act, not the headliner. Before we went onstage I watched from the wings as our opening act performed. It was a group of young comedians doing improvisational comedy routines in a style I had never seen before. They didn't seem to have prewritten routines but instead appeared spontaneous, which was unique for the time. They were doing situations instead of jokes. There were four performers, and their names were Andrew Duncan, Shelley Berman, Elaine May, and Mike Nichols. I didn't know who they were, but it was obvious to me that they were incredibly talented. I was startled by their innovation and creativity. I was just days away from going to Korea, but my mind began to fill with possibilities. I wondered if I might be able to either perform or write that style of humor, too.

I must admit that when I shipped off for Korea I was a little scared. I boarded the ship with seventeen hundred other soldiers and sailed from Tacoma, Washington, for Seoul, Korea. I had never been to a foreign country before, let alone one that was so far from America.

While on the boat I met Gordon Belson, a round-faced soldier with a deep voice who worked as a professional radio announcer in his hometown of El Centro, California. When I told him I was a comedy writer, he mentioned that he had a younger brother named Jerry who liked to write comedy, too. Gordon also liked music and played the trumpet, with more joy than skill. So we formed a band and started looking for other members. Charlie Camilleri, a hippy, rebellious type and superb musician who played seven instruments, including piano and trumpet, joined us. Charlie got a few of his other friends to play, too. For the two weeks on the ship we entertained the troops and officers in the mess hall.

I also volunteered to write for the ship's newspaper and some of the skits that soldiers performed each night. One of my more popular comedy routines which I rewrote from comic Harvey Stone went like this: "They call this ship a floating city. Well, I live in the sewer. We get six meals a day. Three go down and three come up. You should see what it looks like when a hundred guys are leaning over the ship's railing getting sick. It looks like Niagara Falls in Technicolor. One day I went to take my tray of food to throw it overboard. Another officer asked what I was doing with the tray. I said I was eliminating the middleman."

One night I met a corporal with a shiny personality, and I typed him up a skit to perform. But I noticed during rehearsals he was having trouble finding his way with the dialogue. I worked with him for a few minutes and he was still speaking gibberish. That was when I realized he was illiterate. I was pretty naïve back then, and I had never met anyone who couldn't read. But I worked with him and he ended up doing a great job with the skit.

After the ship crossed the Pacific it made a stop in Okinawa, Japan, to unload soldiers who were assigned to serve there. I went out to the deck to wave goodbye to them, and as they stood on the dock they took their instruments and played the Dixieland song "When the Saints Go Marching In" especially for me. It must have pained them to play it because they all preferred jazz music, but it made me smile big. I discovered that day that the army was a place where you met people, found true friends, and soon had to say goodbye. I would not see Charlie again for four years.

Gordon and I, however, were both headed to Seoul to work in the radio and television station together. They made us disembark in the middle of the night. We had to climb down army ropes hanging from the side of the ship in the pitch black. Then we got into little boats like the ones I had seen in pictures of Normandy from World War II. As we were climbing into the boats, I approached my commanding officer.

"Why do we have to arrive in the dark when there is no one here who will shoot us?" I asked. After all, we were no longer at war with Korea.

"Who said so?" said my officer.

I hugged my duffel bag and snare drum and wondered what exactly I had signed up for.

I knew only one other person who had ever served for the United States in Korea. His name was Sandy McMillan, and he was a counselor at Camp Greenkill, my YMCA camp. Sandy had shipped off for Korea while I was still in high school, and within a year he was dead. So I guess in the back of my head I knew that danger was always a possibility.

The corporal in charge of our radio station was a somber, no-nonsense man named Mark Smith. He looked at my résumé the day I arrived.

"Says here you are a TV cameraman?"

"Yes," I mumbled. "Correct."

"We have no TV station here yet," he said.

My father was right about the future of TV, but he was a little ahead of the army.

"Says you are also a writer. What do you write?"

"Jokes," I said.

"Jokes?" he asked.

"You know, skits, little bits, funny things," I said.

"We don't need jokes here," he said seriously.

"Okay. What do you need then?" I asked.

"We need you to write serious material about the country of Korea. Radio documentaries," he said.

For the next twenty months I would try to write seriously about Korea for my radio station—the Armed Forces Korean Network.

A typical day for me involved a combination of guard duty, meals, marching, and work at the radio station. Eventually I became the head of the six-station radio network, and I was in charge of picking the songs and the shows. I taught them how to do comedy shows. In between meals and work we sometimes had to go to classes and listen to presentations about things the army was introducing, such as new weapons, equipment, and strategy. I mastered taking apart a gun while blindfolded, a skill I had never imagined a stickball-playing kid from the Bronx would need. What I was very good at was shooting while resting on the ground. I had talent as a resting sniper, not a standing or kneeling one. So the army gave me a certain confidence and feeling of success.

Sometimes on Sundays we would get the day off and go into the city of Seoul to buy cigarettes and stationery to write letters home. On the walk into town I would daydream and think of new radio shows we could put on the air. I came up with *Evenings with Elaine,* which would become one of our most popular shows. I found an American girl who was working at the officers' club and convinced her to come down to the station and read letters written to the soldiers by their girlfriends back home. The show was a big hit until some officers discovered that the girl I hired was African American. They shut down the show immediately. When I asked why they said it was because they couldn't have a black girl on their network.

It was one of my first experiences of censorship, and I thought it was ridiculous to pull someone off a popular show just because of race. Censorship seemed incompatible with creativity to me, but I had bosses I needed to answer to and salute to, so the show went off the air permanently.

We all had to get special security clearance to write the news and work for the radio station because sometimes we would handle sensitive and secret information. This required filling out a series of forms and questionnaires that seemed cumbersome but essential. One day Gordon, who was now our news announcer, received the paperwork for his high-level security clearance. He called me over to look at it with him.

"Well, would you look at this," he said.

I looked at the form but didn't see anything unusual.

"What's wrong?" I asked.

"Says here I'm adopted," he said.

"So, what's wrong with that? Plenty of people are adopted," I said.

"This is the first I've heard of it. My parents never bothered to tell me," he said.

Getting security clearance turned out to be quite a surprise for Gordon, who was more fascinated than disappointed by the revelation. While he was adopted, his sister, Monica, and brother, Jerry, were biological siblings. Gordon finally figured out why he didn't look like his brother and sister.

I worked with another writer named Fred Roos (who later became one of the producers of the *Godfather* movies). Back then he was just a recruit from Los Angeles. When we weren't writing material in the station, we sometimes sat on guard duty together on the night shift for the TV station they were building. I would make up jokes and tell them to Fred to pass the time.

"I think we need a password," I said.

"What kind of password?" he asked.

"Something that people need to say in order to walk by us," I explained.

"Okay. What is the password?" he asked.

"Matzo. Now you say the password," I said.

"Matzo," he said.

"You may now Passover," I said.

Fred laughed and he wasn't even Jewish.

The TV station contained so much expensive equipment that our bosses worried it might get stolen in the middle of the night. We were on guard to protect it. Although we had guns, we didn't usually shoot at anyone, because if you shot your gun you had to fill out a lot of paperwork afterward. However, if you just threw rocks at the intruders, they usually ran away in fear and no paperwork was required. So we ended up saving our bullets and throwing a lot of rocks at people and at sounds in the dark.

The winters in Korea were terrible, even worse than the winters I spent in Chicago. I remember freezing while Fred and I sat diligently outside the base of the TV station with our rifles and rocks.

"What are you going to do when you get out of here?" said Fred one night.

"I want to write jokes," I said.

"Really?" he asked.

"Yes. I went to journalism school, but I don't do 'serious' well. I do 'funny' much better," I said. "I think I could be an entertainer."

"Well, give me a call in Los Angeles," he said. "Maybe I can help."

"What do you do?" I asked.

"I work at the William Morris Theatrical Agency."

"Are you an agent?" I asked.

"I work in the mail room. But not for long," he said. "If you ever get out to Los Angeles, I can introduce you around to some show business people. I'm going to be a producer."

Walking on the midnight-to-8:00 A.M. shift with a gun in the middle of Korea, I had made my first real-life Hollywood contact.

Shortly after I arrived at the radio station, another soldier, named John Grahams, joined our group. He was from Milwaukee and had graduated from Marquette University. He was a professional radio announcer and a professor of radio history at Marquette. We hit it off right away. He had a great radio voice, and although I didn't have the best voice, I could write for the two of us. It took a long time, but we finally convinced the army brass to give us our own show. We created the *Uncle John and Uncle Garry Radio Show*, in which we discussed different army topics and news of the world. We did radio salutes with a comedy twist to Valentine's Day, Memorial Day, Labor Day, and other holidays. Whatever holiday it was back in America, we would do a tie-in for the troops in Korea. We also did a sports-style play-by-play of a chess match that was quirky but the troops liked it. Finally the AFKN network was known for comedy.

From time to time, like in journalism school, I made mistakes when trying to be funny. Our boss, Mark Smith, told me one day that one of our radio shows was too long. He wanted me to cut our material down to make it fit. But I thought, Why cut our funny material when it is easier to cut the endless Korean song we were required to play in the middle of the show? So I tightened up the song. What I didn't know was that the song was the Korean national anthem, and I'd offended a whole country. Instantly I was demoted for a few weeks. I had learned a valuable lesson: Ask for help in translation before cutting anything.

I redeemed myself during the Academy Awards a few weeks later. Sometimes when we were broadcasting a particularly popular show, the North Koreans would jam our airwaves just to frustrate us. This is what they did the night we were to air the Oscars. Everyone on our base was looking forward to Bob Hope's opening monologue, but I knew ahead of time that the North Koreans had messed up the broadcast. So I tried to come up with some way to fix it. As I sat down to listen to it, Bob Hope's opening monologue was completely chopped up by dead air. However, I already knew from experience how the jokes went from hearing them performed in clubs. So I was able to re-create the punch lines or straight lines. Then I hired a local guy who could imitate Bob Hope and had him fill in the blanks. Suddenly we were back in business broadcasting the opening of the Academy Awards. The other guys in the station thought I was a wizard, and they loved what I had done. So did my commanding officer.

I was always looking for a new project to work on. Another

soldier I made friends with was Jimmy Anglisano, who also was from New York. Jimmy was a pleasant type who later became a banker. He wanted to form a band and heard I played the drums. I told him all I had to offer was the snare drum I had brought with me, not a complete kit. This information did not deter him. One night he picked me up in a jeep. We crawled under barbed wire and entered the back door of a large building. When he turned on the lights I saw the entire room was filled with musical instruments. He helped me carry out a complete drum set, and we transported it piece by piece underneath the barbed wire back to our jeep.

"I'm a little nervous," I said.

"Why? What's the problem?" Jimmy asked.

"I want to form the band, don't get me wrong. But won't we get in trouble for stealing? There are people in charge of this building."

"The person in charge of this building is me," he said. "And I'm fine with us taking it."

Jimmy played the accordion and was also a good leader. He also found a good guitar player to join us. He said our band could benefit from a southerner, so we recruited Marv Dennis, who was from Nashville. To round out our band Jimmy brought in a soldier who was known for doing Elvis Presley impersonations. His name was Jack Larson, and he often performed at the officers' club. Jack, an energetic, gyrating kid with the moves of Elvis Presley, later changed his name to Lars Jackson to give himself a more European flair. As a band we did very well with Jack. Eventually, however, Jimmy and I made the decision to reinvent ourselves as a two-man team so we could enter the army's network of variety contests. Jimmy did mime-style humor while I narrated like a circus barker with a metal crowbar instead of a cane. For some reason, our act was a big hit with the soldiers. They seemed to find it not only funny but also unique. Maybe they wanted to laugh more than they wanted to listen to music. We entered our act in a few contests. Much to our surprise we won the All-Korea Event, followed by the All–Far East Competition. Before we knew it we were being invited to fly to Washington, D.C., to compete in the All-World Entertainment Competition.

I never thought doing the act with Jimmy would be a way to get out of the army. I just thought of it as a way to make my time in the army more interesting. However, once we were in Washington, we found ourselves performing for the secretary of defense. I had only two months left on my two-year service contract. Jimmy and I did our routine in the All-World event, and we came in third as a specialty group in the nonmusical grand finals of 1958. We celebrated, and then they offered us the opportunity to continue in an army show called *Rolling Along,* which would tour all over Europe. The catch was that I had to sign up for another two years of service.

Although I liked performing, I did not want to do two more years in the army. I was just months from getting out, and I wanted to be done and go home. When I declined, I think they didn't see the point of sending me back to Korea, so I was restationed to Fort Belvoir in Alexandria, Virginia. At my new post I met Barry Kurtz, who was a good basketball player from Hostra University. Barry helped me get on a basketball team at Fort Bevoir, and I volunteered for the newspaper, where I wrote a sports column. I got up every day and wrote about national sports and played basketball. Not a bad job in the army during peacetime.

I wanted to get out of the army, but I have never been the best at navigating paperwork. One day on the basketball court I started talking to Barry Kurtz, who was the company clerk. Barry was an athletic con man always looking for a deal. He told me that because of my service and circumstances, if I filled out the right paperwork I could get out by springtime. So that's what I did after two years of service. In the spring of 1959 Barry helped me fill out the proper forms and I was released. I grabbed my duffel bag, snare drum, and the plaque Jimmy and I had won, said goodbye to my friends, and headed off on the next train bound for New York City.

I arrived at Penn Station and then boarded another train for the Bronx. I got off at Bedford Park on 204th Street and walked the five blocks to my house. By the time I got home, dragging my duffel and drum, it was 11:00 P.M., but I remember feeling so happy to finally be home. I rang the bell of my apartment, and my mother and father opened the door to welcome me. Then Dad said, "It's late. Go to bed," and we all went to sleep. But as I got undressed in my room, with my dog tags and army uniform, there was only one thing on my mind: How was I going to make a living now? In the army, I could play sports, write articles, and perform music. But now, without the clear structure of camp or the army, I wasn't sure where I fit in or who would pay me to fit in.

That night I lay awake looking at the sports stars who still lined the walls of my childhood room. It was obvious that a career as a professional athlete was still not a possibility for me, but maybe I could forge a career as a sportswriter. After all I did have a degree from Medill, Northwestern's journalism school and one of the best. The problem was that most of the top-notch Medill graduates got sent right out of college to small-town newspapers in places like Boone, Iowa, and I didn't really want to live in Boone, Iowa. So I came up with another plan. I would apply as a copyboy at the New York *Daily News*. I also decided that I would call my college writing partner Fred Freeman and tell him I was back in town, ready to write some new comedy material. I wasn't sure whether journalism or comedy writing was going to be a profession for me, but I knew I had to try to make a living at something.

4. NEW YORK CITY

★

Writing for Stand-Up Comedians
and Being Paid in Corn Beef

W HEN I CAME back from Korea I lived in my parents' house in the Bronx and I was out of work for two weeks.

That was literally the only time in my life that I was unemployed against my will. I hated it. I felt lost. I didn't want to rely on my parents to support me, so I felt constant pressure to find work. I decided right away that the best road would be to get a newspaper job and save money by moving in with my writing partner Fred Freeman, who had an apartment in the East Village. I went to *The New York Times* and was told they wanted only journalism graduates from Ivy League schools. So I headed over to the *Daily News,* where I was hired right away. They didn't even care where I went to journalism school. As long as I could carry a cup of coffee without spilling it, I could be a copyboy at the *Daily News.*

Fred worked for a vanity press called *Exposition,* which published writers' books for a fee. He got paid a hundred dollars a week, compared to my thirty-eight dollars a week at the newspaper. With low-key day jobs, we both had time and energy to work on our comedy writing at night. Just as Fred had planned before I went to Korea, we put our heads together to write and sell jokes and sketch material to stand-up comedians. To make our venture professional, we had business cards printed up that read "Freeman & Marshall—Comedy Writers 100 percent Virgin Material." We would go to nightclubs and hand out the cards to anyone who would take one. With my confidence from performing stand-up in the army, I began to step up to the mike in small New York nightclubs as well.

The story I told that got the most laughs was about how my first job straight out of college was as a fox-face stuffer in a factory that made ladies' fur coats and stoles. The routine went something like this. "So in the factory the fox stoles would come to me and the foxes' faces would be down and droopy because the fox was dead, of course. However, no fancy rich lady wants a droopy-nosed fox hanging down looking sad over her shoulder at a cocktail party. So my job would be to shove a piece of firm cardboard into the nose of each fox face to make it turn upward. So the cardboard would take each nose from droopy and sad to perky and fun. Women all over Manhattan were wearing perky-nosed fox stoles because of me."

The truth was, that I never really worked as a fox-face stuffer. My friend Harvey Keenan from the Bronx did it, but it was such a funny story I put it into my act. He worked down in the Garment District for a company that sold fox stoles. And he really did shove a small piece of cardboard into the nose of each fox, and make it cute instead of droopy. I did a whole routine about stuffing the fox faces. And then I riffed on what it must have been like for my friend Harvey to pick up girls at bars with the line "I'm a fox-face stuffer. What do you do?" I got some big laughs with that routine, and I still perform it from time to time. It taught me an important lesson: You can hear a funny story from a friend and then make it your own.

Just as I had done in college and the army, I joined a band to make some side money. When you have a thirty-eight-dollar-a-week job, you need to make extra money. Jimmy Anglisano was back in New York, too, and we formed a group called the Mayfairs. We played in nightclubs all around Times Square. We hired a bass player named Richie McCormick, who had gone to Northwestern with me. Sometimes I would have to work late at the *Daily News* and then go right to my band job. So I taught my partner and roommate, Fred, how to set up my drum set so I could go straight from the newspaper to the nightclub and grab my drumsticks as the show started.

While back in New York, I reconnected with some of my

childhood friends from the Bronx. Marty Garbus and Joel Sterns were both going to law schools nearby. I dated a raven-haired secretary named Sandy Brooks, whom we all called Babbling Brooks because she never stopped talking. Eventually Fred decided that he liked collaborating with me but not putting up with my late-night schedule or assembling the drum kit, so I moved out of his apartment into a five-floor walk-up on West Sixteenth Street. I lived there with Bob Brunner, another copyboy I met at the *Daily News*. Bob was a stocky, tough former high school football player with dark circles under his eyes. He would later become a top Hollywood comedy writer-producer. We split the rent of $150 a month. Carrying my snare drum, bass drum, tom-tom and cymbals up and down the five flights of stairs many nights was challenging, but I felt young and excited to be finally living on my own away from my parents.

Despite being the time when I gained my independence, which I cherished, this period in my life was when I struggled to find a way to support myself. On Mondays and Tuesdays, my days off from the *Daily News,* I could work on my comedy writing with Fred. Sometimes when I played in a nightclub as a drummer or stand-up, I would pass other comedians jokes for free. Most of the time they liked my material and thanked me. But one time I passed a joke to a comic and he didn't like the joke so he set it on fire and gave me my first flaming rejection.

Another place to sell material was a comedy hangout, the Stage Deli. Fred and I would go there and hand out jokes to the comedians as they ate lunch. We would write them on little slips of paper and give them to guys like Jack E. Leonard, Jack Carter, Joey Bishop, and Buddy Hackett. Although once in a while someone would pay us fifty or a hundred dollars for a page of jokes, most of the comedians just paid in food. They bought us sandwiches and called it even. When you are a young single guy without a family to support, living on corn beef sandwiches doesn't seem so bad. It was exciting for us just to sit at a deli table with working comedians and talk about comedy.

To pay our rent, however, Fred and I found side jobs. We were freelance writers for *Rogue* magazine, a men's magazine that ran features on food, entertainment, and world travel. A former teacher of mine named Frank Robinson was the editor, and he hired Fred and me to write reviews of movies, plays, and restaurants. *Rogue* paid ten dollars for each review, and we wrote a lot of them. We didn't tell Frank, but most of the movies and plays we never saw, and the restaurants we never ate in. To save time and money, we would interview our friends and find out what movies and plays they had seen. And for restaurants we relied on several stewardesses who lived in my building. The girls told us about cafés and bistros in places such as Belgium and Austria, in colorful detail, from the appetizers right on through to dessert. Frank loved our pieces because we seemed so well-traveled. We worried all the time that our scheme would be uncovered, but the money was too good to turn down.

While our day jobs were fine, we both knew that we needed to get a lucky break in order to make a living as comedy writers. One day when we least expected it, our break came. Fred and I bumped into a guy coming out of an elevator named Muttle "Mutt" Tickner, who was friends with my army buddy Charlie Camilleri. Mutt, it turned out, worked as the receptionist at a management office called Berger, Ross and Steinman, which handled top comedians. Meeting dry-witted Mutt was the big break we had been waiting for.

Phil Foster was the first A-list comedian Mutt introduced us to. Phil was a mean-looking cross between a bouncer and a baseball catcher. He would also turn out to be a very loyal and charming man. Phil came to see me at a comedy club one night. When I finished my act, he said my material was great but my delivery was not as strong. So he suggested that I forget performing and stick to writing, which I did. He then invited us to his house to work for him, and he would say "Wake me when it's funny," and go into his room to take a nap. We would work on some material, and when it was ready we'd wake him up to review it. Phil was a great client to have because not only was he a regular on *The Ed Sullivan Show,* but he also had a radio show. We would write him routines and social commentary along the lines of Andy Rooney on *60 Minutes.* Our relationship with Phil Foster opened doors to other comedians, such as Joey Bishop, a dead-pan somber-looking man who rarely seemed happy.

The day I went to have my first meeting with Joey Bishop, I handed him my diploma from Northwestern.

"What's this?" he said.

"My college diploma," I said. "I thought you would be impressed I have a writing degree."

"Interesting. But write some jokes on the other side of it and then I'll really be impressed."

Joey was a big deal in comedy because he was a guest host on Jack Paar's *The Tonight Show*. Phil convinced Joey that he should have his own writers for the show and that Fred and I would be perfect for the job. Joey agreed and paid us three hundred dollars a week, which we split. Suddenly, Fred and I were working as a television writing team for a comedian on *The Tonight Show*. Soon a man named Frank Cooper contacted us and said he wanted to represent us. Once you started making money back then, you didn't need to look for an agent. Agents found you. That is still true today.

Writing material for Joey wasn't an easy job. He was a comedian of few words and known as king of the deadpan. If a joke wasn't working or didn't get a laugh quickly, he would say "son of a gun," which was his catchphrase. In the general scope of comedy, he was not as funny as Don Rickles and Jack Carter, but he was more connected. Stars like Frank Sinatra and Dean Martin liked him and considered him a member of their Rat Pack. Joey's style was unique. He liked to assume the part of the sullen Rat Pack comedian and often had the audiences overhear his jokes instead of hearing them dead-on. To achieve this, he would even perform with his back to the audience, playing his material directly to the band. What we found the most difficult to deal with was that he didn't respect writers. He rarely introduced us formally. Among the staff of *The Tonight Show,* Fred and I were known as Joey's Kids.

The first year we wrote for Joey whenever he substituted for Jack Paar, which was about seven times. The second year we signed with an agent who negotiated a deal for us to write for Jack Parr as well, full-time as staff writers. We joined Paul Keyes, Bob Howard, and Walter Kempley on the writing staff for *The Tonight Show* in 1960. We wrote about five pages of jokes each day, four days a week. Joey or Jack might use one or two of our jokes each day, and each time it felt like sweet victory to us. Jack was a paranoid yet dapper type with an obsessive curiosity about life. That's what made him such a good talk-show host. We wrote jokes about being stuck in rush hour such as "Traffic was so heavy that I drove from Long Island to Manhattan in neutral." Joey loved that joke and asked for more like it. Both he and Jack wanted material that appeared as if they had just thought of it spontaneously. One day Fred and I and the other three writers were standing in the hall talking. Jack saw us and looked annoyed. "Don't bunch up," he said. "I don't want people to think I have so many writers." Basically the comedians paid us to write funny material for them and remain anonymous.

One of the reasons the audience had an affinity for Jack was that he liked to tell stories about his family. However, one night his material backfired. He described how his daughter had just gotten her first training bra. His daughter, about twelve years old at the time, heard what he said and was mortified. That incident resonated with me. I vowed then and there that if I ever had children I would not embarrass them in public or on television. Jack defended his jokes because he said they were not only true but also funny. But to embarrass your child in the service of comedy didn't seem right to me. Even if such a story was true, it caused too much hurt to be worth it.

The talent coordinator on *The Tonight Show* was a very bright young man named Dick Cavett. His favorite guest to book on the show in those days was an up-and-coming comedian named Woody Allen. Jack didn't understand Woody's humor because it was so different from and edgier than his own, but Fred and I loved his material because it was so fresh and different. Woody also told us a story that has stuck with me. He was writing for comedian Garry Moore and making fifteen hundred dollars a week. Garry was very social and liked to have his writers over to his house on Sundays for barbecues. But Woody refused to go, so Garry fired him. I was amazed that Woody wouldn't just grin and bear the barbecue, especially for a job that paid fifteen hundred dollars a week. But socializing just wasn't Woody's favorite thing to do, and he was willing to be unemployed to avoid it. Woody had no wife or children at the time. I felt conflicted. I admired Woody on the one hand for standing up for what he believed in. But on the other hand, I knew when I got to be a husband and father, I would go to every barbecue I was invited to just to keep my job.

The longer we wrote for *The Tonight Show,* the more comedians we met. Often they would ask us to write for them, too. The other guest hosts on *The Tonight Show,* such as Sam Levenson and Hugh Downs, were not as quick as Joey. So sometimes we would stand to the side of the desk off-camera and feed the guest host jokes about products and toys he was riffing on. Fred and I learned immediately that it was an asset to master the art of writing under pressure. When we told our friends we were writing for *The Tonight Show,* they were all very impressed. Only on Friday night the writer's credit would roll across the screen and my parents would stay up to watch it. To get an on-screen credit for a job I loved doing seemed thrilling.

Just to be on the safe side, I kept my job as a copyboy at the *Daily News.* I wanted to have something to fall back on if we lost our *Tonight Show* gig. However, when Jack Paar found out that I was also working for the newspaper, he worried I might be a news spy plotting to expose the show's secrets. The truth was, the only time I got a byline was in a story about a stamp collector. Eventually the paper raised my salary from thirty-eight dollars a week to forty-five where I worked eight hours. A forty-five-dollar-a-week job as copyboy and freelance writer didn't compare to the four hundred dollars a week I had worked my way up to on *The Tonight Show.* So I quit the *News.*

I honestly thought *The Tonight Show* gig was the best job in the entire world, and I wanted to do it forever. Fred, however, seemed unsatisfied. He liked writing jokes, but he had dreams of bigger things. He talked about writing plays and books and material more erudite than television.

Fred's ambition and passion for something other than *The Tonight Show* skits convinced me it was time to seek something else, too. That's how we decided to take a job in Miami Beach one winter writing for comedian Alan Gale. It paid great money, and we liked the idea of leaving New York to spend some time in Florida. Alan had a revue that included other celebrities. It was a growing experience for us because they wanted a different, esoteric type of humor. For example, comedian Arthur Treacher had a line in the show that went "I got up this morning and my mouth tasted like Harrisburg, Pennsylvania, after a heavy rain." I liked that type of writing, which used obscure images, and I tried to duplicate it.

We were supposed to work on Alan Gale's show for ten to twelve weeks, but it closed after four weeks. We didn't have money to fly home for Christmas, so Fred and I stayed down in Florida. While it was depressing not to be in New York for the holidays, I did get to play in a band for comedian Lenny Bruce. I was part of a trio that played behind him. He didn't use any writers, but Fred and I learned a lot from watching him. He swore something like a hundred times in his act, and audiences in Florida knew they were watching something special and irreverent.

It was when we were in Miami Beach, laid off from Gale's show, that we got a call from Joey Bishop. He was in Los Angeles starring in his new sitcom, *The Joey Bishop Show,* which Danny Thomas had created for him. After a few episodes, however, it was clear the show was not going well. The scripts were not strong enough. Joey wanted Fred and me to move to California to write for his sitcom. While I was weighing the pros and cons of moving across the country, Fred answered for both of us: "Yes." Another lesson learned: Sometimes it is important to have a partner more ambitious than you are. Fred said it would be the perfect opportunity for us to move up. In his mind returning to *The Tonight Show* in New York would have been a step backward for our writing careers.

Before we made the final decision to move to California, we wrote for the lovely and talented comedian Shari Lewis and her puppet Lamb Chop, who communicated with us in a strange, calculated manner. Shari was very nice to us as writers, always offering coffee or tea and saying our jokes were funny. Her puppet Lamb Chop, however, would yell at us and say, "Boys, these pages are not funny at all. You can do better than this." And then at the next meeting

Shari would say, "Boys, would you like more donuts?" And then Lamb Chop would say, "We don't do satire. Write better!" Fred and I would sit staring at a screaming puppet as he tore us apart. One evening when we were leaving from a big meeting with Shari and Lamb Chop, Fred said, "We are done. I can't write for a piece of cloth any longer." I agreed.

Still, I remained on the fence for a few weeks. I needed more information before I would make the move to California for a new job. So I consulted some other people for advice. Our agent, Frank Cooper, said "Definitely." He said the future was in sitcom and sitcom was in television, so we should make the move. My own father said I should go because the future was anywhere other than in the Bronx. Jack Paar could have said no because he had us locked into a contract, but he let us out of our contract and told us to head west. He liked Joey and thought we would be a good fit to fix the new sitcom.

The night when everything changed was when we met Phil Foster at the Latin Quarter. Fred and I went right up to the maître d', and he asked us if we had a reservation. We said no and then sheepishly went to sit in a dark corner to wait for Phil. It was a fancy club and we felt uncomfortable. When Phil arrived he was mad that we were hiding. He thought we should be sitting at a good table. So he chewed the waiter out.

"Do you know who those two men are?" asked Phil, pointing toward us.

"No," said the maître d'.

"That's Garry Marshall and Fred Freeman," said Phil.

"I still don't know who they are," said the maître d'.

"That's why you're still a waiter," said Phil.

It was the nicest thing anyone has ever said for me. If Phil had that kind of confidence in us, I thought, then we should have it in ourselves.

We finally moved to Los Angeles in the fall of 1961. Joey said he would pay us two hundred dollars a week for six months, and that's as far as I planned.

There was only one slight catch: I had a girlfriend I had met while writing for *The Tonight Show,* a singer named Ann Merendino.

A sultry, chestnut-haired Italian girl, Ann was an only child, and she sang in our band. I was never very good at dating, and the fact that she was nice and didn't have any money made me think we should get married. She got excited and planned a gigantic wedding with 400 people. My friend Bob Brunner was also dating a girl named Ann, and they were planning to get married, too. So I told my Ann as well as Bob and his Ann that I would go to California for a little while and then when I came back we would have a double wedding. Little did I know that I would never move back to New York. I called Ann a few months later, and we agreed marriage was not for us and called the engagement and the wedding off.

In November 1961, Fred and I ate Thanksgiving turkey at Schwab's drugstore restaurant on Sunset Boulevard. I was scared.

"So what if this doesn't work out?" I asked Fred.

"Then we'll find another job," he said.

"But we don't know anyone in Hollywood except Joey," I said.

"It doesn't matter," Fred said.

"Do you think we're as good as those Hollywood writers?" I asked, sharing my fear with Fred for the first time.

"We're going to be better," he said.

"But we don't have the experience yet," I worried.

"That's the point. We're going to learn from the guys with experience and then teach ourselves to write better than them," he said. "We're going to write for Danny Thomas. We're going to be that good!"

"You are right," I said with new confidence in our writing skills.

The last thing my mother had said to me before I left was "If you get sick from the heat, you can always come home."

5. HOLLYWOOD

★

Finding Love, Laughs,
and Lucy in California

AT FIRST, I FELT like Los Angeles was all a dream. I didn't unpack my suitcase for at least a month for fear the job wouldn't work out. I started to take pictures of every star I met. Joey Bishop. Abby Dalton. Milton Berle. Jack Benny. Zsa Zsa Gabor. I had a plan that if our sitcom got canceled and we were out of work I could open a restaurant and put these pictures of the stars on the walls to attract patrons. That, of course, was a pipe dream because I didn't know how to cook and had no vocation for business. But still, I sent the pictures home to my parents because I wanted my mom to be proud of me and tell her friends on the Grand Concourse that her son had amounted to something. "My son, the show biz writer, lives in Hollywood," she would tell the people in our basement laundry room.

Fred remained the confident one while I worried quietly. Fred and I began our staff writing job on *The Joey Bishop Show* in December 1961. We rented separate apartments; mine was just a short bus ride away from the Desilu Cahuenga Studios. I found Los Angeles a strange place because you couldn't walk anywhere. In New York everybody walked, but in Los Angeles, I had to learn how to take the bus while I saved money to buy a car. So, as in college, I dated only girls who knew how to drive and had cars. One night I went out with a girl and we parked her car near my house. I leaned over and blew in her ear. She freaked out.

"What's wrong?" I asked.

"Ouch!" she said.

"What did I do? You don't like it when a guy blows in your ear?"

"I have a hearing aid," she said.

Who knew? The relationship didn't last long even though she was a nice girl with a good car.

Jumping into the writing staff of a struggling sitcom is never an easy job. We had to quickly get up to speed on the characters, as well as on the politics between the writers and producers. The most important information we learned was that producers Danny Thomas and Sheldon Leonard were the most powerful people on the lot. Danny was a devout Catholic of Lebanese decent, and Sheldon was an intimidating man and an impeccable dresser. If they didn't like you, your job there was history. If they liked your work and your personality, they would open doors to greater things for you. I was nervous that people in Hollywood wouldn't like me because of my heavy Bronx accent. But the day I met Sheldon Leonard I realized he spoke just like me. When we had a conversation, we sounded like two New York gangsters. He liked me from the start.

It was pretty clear that *The Joey Bishop Show* was not going to be on the air forever. So Fred and I quickly started looking around to see what other shows we might be able to write for. We decided that our goal should be *The Dick Van Dyke Show,* which starred Dick and Mary Tyler Moore. However, the show's producer Carl Reiner knew us from New York and had us pegged as punch-up writers and joke meisters. Carl didn't know yet that we could write a solid story. So Fred and I had to find a way to convince Carl that we could write big jokes as well as strong plots for the show. Carl was a fatherly type with an original mind. He could think on his feet better and faster than anyone I had ever seen.

In the meantime we stayed on Joey's sitcom and traveled with him to Las Vegas when he opened at the Sands Hotel for Frank Sinatra. We made friends with Sinatra's conductor, the young and talented Quincy Jones. Quincy said he wanted to compose music for sitcoms and we should remember his name if we ever had our own shows. I couldn't imagine back then being the show runner of my own show. When I looked at Danny Thomas and Sheldon Leonard, I saw an inner confidence and wisdom that I had not yet developed. Inside I still felt like a wisecracking, fast-talking kid from the Bronx who might eat something I was allergic to and at any minute be rushed to the hospital.

I was, however, always good at recognizing an opportunity for humor. That was the case the night Fred and I went to a cast party on the Desilu lot. The party was held in the commissary, and writers from all the different shows stood up and told jokes. Fred and I knew the writing team of Bill Persky and Sam Denoff and a few other writers, but most of the people in the room were strangers to us, so it was intimidating. But I stood up and took the mike. There was a head chef named Hal who ran the kitchen where we usually ate lunch. Day after day he wore an apron that looked like it was covered in blood. That night I said, "Hal was going to be here tonight, but he couldn't make it. He's in Mexico, where they are having a cockfight on his apron." That single joke brought down the house. I looked over and saw even Carl Reiner laughing. Months later writers and producers would come up to me and say, "You wrote that joke about Hal's apron. Funny!"

During our first year writing for Joey Bishop began to take its toll on us. Fred and Joey would fight. Fred wanted more respect. Joey never had the highest respect for writers, so they were constantly getting into battles. One night Fred was explaining to Joey that we needed to strengthen the "protagonist" in the show to make him more compelling. Fred went on to define the word *protagonist* when it seemed clear Joey didn't know what it meant. The fact that Fred was talking down to Joey made the star come completely unglued.

"If you don't like it here, then get out," said Joey.

Fred said "fine" and quit on the spot. I was stuck. Should I quit, too, in solidarity with my partner? In truth I didn't want to quit. I was starting to like California, and I was just beginning to date a girl named Barbara Sue Wells, who worked as a nurse at Cedars of Lebanon Hospital and happened to live in my apartment building. Barbara was a long-legged very pretty Midwestern girl with the warmest smile I had ever seen. But I didn't know what it would be like to write a sitcom without Fred. I weighed the pros and cons. I didn't want to move back to New York and write for *The Tonight Show* anymore. And I certainly didn't have a future back at the *Daily News*. So Fred and I talked. He said it was okay to stay in California and find another writing partner. I said goodbye to Fred, and he moved back to New York and got a job on *The Jackie Gleason Show*.

Joey hired me to keep writing scripts for him and paid me more money. Milt Josefsberg took over as head writer on the show and Milt liked me. So I was on my own in Hollywood, without a partner but with a steady paycheck. Fred and I had been paid $300 a week, which we split. After he left I got the entire $300. I tried writing alone for a while, but I didn't feel as productive. So I took $150 of my money and hired two writers I liked to create a team. That's how Dale McRaven and Carl Kleinschmitt joined the staff of *The Joey Bishop Show*. Dale was a hippie with a long black beard, so he sort of stood out from the rest of us. Carl, on the other hand, was a redneck political speechwriter who wrote for both Democrats and Republicans.

After they'd been on the show for eleven weeks, Joey called me into his office to ask me about Dale and Carl.

"Who are those two kids hanging around the writers' table?" he asked.

"McRaven and Kleinschmitt," I said. "They help punch up the show."

"Who pays them?" he asked.

"I do," I said.

"With what?"

"You give me three hundred dollars a week, and I pay them one fifty of that money. It's worth it because they make the show better."

Joey said I didn't have to pay them anymore and he would put them on staff. But Dale's long black beard still made Joey nervous.

"That kid looks like a hippie," Joey said to me one day.

"He is a hippie. But he's a good writer, too," I said.

"Have him shave his beard," said Joey.

At the next writers' meeting I told Dale he had to shave his beard. Later that night Barbara was hanging out at my apartment and we heard a loud bang on the door. Barbara was afraid, and I was, too. But I opened the door to find an envelope pinned to it with a knife. I took out the knife and opened the envelope. Inside was Dale's shaved beard. He was giving me the proof that he had conformed to Joey's clean-cut look. I thought it was pretty funny, but my girlfriend was not amused. "It is hard to date someone who has hippies throwing knives at his door in the middle of the night," she told me. Barbara later became good friends with Dale, but it was clear I needed a new partner at the time. I called the first person I could think of who might know someone.

"Gordon, hi. It's Garry Marshall. Remember, from Korea?"

"Garry. Yes! How are you?"

"Remember you said you had a funny brother?"

"Yes. Jerry. But not adopted."

"When can I meet him?" I laughed.

I met Jerry Belson the next weekend. He was four years younger than I was. He had never been to college, and had never seen a stage play. But he had a darker, hipper sense of humor, which complimented my upbeat one. Jerry was a smiling, out-of-shape ex–fat kid with one of the most brilliant comedy minds I had ever met. I talked to Sheldon Leonard, who was in charge of all the shows under the Danny Thomas umbrella, and told him about my new partner. Sheldon knew that Joey Bishop was a tough person to write for and he admired me for sticking with Joey and his show. So he gave Jerry and me a script to write on *The Danny Thomas Show*.

Our first script for *The Danny Thomas Show* was about his daughter Linda developing a crush on a boy we named Wendell Henderson. She liked him so much that she would scrape the dirt off his Little League cleats and keep it in her room. The script was successful, so Jerry and I formed our own production company and called it Wendell Henderson. (Years later when we split up, Jerry took Wendell and I became Henderson Productions, which I remain to this day.) Jerry was a great partner because he was so productive and driven. When I got a good idea it was usually my third or fourth try. But with Jerry the first words out of his mouth were often the funniest of the day. I liked that we worked differently. Sheldon recognized our compatibility, too, and gave us another script, this time on *The Bill Dana Show*. After that the work did not stop coming our way.

Writing for these shows gave us the chance to get to know stars like Danny Thomas. Danny was an odd fellow. He was a great comedian who excelled by telling funny stories rather than punch lines. He was folksy in a family way, like Bill Cosby later was on his television show. Danny was also the most religious comedian we ever worked for and a legend for his charity in founding the St. Jude Children's Research Hospital. One day he invited Jerry and me to his home and showed us his beautiful swimming pool. At the end of the pool was a statue of Jesus. Jerry said, "Well, you have a good lifeguard, Danny." I chuckled inside, but Danny didn't laugh at all. We never joked again about religion around him. He was gracious and sweet and always so good to writers. But he was complex in a way that we sometimes couldn't understand. One night we went to a charity event with him in a kind of seedy neighborhood of Los Angeles. He lifted his pant leg to zip up his boot, and we saw a gun sticking out.

"Danny, you carry a gun?" I asked.

"Always," he said.

"Why?" I asked.

"I do charity work in many neighborhoods that aren't safe. You have to protect yourself," he said.

It made sense but seemed at the same time incongruous for a religious man to be packing a pistol in his sock.

Danny had a great influence on me because he was such a family man; he had a wife and kids. I wanted that, too. So with my career going so well, I decided that it was time to make a commitment in my personal life. On New Year's Eve, 1963, I became engaged. On March 9, 1963, I married Barbara Sue Wells, whom I had been dating for over a year. We were a perfect match. I was a sick hypochondriac and she was a nurse. Originally from Cincinnati, she had moved to California in 1961, after another boy left her standing at the altar. She and her friend Donna Parmer both worked at Cedars, and before they started making money they would eat the patients' pudding and custard in the hospital refrigerator just to save money. When you went over to their apartment, they would serve it to guests.

We got married in Las Vegas. We didn't have enough money to fly our parents out, so we just invited our California friends. My father and her mother were mad about the fact we did not include them. Her father was fine with it and wished us well. My mother was only disappointed I didn't marry a doctor, but I told her a nurse would take care of me just as well.

Our best man was Tom Kuhn, and Donna Parmer was our maid of honor. They were dating, and they were the ones who'd introduced us. Joey Bishop paid for our hotel room at the Sands, and Phil Foster paid for us to see a show. We paid for the rest of the wedding. Our wedding party included about twenty people altogether. To us it was perfect, but to our parents, to have their two oldest children get married without them in attendance was an eternal disappointment. We didn't have time or money for a honeymoon, and on Monday morning we were both back at work.

Now that I was married, my job, salary, and responsibilities were carried to a whole new level. When Milt Josefsberg was head writer on *The Joey Bishop Show,* he was very generous to me. He gave me the credit as "script consultant" every sixth show. He taught me everything he had learned from writing for Jack Benny. Then one day, seemingly out of the blue, Joey fired Milt. I couldn't imagine why Joey would do such a thing, but again, he asked me to stick around. Joey was very combative with other people, but not with me. So I brought in Jerry Belson, and together we wrote scripts for Joey. Just when I was starting to really make a living, my mother and my blind grandmother moved to California. My mother had not gotten along with my father for years, and she heard that California had some nice retirement homes for the blind, where Nanny could live for next to nothing. They arrived shortly after Barbara and I got married. Unfortunately for my mother, my dad followed her out west a few months later. I told them I could help them out with rent, but I didn't have enough money for them to have separate apartments. So they would have to find a way to live together. My mother joined a group called Mothers of the Stars and made fast friends with Lucille Ball's mother and Carol Burnett's mother.

In December 1963, my wife gave birth to our first child, Lorraine Gay Marshall. The night before the baby was born I stayed up writing a charity skit for Lucille Ball. I remember thinking that now that I was going to be a father, I needed to step up the pace and work harder than ever. I was responsible for a wife and a daughter, and writing for Lucy seemed like the steady dad kind of job I should have. But again you couldn't just send in your résumé and get a job on these shows. You had to prove yourself and be handpicked by either the star or the producer. And luckily, Milt Josefsberg liked me and was running Lucy's show.

Milt had landed as head writer on *The Lucy Show*. Immediately he called and asked if Jerry and I could write some episodes, and we jumped at the chance. At the time we wrote for Lucille Ball, she was divorced from Desi Arnaz and married to Gary Morton. Gary was a comedian we had met before; he showed us his closet, in which he had over a hundred pairs of shoes. I couldn't imagine wanting or needing that many shoes, but Gary acted like it was a dream come true. When we wrote scripts for Lucy, she was funny and talented but sometimes also difficult and hard to please. She was at a vulnerable point in her career because she had never run a show without Desi. So I think part of her wanted to appear tough, and the other part was scared and ambivalent about being the boss. I was fortunate that she remembered me.

"Garry, you're the one who wrote that funny skit for me at the Writers Guild charity event last year," she said.

She was right. I wrote that script for no money because I hoped the more I wrote for charity the more people would know my work and hire me. My plan had clearly worked with Lucy. However, the first script Jerry and I wrote for her didn't go over as well. She wrote on the front cover THIS IS SHIT and gave it right back to us. Jerry and I were in shock. We had wanted to please Lucy and had ended up offending her in some way. Milt told us not to worry. Sometimes the pressure of running her own show made Lucy cranky. So we rewrote the script with a fresh cover, and she liked the second draft.

We quickly learned the key to writing for Lucy: start with a funny situation and then build the whole script toward it. We wrote the episode in which Lucy ended up at a fancy banquet wearing a ball gown with roller skates. As the story went, her feet were swollen and she couldn't get the roller skates off. The script called for her to go through a reception line with the roller skates on. During rehearsals she crashed into a row of waiters. The sight of this threw Jerry and me into a complete panic. He said, "Do you think we've killed Lucy?" But she quickly got up and dusted herself off as we ran over to apologize. "No. No. I'm fine," she said. "It was my fault. Keep writing this kind of script and I'll keep going at it." She was brave and strong, and she could tell what was funny and what would fail. She didn't care so much about plot; she wanted that big comedy scene that fans would remember, so that's what we gave her.

As much as we liked writing for Lucy, we still wanted to break into *The Dick Van Dyke Show,* because it was a classier show. We were going to leave Lucy completely, but Milt cautioned me. "You have a daughter now, Garry. You need security. Writing for Lucy is like taking out an insurance policy. Lucy's shows are going to run forever."

Milt was right. Residuals were the new way to make money, and he knew Lucy would be a residual gold mine. So instead of six scripts for Lucy that year we wrote three, and at the same time we wrote episodes for *The Dick Van Dyke Show.* Writing for Van Dyke was not always easy either. We broke into the show by doing scripts for Mary Tyler Moore because the veteran writers only wanted to write for Dick. But one of our first scripts Mary read she threw across the room, nearly hitting us in the heads. It turned out it wasn't so much that she didn't like the script as it was that she was trying to quit smoking. Jerry and I learned early on that you can't take stars' anger personally. You have to write and rewrite until you can make them smile instead of scream.

While I was busy working my sisters were both having a hard time. Ronny had three little girls and had decided to divorce and leave her husband back in Illinois. She came out to California with her daughters. As if that wasn't enough, Penny arrived from New

Mexico with a baby and no husband. So in one year my entire family moved to California and I was the only one working. I felt pressure and shared it with Jerry. We stayed up late into the night writing scripts. He took pills and smoked pot, and I ate Fig Newtons and Oreos.

Shortly after, Jerry got divorced and had to pay alimony. So we had to make even more money. We decided to write some scripts using pseudonyms. I became Samuro Mitsubi, and Jerry was Tawasaki Kwai. We took the names because our agent said we were too big to write under our own names for so many shows. He wanted us to remain in high demand for the top-rated shows.

Whenever someone asked us to write a script, we said yes. Sometimes we had ten scripts going at once. We even ghostwrote other people's scripts and they would pay us cash in brown paper bags. Later on when my wife was making dinner I would put four hundred-dollar bills underneath her dinner plate. All through dinner the baby and I would wait for her to lift up the plate and then laugh out loud. We were a team in demand. By the end of the 1963 television season, Belson and Marshall (using our real names) had written thirty-one produced sitcom scripts, which was more than any team had ever written before. After writing that many scripts, when my hands weren't typing, they were shaking with exhaustion. And that is when I looked at my wife and baby girl and said, "We need to take a break or I could die."

We decided to move to Palm Springs, just two hours south of Los Angeles. I didn't know how long we would be there, I just knew I had to go someplace and rest. Barbara had quit her nursing job right before the baby was born, so it was easy for us to pack up for a while. We rented a small house with a swimming pool, and friends from Los Angeles, including my parents and sisters, would visit us on the weekends. I decided I wanted to write a play about my mother and how she was never able to fulfill her dreams professionally or personally. I called that play *Shelves,* and after I finished it I put it in a drawer. I didn't know if I was ever going to do anything with it, I was just happy I had written it. After six months of swimming, sleeping, eating, and pushing my daughter's baby carriage along the streets of Palm Springs, I felt rejuvenated. That's when I got the call from Jerry.

"Garry, we sold a pilot," he said.

"*Hey Landlord!*" I asked.

"Yes. The network wants us to executive-produce it. Can you come back?" he said.

"We're packing up now," I said.

So Barbara, Lori, and I headed back from Palm Springs to produce my first television series. Sheldon Leonard had told me that, to be successful, Jerry and I needed to create our own series so we could own a piece of it. Having our own show also allowed us to give other people writing, producing, and directing jobs. It was a watershed moment in my career because as one of the producers of the show, I was allowed to hire myself as one of the directors, too. I had never directed anything aside from my home movies, but I had learned from watching others. Our first director on the show was John Rich, a well-known television director who had done episodes of everything from *The Twilight Zone* to *Mr. Ed.* John was one of my early directing mentors. But he soon got another job, so we hired Jerry Paris, who had been an actor and director on *The Dick Van Dyke Show.* Jerry took me under his wing and taught me everything he knew about directing.

Hey Landlord! starred Sandy Baron, Will Hutchins, and Michael Constantine. The NBC series premiered in 1966, after it took us more than a year to develop, write the scripts, and cast the show. *Hey Landlord!* was about a young man from Ohio who inherits a New York brownstone from his uncle, then shares it with a stand-up comedian. To write the show we hired people we knew—Arnold Margolin, Dale McRaven, Carl Kleinschmitt—and young actors, Richard Dreyfuss and Rob Reiner, who was Carl's son. We used to see Rob hanging around the set of *The Dick Van Dyke Show* and thought he was funny, in a dark and hippie comedic sort of way. Once we were able to hire Quincy Jones to do the music for *Hey Landlord!,* we were on top of the world.

With Danny Thomas and Sheldon Leonard as our producers, we thought we had all the makings of a hit sitcom. While the scripts were funny, Sandy and Will didn't have the experience to carry a whole show. Only Michael Constantine got big laughs, and his was a small part. One night Will was appearing in a musical and Jerry and I were supposed to attend to be supportive. But on our way out the door our daughter pulled away from the babysitter and ran after us. She fell and hit her eye on the front door, and we had to take her to the hospital for stitches. When I called Jerry at intermission from the emergency room to tell him our daughter had fallen and needed stitches, he said, "You're having more fun than me." The show was canceled after one year, but we didn't regret getting our feet wet. It was a lesson in how to be show runners, and Jerry and I had a lot to learn. I found it similar to being the captain of a baseball team. People's feelings got hurt, but at the end of the day the buck stopped with me and I was fine with it, or at least secure.

Then, the final ratings came out; we were ninety-ninth out of a hundred shows. I clipped the ratings from the newspaper and kept them in my wallet to remind myself that I had no place to go but up. Failure wasn't going to ruin my career just yet. It made me a little sad and depressed, the same way I felt when Lucy wrote THIS IS SHIT on our first script for her. But I knew from that experience there was no need to dwell. We just had to write and rewrite something new.

Jerry and I next created a television movie called *Evil Roy Slade,* the tale of a notoriously mean villain in the Wild West who tries to give up his life of crime when he falls in love with a schoolteacher. While *Evil Roy Slade* got a great review in *Life* magazine, we were unable to sell it as a television pilot called *Sheriff Who?* Once again we were at a crossroads. What should we do next?

We decided to write a few comedy specials for Danny Thomas's company. One was called *The Road to Lebanon,* and the other was called *It's Greek to Me.* When we handed in the specials Danny wasn't totally happy with them, and he asked for a lot of rewriting. Jerry and I were grumbling about the rewrites one day in the writers' room, where there were coffee and donuts. An old writer, Harry Crane, heard us complaining. He came over, took my face and Jerry's face, and pushed them together.

"Look out the window, boys," Harry said. "There are men

outside wearing hard hats. You could be outside wearing hard hats and working in hundred-degree heat. Instead you're inside with air-conditioning, donuts, and coffee. So shut up. Do the rewrite and stop complaining!"

Jerry and I exchanged a quick look of recognition and headed right back to our typewriters.

My wife and I wanted to have another baby, but we were having trouble getting pregnant. So we took our daughter, Lori, to Ohio to stay with Barbara's parents and we went to England and Ireland for a month and came back pregnant. Europe gave us fertility. With a second baby on the way, I felt the need to get back to work right away, so Jerry and I moved into the movie business. If we could produce a television series, we thought we could produce a movie, too. How different could they be? The first movie we produced was called *How Sweet It Is!* and starred James Garner and Debbie Reynolds. The film was bankrolled by a company called National General. It was a fluffy romantic comedy about a professional photographer who takes his wife and hippie son on a work assignment in Paris. We hired Jerry Paris to direct.

There were so many differences between writing for a television show and writing for a movie. We got paid $3,500 per episode for a television script, and $75,000 for our movie script. When we wrote for television we had to answer to producers and show runners. But on *How Sweet It Is!* we were the writers as well as the producers, so Jerry and I had to learn to step up and be bosses. On television we worked during the day and worked late only on the nights we shot the shows. On the movie, however, we seemed to be working all day and night. The pace was tiring but also invigorating for us creatively.

My wife gave birth to our second daughter, Kathleen Susan, on December 16, 1967. On January 17, 1969, following the release of *How Sweet It Is!* our son, Scott Anthony, was born. All three of our kids were conceived in the late spring, typically hiatus time for television, which makes sense because there isn't a lot of time for making babies during the regular season.

Jerry and I liked the experience on *How Sweet It Is!* even though the picture wasn't a hit. So we approached National General about making another movie. The script was called *The Grasshopper* and starred a very young Jacqueline Bisset and the former football player Jim Brown. It was a tale about a nineteen-year-old girl from Canada who lands in Las Vegas, becomes a showgirl, and falls into a relationship with a former NFL player. While Jerry Paris wanted to direct the movie, we decided we wanted to go with a more famous and edgier director, someone who had more clout and more movies under his belt. So we hired Don Medford.

There was trouble from the start. Every time we got ready to start, he said he needed another week to prepare. After five weeks National General said we had to fire Don. Jerry and I were nervous wrecks because we had never fired anyone before. I don't love confrontations, but I learned to deal with them. After we broke the news to Don, we left in a hurry. I realized when we reached his apartment lobby that I had forgotten my glasses; we didn't dare go back. It was easier for me to buy a new pair.

We knew we had made a big mistake, and we wanted to get Jerry Paris back. However, Jerry was in Italy with his wife and three kids. My wife thought it was very poor taste to call and interrupt his family vacation, but we felt we had no choice, and Jerry was the only director we knew. So we called him in a remote village in Italy and explained our problem. He left his wife and kids and jumped on the first plane out. Two days later he was on our set as the new director. He said his family understood.

The movie was plagued with production problems from day one. One day my wife brought all three kids to the set, and things were behind schedule.

"Garry, the kids can't stay all day. When are you going to start?" asked Barbara.

"As soon as I get my star out of jail," I said.

"What?"

"Jim Brown had an altercation with his girlfriend. I have to go and bail him out." Jim was not a bad guy. He was just going through a rough time.

Despite our hard work *The Grasshopper* got mixed reviews. But

I was still proud of what we had done. I liked movies. The problem was that making movies seemed like a bad fit for a dad. The kids had events at school and activities after school that I was unable to attend because I had to be on location. So my mind started drifting back to television. Working as a television producer and show runner seemed much better for a father of three.

In 1969 Jerry and I got a call from Paramount and ABC to produce *The Odd Couple* for television. I remembered what Sheldon Leonard had told me a few years earlier. "Write your own shows, boys. That's where the money is." But Jerry had stomach problems, and he didn't like the idea of doing a weekly sitcom. He wanted to pursue movies. Still, I convinced him that now that we both had kids, television was where we wanted to be. So we became the producers of *The Odd Couple*. It would mark the first sitcom hit of my career as a producer. The day we reported for work we opened the newspaper and found out that Neil Simon was furious that we were making a television show of his play. It was not the best news to get on your first day of a new show, particularly because we both idolized Neil Simon.

6. THE ODD COUPLE

*

Running My First TV Show with Oscar and Felix

THE YEAR WAS 1970, and I found myself, along with my writing partner, Jerry Belson, the producer of ABC's much anticipated new comedy *The Odd Couple*. This show took me from being a producer of pop art to being the critics' delight. Not only was *The Odd Couple* my first critically acclaimed show but it also made me the envy of other television producers. Holding a job that others desired made me almost overnight someone people wanted to talk to and work with on other projects in development. One well-respected show, and suddenly I was a player in show business. To this day when I tell people I produced *The Odd Couple,* they are impressed, which always makes me smile inside because it was a show that impressed me, too.

People are also amazed that I produced *The Odd Couple* when I was only thirty-six years old. Barbara and I had bought our first house, in the San Fernando Valley community of Toluca Lake. The single-level home, on a corner with a broad front yard, cost $50,000. We were looking for something in the $35,000 to $38,000 range, but we just fell in love with this house on Arcola Avenue. Bob Hope and his wife lived across the street, and I thought living across the street from a comedy legend would be lucky. Also, my new office at Paramount was just a short freeway hop away. I loved the neighborhood's small-town feel and was comfortable buying a house because my career was finally taking off. Some of my friends were buying houses in Brentwood, Westwood, and other cities on the Westside.

But those neighborhoods were not for us. Barbara and I were both low-key, low-maintenance people, and Toluca Lake seemed like a great place to raise children. After we moved in I would take my three kids to the local miniature golf course on Riverside Drive and teach them to hit golf balls just as my dad had taught me.

It also was an exciting time because on *The Odd Couple* I was finally the boss. When I was working for Joey Bishop, Danny Thomas, and Lucille Ball, I was always a "writer for hire" and told what to do. But on *The Odd Couple,* I was the producer and show runner, equivalent to my mentor the great Sheldon Leonard. Producing *Hey Landlord!* had merely been a test drive in producing television. *The Odd Couple* was, from anyone's vantage point, the big leagues. Would I make it? Or would I fail? And if I failed, where would I go? Could I pay my mortgage on the new house? On the first day of shooting that summer in 1970, all I knew was that Neil Simon was telling the press how much he hated the show. It was not the best way to kick off a new TV series.

Neil was mad because he'd gotten a raw deal from Paramount. The studio had given him money to do *The Odd Couple* as a Broadway play and movie but had stiffed him on the television rights. Neil had no creative control over the project, and we felt bad that he was getting the short stick. However, Jerry and I didn't feel bad enough to turn down the job of running and developing our first major television series. Neil had done the hard part of creating well-written and complex comedic characters that we knew would translate well to the small screen. There was no need for us to improve on his finicky Felix Unger and messy Oscar Madison. The ever-bickering duo were the picture-perfect tribute to male friendships everywhere. At first the challenge for us as producers was not further character development, but casting.

The studio pitched Jerry and me some possible combinations: Martin Balsam and Eddie Bracken, and Dean Martin and Mickey Rooney. But no combination seemed up to snuff compared to Walter Matthau and Jack Lemmon, who had done the movie. We needed to get closer to Matthau and Lemmon. I remembered an actor I had seen opposite Ethel Merman in the Broadway production of *Gypsy*.

He played the stage manager, and basically for two hours Merman sang loudly and sprayed saliva on him while he faced her with his back to the audience. At the end of the show the people in the audience were in love with him. I had never seen such stage presence before, nor a more expressive, regular-kind-of-guy face. I asked the casting department at Paramount to find Jack Klugman, and they sent me a man named Jack Kruschen, who had a mustache.

While Klugman and Kruschen are similar names, the appeal didn't compare and only one had a mustache. So when Klugman finally came into my office, I knew I had my Oscar. He had what you need more than anything else in television—likability. Audiences would want Jack Klugman to walk into their living rooms once a week. Finding our Felix was not as difficult. Tony Randall had been in dozens of films and was known for his comedy timing and elegance. We had to convince Tony to move to Los Angeles from New York in order to shoot the show. But once he agreed to move we had our cast. Tony and Jack were reluctant to step into Matthau's and Lemmon's shoes, though. Who wouldn't be? We convinced them we would protect them and not let them fail. Who knew if that was true? But Jerry and I were optimistic and eager to get the show off the ground, so we promised whatever it took. Jack was a man's man with crumpled clothing. Tony was an opera-loving guy with a suit and tie. They were both leery of us and it turns out each other.

We shot the opening title sequence in the streets of New York because the show was a love letter to the city itself and its people, the finicky ones, the messy ones, and everyone in between. As we set up the shots I saw that fans already recognized the stars, particularly Jack, whom many knew from *Gypsy*. I could see it was hard for Jack and Tony to concentrate with so many spectators. So for the setup of the shots, I ordered a limousine where they could sit together and wait. A few minutes after they went into the limousine, Jack came out of one door, and Tony came out of the other door, and both said almost simultaneously, "I can't work with him." I quickly figured out the problem. Jack liked to smoke cigarettes, and Tony was allergic to smoke. In my mind this was not a reason to cancel an entire series before it got off the ground. I simply got a second limousine so they would never have to share air space again. This is what a producer learns to do best: solve problems quickly by throwing money at them. The less money you throw at a problem, the better producer you are.

The casting was perfect because Jack's and Tony's personalities were quite similar to those of the characters they played. Today some people even consider them the finest *Odd Couple* casting of all because they nurtured, developed, and embodied these roles over five years. In TV life and real life Jack liked racehorses, gambling, women, and smoky bars. Tony liked opera, ballet, New York City, and the finer things in life. Jack had an ex-wife and two kids in Los Angeles whom he was very close to. Tony had no children and a wife who lived in New York. The bottom line is that Jack was a messy gambler and Tony was a finicky neat freak.

Their acting styles also were completely different. Tony would ask for changes in the script when he knew something would make it better and stronger. He liked saying, "Change this!" and having us listen to him. In his previous film work—such as *Pillow Talk* and *Send Me No Flowers*—stars Rock Hudson and Doris Day had always said "Change this!" and the director or writer would accommodate them. Tony was just a supporting actor in those films, so he didn't have the same clout. In *The Odd Couple,* Tony was the star, and he liked the power that came with that new role. Jack, on the other hand, simply needed to know what his character "wanted" in every scene. Once he had his motivation Jack asked for little else. Plus you could get any line or joke past Jack if you pitched it to him at 3:45 P.M. because by 4:00 he would be out the door to listen to the racetrack results on the radio. He would come back on the set afterward, and his head would be right back into work.

The first season we shot the show without a live audience, but Tony didn't like it that way, and neither did I. He desperately wanted us to shoot in front of a live audience, which some sitcoms at the time were doing. He found the canned laughter grating, like nails on a chalkboard. We agreed that a live audience would make the show stronger because the laughter would be more spontaneous and genuine, but nobody listened to us. Paramount wasn't rushing to spend extra money to accommodate a live audience on our sound-stage. So Tony decided to take matters into his own hands. He went on Johnny Carson's *Tonight Show* and asked viewers to write in to Paramount and tell them to get rid of the canned laughter on *The Odd Couple*. He said, "If you all write letters, Paramount will listen." And he was right. Shortly after that *Tonight Show* aired, people began to write letters to Paramount asking for the change in format. From the second season on we always filmed in front of an audience, and I think in everyone's opinion it was a better show. The audience could act as a referee between Tony and Jack and me. Having a live audience is a quicker and more definitive way to find out what is funny and what is not.

While Tony liked a live audience, he didn't like live children. He found children a distraction when he was working. Each week we had two run-throughs. One was at 4:30 P.M. and kids could come, and the other one was at night, for adults only. Tony didn't think that kids should be allowed to attend either. He hated the 4:30 one, so we even tried to limit the number of kids in attendance. Whenever my own three children came to visit the set, we hid them under the audience bleachers so Tony wouldn't see them. For the entire run of the show my children were in fear of Tony discovering their secret location and being thrown off the lot. (It is ironic that many years later Tony had two children with his second wife, Heather, and seemed to love every second he had with them.) My daughter Lori later appeared in an episode called "That Is the Army, Mrs. Madison," in which we see Oscar marry his wife, Blanche, through a series of flashbacks. Every day at the rehearsals Lori would dodge around the set trying not to make eye contact with Tony for fear he would fire her. But deep down he was the sweetest of men.

The thing about producing your own television series is that things can go wrong and you have to learn to fix them on the spot. In an episode called "I'm Dying of Unger," the scene was falling flat. The lines were fine, but the comedy wasn't popping. I suggested that Tony and Jack do the scene again, exactly as written. But I added a twist: I had Murray the cop put his nose through the peephole of Oscar and Felix's door. Felix saw the nose and instantly knew who was on the other side. The scene suddenly got laughs and all our problems were solved. Learning to punch up a scene is sometimes as important as writing the scene to begin with, and I learned that from Carl Reiner on *The Dick Van Dyke Show*.

I always try to be sensitive to what the actors think of the material because they are the ones who have to say the lines and performing is a difficult job. Tony got upset about the script called "The Subway Story." He said it was the worst thing he had ever read. I was confused because I'd supervised the script and thought it was funny. So I called up Tony's agent and asked if there was a problem. He explained that Tony didn't like the script because it was about a subway robbery and it made New York seem unsafe. New York City had just appointed Tony spokesman for a new publicity campaign to make it desirable for tourists. He worried that our episode presented a conflict. He didn't think I would have time to change the script. But what he didn't realize is that the way I work, I always have time to change a script when necessary. So the writers and I rewrote it to make Tony more comfortable and make New York the hero in the story.

In that same episode another problem came up suddenly. Gavin MacLeod (who later played Captain Stubing on *The Love Boat*) had an attack of appendicitis the Thursday night before the Friday shoot. We didn't have time to cast another actor, so I decided to jump in. I had acted from time to time in the shows on the Desilu lot, including hiring myself as an actor on *Hey Landlord!* I thought it was important to be in the Screen Actors Guild as well as the Writers Guild so I would have another job to fall back on. Plus, I had a New York accent, which was what the character needed. Writer-producer Milt Josefsberg had been out of work for six years after *The Jack Benny Show,* and I didn't ever want to face a situation like that. With a wife, kids, and a mortgage to pay, I felt pressure to do as many different jobs as possible so I would never be out of work.

Despite the pressure I felt. I was so proud of the work we did on *The Odd Couple*. It was the quintessential New York show before *Seinfeld*. Although we didn't shoot every day in New York, our show was a tribute to the city we all loved so much and many of us had grown up in. I had been a boy in New York. I had been a struggling stand-up comedian in New York. I had been a soldier in uniform in New York. And now I was producing a prime-time television series about New York. Jack liked it when we could experiment and shoot New York outdoors. There was an episode called "The New Car" in which Oscar and Felix win a car on a radio contest. Oscar wants to sell the car but Felix won't let him, so they decide to keep it and deal with New York City's parking laws. Each morning one of them has to get up and move the car to the other side of the street. So we shot a montage of them moving the car in their pajamas. It was a unique New York episode and very funny as well.

During our five-year run many writers worked on *The Odd Couple*. Jack and Tony were not easy actors to please, and thus it was not an easy show to write for. The head writers sat at the table, and the apprentice writers sat around the outer circle in chairs without desks. I always thought the apprentice writers dreamed of one day being promoted so they could see their names on the credits as writers on *The Odd Couple*. But the truth involved food more than prestige. The head writers got their trays from the commissary and could eat at the table. The apprentice writers had to eat with the trays on their laps. The apprentices dreamed of moving up so they could place their trays on a table. They were motivated to write better so they could eat more comfortably.

One of my favorite writing teams who got their big break on *The Odd Couple* was Lowell Ganz and his partner, Mark Rothman. Lowell was a skinny guy with a brilliant memory. Mark was a tall, outgoing writer who loved gambling. Mark's father was a chauffeur named Abe Rothman, and one day Abe was driving Jack in New York City on a publicity junket. Abe gave Jack some pages of jokes that Mark and Lowell had written. Jack liked the material and sent it to me. Despite the fact that Lowell and Mark were dropouts from Queens College, I liked their material, too. You don't necessarily need a college degree to write comedy. So I flew them out and gave them some work as punch-up writers. They lasted a little while, and then Jack and Tony asked me to fire them, which was sad but not unusual. So I thought we had heard the last from Lowell and Mark.

A few weeks later, however, I was sitting in the live audience watching a run-through when I saw them in the stands, watching the rehearsal.

"Didn't I fire you?" I asked.

"Yes," said Lowell.

"Then what are you doing here?" I asked.

"We have no place else to go," said Mark.

"We don't have enough money to fly back to New York. So we're trying to watch the show and learn how to improve our writing," said Lowell.

I was amazed by their patience and persistence. They eventually wrote another script on spec, and I bought it. Jack and Tony liked the script so much that we rehired them.

I grew closer to Jack and Tony each year. Every Monday the three of us would go to lunch at a Hungarian restaurant on Melrose where Tony loved to eat. Jack was always starving and would eat anything. But with my allergies the only thing I could eat on the menu was eggs. So every Monday while I ate scrambled eggs with toast and they ate more adventurous Hungarian food, we would discuss *The Odd Couple* and where we wanted it to go. Jack wanted athletes and sports announcers to appear as guest stars, while Tony was always trying to get opera stars onto the show. One time he convinced the great opera diva Marilyn Horne to guest-star. I met with Marilyn and asked her what she would like to do on the show. She said ever so sweetly, "I would like to get kissed at the end." In most of her operas she had to die by the final curtain. So in her *Odd Couple* episode she got her kiss from Jack Klugman.

In addition to opera stars, Tony liked pretending to be a lawyer. We had several episodes in which he said lines like "I'm defending myself" or "I'm defending Oscar." He also liked to have a sidebar with the judge and have us write schtick for him—like playing with the judge's gavel. His most well-known courtroom episode of *The Odd Couple* was called "My Strife in Court." In the episode, now even featured on youtube.com, he gives advice to the jury not to "assume" anything because when you "assume" you make an "ass" out of "u" and "me." Another funny thing Tony liked to do was jump onto a desk from the ground. So whenever we didn't have an ending, he would suggest that he jump on a desk, and he was able to do it well into his sixties.

Tony knew when a script was funny and he knew when it was not. He wanted every script to be top-notch. He would give a speech to the writers each year that basically said this: "Soon Jack and I will be at the home for aging actors and there will be people at the home with us. We will invite them into our rooms to see old episodes of *The Odd Couple*. When I'm showing my friends these episodes at the home, I don't want to cringe. I want to be proud and say that we did the best we could do with this show. This was our best work and we are content." Whenever Tony gave this speech we could not help but be inspired. We wanted Tony and Jack to be proud of all of us, and the shows that we were producing and writing. The image of them not cringing at the old people's home always stayed with us.

While the writing for the show improved with each episode, unfortunately, my partner, Jerry Belson, got sicker. For as long as I had known him he'd suffered from ulcers. But as the years went by they got worse and he began to rely on drugs for relief and escape. Sometimes he was so sick that he was unable even to get in the car to drive to our set. When Jerry did show up his comments were always the best and most insightful in the room. But when he wasn't there the responsibility of running the show was on my shoulders. I felt invigorated by the new power, but with each visit Jerry seemed to grow more bored. He was losing interest in the show, in television in general, and had already started talking about going back to movies. I convinced him to hang on, that *The Odd Couple* was a show worth the trouble. As a dad and a father I felt the show was a perfect fit for me, and I didn't want anything or anyone to jeopardize it. I would do double the work if I had to, just for Jerry to remain onboard. However, the thought of producing it alone didn't appeal to me. I knew I always did better work with a partner to bounce ideas off of and be inspired by. I brought in Bob Brunner, my old friend from New York, to be on staff.

Another headache I had on *The Odd Couple* was with my family. They all needed jobs because they now had families. Penny had a daughter, Tracy, and Ronny was a single mom with three daughters:

Penny Lee, Judy, and Wendy. I cast Penny as Jack's nasal secretary, Myrna Turner. Occasionally I would play her brother, Werner Turner. And in one big episode my sister Ronny appeared with us as Verna Turner. In an episode called "The Rain in Spain," we cast Penny's husband, Rob Reiner, as her TV boyfriend Sheldn (a clerk left the *o* off his birth certificate). The first time Penny appeared on *The Odd Couple* as Myrna I could tell she had real talent. She had not done much acting in high school or college, but she was naturally funny on-camera and she was a quick learner. Most of her scenes were with Jack, and he was gracious enough to teach her about acting. Along with Penny my dad became an associate producer on the show, and my mother even appeared as a tap dancer in one episode. This is when I began to make nepotism an acceptable art form.

While I was the boss of the show, my dad could still teach me things because he had a better head for business. He taught me that each episode didn't need to cost the same. If I wanted to spend more money producing an episode, I could do that. I simply had to make another episode in that season for less. The budget had to balance at the end of the season. So I started doing some shows that I called stuck-in shows, which I had first learned about on *The Dick Van Dyke Show*. The stars would get stuck in an elevator and we would save tons of money on building sets for that week. The episode called "Trapped" was the quintessential example of a stuck-in show. In that episode Felix and Oscar and a date were on their way to a costume party when they got trapped in the building's basement. It was great to experiment with smaller-budget and bigger-budget script ideas.

Most of the studio notes we got on *The Odd Couple* were about the lack of women in the show. The executives worried that people might think Oscar and Felix were gay because they didn't have girl-friends or dates in every episode. We used to shoot extra gag footage of Jack and Tony hugging and kissing each other and send it to the network just to agitate them. We were a sophisticated show, but we loved to drive the network suits crazy. In the meantime, behind the scenes, the network and Paramount began to put pressure on me to create other sitcoms while *The Odd Couple* was still on the air.

I wanted to bask in the excitement of being the producer of *The Odd Couple,* but they kept calling me and saying, "What's next?"

I finally gave in to the pressure and created another show, called *The Little People,* with Brian Keith. He played a doctor who worked with his daughter in Hawaii. My motivation for creating the show was twofold. I thought it would make an interesting series, and it would let me take my wife and kids on vacation to Hawaii. My wife supported me in working as hard as I wanted during the television season, but in the off-season she liked us to take family vacations to Carmel Valley, visit her parents in Ohio, or go someplace entirely new, such as Oregon or Canada. We would put the kids in the car, and I would sit in the front seat penciling up scripts of *The Odd Couple* and then *The Little People.* As much as we liked our family vacation to Hawaii, *Little People* was not a hit with television audiences. So the network pressured me to come up with another idea. Network and studio executives said they liked the way I worked. I took care of the stars and relied on diplomacy. I was not arrogant. I was basically sane, and I didn't pick fights with anyone. Plus, I had no ambition to head up a studio or production company. I just wanted to produce a good sitcom every week and go home to my wife and kids.

Another family man was Jerry Paris, whom Tony and Jack liked as a director for *The Odd Couple.* Jerry had directed some episodes of *Hey Landlord!* as well as *How Sweet It Is!* and *The Grasshopper.* I had known him since he was an actor on *The Dick Van Dyke Show,* where he played Jerry Helper, Dick's neighbor and a dentist. He had three children, and his youngest son was the same age as my older daughter. I learned a lot from Jerry because, unlike some of the other people on the lot, he prided himself on being a good dad. It was on *The Odd Couple* that he taught me the basics of how to direct a weekly sitcom. He had a positive energy that seemed to mesmerize the actors. Also, he had a lovely wife, Ruth, who had gone to Northwestern. I used to sit in the stands of the show and watch Jerry direct, taking notes on his choices and on his relationship with the actors.

Directing, however, was still not on my radar because I was so busy writing. I loved the creative excitement of producing *The Odd Couple* and from time to time writing scripts, too. Jerry and I wrote the first episode, "The Laundry Orgy," together, as well as "Oscar the Model," in which an executive insists Felix shoot Oscar's face in a big cologne ad. We had a formula in which we would put Oscar and Felix in different situations to showcase their differences. By myself I wrote the episode "Hospital Mates," in which Felix and Oscar shared a hospital room. Felix was in for nose surgery and Oscar had hurt his knee. Phil Foster, who gave me my start in the comedy writing business, played the doctor. The classic button on the plot was that when Felix and Oscar went home from the hospital, Felix couldn't see because of his bandages and Oscar couldn't walk because of his knee. But still Felix insisted he could hear Oscar flicking cigarette ashes on the carpeting.

Many *Odd Couple* fans have their favorite episodes, whether they be "The New Car," "Let's Make a Deal," "That Is the Army, Mrs. Madison," "Password," "The Ides of April," "It's All Over Now, Baby Bird," or "The Rain in Spain." My favorite is called "The Odd Monks" because I wrote it out of desperation. With my journalism training from Northwestern, I was not a fussy or picky writer, and on TV you need to be on deadline. But after spending so many years writing with Jerry Belson, I worried I might be too lazy to write alone. So sometimes I looked for opportunities to make sure I still could. This episode came at a point in the season when Jack and Tony said they were getting tired of the long, complicated scripts we were giving them. The truth was they didn't want to memorize so many lines. So I offered a compromise. I said, "Everybody take the week off. I'm writing the script this week." In the script Felix and Oscar go to a monastery and have to take a vow of silence. For nearly forty pages there was no dialogue, thus eliminating the need for the two stars to memorize anything. The entire script was based on physical and visual humor, which I had learned from the scripts I had written for Lucille Ball. I think it was not only a funny script but one that varied the rhythm of the show. Sometimes when I watch TV with my wife I'll come across "Odd Monks" on cable, and I have to sit and watch it through to the end. Jack and Tony, in my opinion, knocked that episode out of the ballpark.

Jack and Tony were excellent costars on *The Odd Couple,* but I don't think they were true friends until years later. There was tremendous pressure on them, so there honestly wasn't time for them to just hang out and chat. Even when they were at cocktail parties, they were constantly meeting people and asking them to be on our show. One night Tony went to a party and the next day he said he'd met Allen Ludden and Betty White. So we wrote an episode for them with Jack and Tony called "Password." Aside from the show the only thing Jack and Tony shared back then was an agent named Abner "Abby" Greshler of the Diamond Artists talent agency. When we filmed the show in front of a live audience, we would throw bite-size candies into the bleachers during intermission. Abby was so cheap that at the end of the night he would collect the candy that had fallen through the bleachers and take it home and serve it to guests.

The Odd Couple was never number one in the ratings, but it was always in the top twenty. It won awards and received critical acclaim but was not a ratings superstar. That didn't bother us. After four years we looked toward the fifth season as our last because we just all felt it was time and wanted to do other things. Jack, Tony, and I made a pact at one of our Hungarian Monday lunches that we would leave after five years. Most shows today run much longer, but to us quality was superior to the number of years we wanted to be on the air. I knew it was time for The Odd Couple to come to an end, but I was not ready to leave television. Another producer on the lot, Tom Miller, and Michael Eisner, who ran Paramount, and I had an idea about a show that took place in the 1950s. They thought I should pursue it. It was about young people, and I thought that sounded like a good show to follow The Odd Couple. I had done a show about older men, now it was time to tackle youth.

As it came time to film the final episode of The Odd Couple, in the spring of 1975, we performed a prank. Early on we all took an oath never to do any spitting in the show. Comedians on television shows often did "spit takes" to get an easy laugh. So we vowed to take the more sophisticated road. For 114 episodes no one on The Odd Couple spat. But the last show we shot a series of outtakes in which we did a salute to the spit take. It was a montage of Tony, Jack, and other cast and crew members spitting when a funny line was said. It was one of the funnier behind-the-scene things we did as a cast and crew.

During *The Odd Couple* my daughter Lori attended the Westlake School for Girls, where Neil Simon's daughter Nancy also went. One day, around the third season of the show, I received a letter from Neil. He said his daughter had told him to watch our show because she thought it was funny. He watched a few episodes, and much to his surprise, he liked it. He wrote that he thought we were doing a good job. So after I received his letter, I called him up and invited him to guest-star on the show, and he did, playing himself. We grew from Neil hating the show in the first season to his smiling upon us in the end. He and I have been friends ever since.

The friendship of Jack and Tony grew beyond the final season of *The Odd Couple,* too. Years later when Jack was diagnosed with throat cancer, Tony rallied to his side at the hospital. When Jack got better Tony galvanized a group who with Jack performed a live version of *The Odd Couple* onstage. Then when Tony got sick Jack was right there supporting him in the hospital. Illness brought them closer to each other than the television show had. They talked on the phone every day when they were ill. They were there for each other until Tony passed away, in 2004. They were an odd couple, but in the end the portrait of a true and lasting friendship. And I am so lucky that I got to know and work with them both because they also changed my life. After running *The Odd Couple,* I had confidence for the first time. The insecure "what if we fail?" "How will I make a living?" guy had gone away. I was responsible. I could deal with big-time people like Tony and Jack, and the networks. I understood the "game." After *The Odd Couple* I could play with whoever, wherever, whenever.

Tony's daughter Julia is now an actress and had a small role in my movie *New Year's Eve*. With her dark hair and alabaster skin, she reminded me so much of her father the day we shot her scene. I smiled inside, and I hope Tony looked down on us working together and smiled, too.

7. HAPPY DAYS

★

Hanging Out with the Cunningham Family and Friends

HAPPY DAYS WAS a rare show in that it stayed in the Tuesday night time slot all of its eleven seasons. That was a gift from the network gods because audiences always knew where to find us. The fourth, fifth, and sixth seasons *Happy Days* was at the top of the ratings, at 1, 2, or 3, gloriously floating on sitcom air. We remain one of ABC's longest running sitcoms. The success of *Happy Days* gave me more confidence as a creator, writer, and producer. It is my favorite television show that I created because it rarely gave me a headache or a stomachache. *Happy Days* was for me the quintessential television success story. I had followed my instincts, and they had turned out to be right.

Years earlier I had followed my instincts and they were wrong. Jerry Belson and I created a show called *The Recruiters* during the height of the protests against the war in Vietnam. We should have looked out the window and seen people protesting and burning draft cards, but we were too myopic with our idea. I was determined to strike a more successful chord with *Happy Days*. I wanted to write about youth, but our country was still at war. How could I create a comedy about teenagers with Vietnam as the backdrop? I decided to go in a different direction altogether.

I would not create a modern show, thus avoiding the issues of war, sexual liberation, dangerous drugs, and the darker side of rock and roll. I went back to the 1950s, a time that at least in my own life and mind was much less complicated and politically charged.

I based the entire show on the images of poodle skirts, hula hoops, malt shops, bubble gum, and squeaky clean music. The fact that *Happy Days* helped viewers travel to a different era caught people's attention immediately. Only a few other shows, like *The Waltons,* had found success tapping into simpler times. People in the 1970s seemed happier with the past better than the present or future.

People always ask me how *Happy Days* got on the air, and the truth is, it all started with a snowstorm. Snow, it turns out, is lucky for me that way. Snow coated my childhood memories in the Bronx. Snow lined the streets of Sheridan Road when I went to college at Northwestern. Snow fell on my helmet when I served in the army in Korea. And then a snowstorm on the East Coast brought about an idea that would change my life in television forever. During a snowstorm everyone has to take time to pause.

Here's what happened: The year was 1973, and Michael Eisner, then the head of Paramount, was delayed on the East Coast with the up-and-coming Paramount executive Tom Miller. Not sure when their flight would take off, the two men started pitching sitcom ideas that they could develop for ABC, their partner network at the time. Eisner brought up the idea for a family show with the feel of the old show *I Remember Mama,* which was about a Norwegian family. Tom mentioned my name to produce it because *The Odd Couple* was headed toward its final season. When they pitched the idea to me, I was not exactly rushing to do it.

"*I Remember Mama?* The show about Swedish people?"

"Norwegians," said Miller.

"Either way. Swedes or Norwegians, I don't think I can create a show about guys named Lars and Hans in the 1930s," I told them. "I don't know families like that. But what about a family show about the 1950s? That I know. That's when I grew up, and I can give you a nostalgic show about that."

Eisner and Miller liked my idea. So I wrote a pilot episode about a family in the 1950s who were the first in their neighborhood to get a television set. The story was a personal one for me. I remember when we got our first television set, and how special it made me feel. Mel Ferber directed the pilot, which starred Harold Gould,

Marion Ross, and Ron Howard. We pitched it to ABC, and they didn't buy it. They just didn't see the demographic appeal of a show in the 1950s airing during the early 1970s. But I saw beyond their vision: I knew the show had a "dated" feel to begin with, so in the reruns it would never go out of style. ABC, however, was simply not ready for *Happy Days*. So in 1971 Paramount put it on the series *Love, American Style*, otherwise known as the graveyard for dead pilots. The episode was called "New Family in Town," and after it aired we thought *Happy Days* was indeed dead.

But then the tide suddenly turned: My friend from Korea Fred Roos was producing a film with George Lucas called *American Graffiti* about the 1950s. They wanted to see my 1950s pilot because they were thinking of casting Ron Howard as the lead of their movie. They liked Ron, cast him, and *American Graffiti* was a big hit. Then a play called *Grease* hit Broadway, and it further reinforced the popularity of the 1950s. The executives at ABC called Eisner, and he remembered my pilot about the 1950s. *Happy Days* was repitched as a midseason replacement and given a second life three years after it appeared on *Love, American Style*. Television is a derivative medium. If something is hot, television will copy it and frequently make it a success.

Money became a big issue when I created *Happy Days*. I began working with a young agent named Joel Cohen, who worked for my previous agent, Frank Cooper. Joel was a serious man who told boring stories but that is what made him such a great agent. He would bore people to death so they would give in and make a deal. Together Joel and I crafted my deal memo for *Happy Days*. He asked me what I wanted. I said I would like a basketball court on the Paramount lot, and a malted milk machine in my office. I was serious. That's what I knew would make me happy. I also said maybe a car. At first I said a Volkswagen, because it was the first name of a car that popped into my head. But then my clearheaded wife called Paramount herself and said, "Garry doesn't know anything about cars. He meant to say a *Mercedes*." As far as salary went, I thought I should ask for the same amount I got on the fourth season of *The Odd Couple*. But Joel had another idea up his sleeve.

"This new show, *Happy Days,* do you believe in it?" he asked.

"Yes," I said. I would have given a more ambivalent answer about a show like *Hey Landlord!* but I knew *Happy Days* was good from the moment we sold the pilot. And for me the show also was important because I was writing about my own childhood, and I knew I would never run out of stories.

"Well then, why don't we shock them?" Joel said. "They are fighting about giving you a raise on *The Odd Couple,* so we will say fine to that. We won't even put up a fight. They've offered you average money per episode on *Happy Days.* So let's shock them even more, and say you'll take less per episode on *Happy Days.* In exchange for that, you will ask for a larger ownership piece of *Happy Days.*"

It was a gamble for sure. We were betting on the fact that *Happy Days* would turn out to be a hit, and we were right. I never had a strong head for making deals, but Joel was brilliant at it. Jack and Tony owned most of *The Odd Couple,* and I owned very little. With *Happy Days,* however, I had much more to gain. We didn't know the show would run eleven seasons, but I did have a feeling from the beginning that it was something worth betting on.

I also loved the creativity involved in launching *Happy Days.* In *Grease* and *American Graffiti,* there were clearly identified bad guys. Eisner wanted me to have a gang element in *Happy Days,* but we couldn't afford a whole gang. So I created a character who could be a one-man gang. I based him on a few guys I had known growing up, namely Peter Wagner, who had owned a motorcycle and had gone to YMCA Camp Greenkill with me. All the guys in my neighborhood thought Peter was cool. Even when he wasn't riding his motorcycle we knew he had a bike, and that was cool enough. He could just be leaning against the bike and he was tough. While we were all fast-talking, wisecracking kids, Pete was a man who said few words, but each one packed a powerful punch. Also, he was from a mysterious land called Yonkers, where few of us had ever been.

On *Happy Days,* I wanted to call my cool character Mash after my Italian name, Masciarelli, but Larry Gelbart already had an army hospital show called *M*A*S*H,* so that seemed too confusing. Bob Brunner, my writer friend from the *Daily News,* suggested we call him Arthur Fonzarelli, Fonzie for short. I liked the sound of that name. (I had brought Bob out to Hollywood earlier to help write on *The Odd Couple*. Bob went on to be the show runner and producer for two series called *Webster* and *Diff'rent Strokes* and did quite well for himself.)

I created the characters for the new sitcom and we launched a major casting search for likable actors, but one of the keys to the success of *Happy Days* was director Jerry Paris, who directed for us on *The Odd Couple*. During the first year we shot *Happy Days* with one camera and he directed some of the thirteen episodes. In the second year, when we went to three cameras and a live audience, he became our series director, a job he held for the next ten seasons. To have a nurturing father figure like Jerry Paris as director on a series that starred so many young people was invaluable. It allowed Jerry to form close working relationships with all of the actors. This is not to say that Jerry couldn't drive us all crazy. Whenever his daughter was selling Girl Scout cookies, he would bug every single cast and crew member until all the boxes were sold. But most of the time Jerry was everything we wanted him to be as a director: sensible, stable, reliable, and funny. Wearing his famous red V-neck pullover sweater, Jerry was at the helm every Friday night. He had more energy than any person I had ever worked with. We filmed in front of a live audience. Unlike *The Odd Couple*, which had primarily an adult audience, *Happy Days* had an audience filled with little kids, teenagers, and adults. The energy was exciting, festive, and always fun.

I was forty years old when I started producing *Happy Days*, and I reached a defining point in my relationship with my writing partner Jerry Belson. We decided to go in different directions. After *The Odd Couple*, Jerry didn't want to produce *Happy Days* with me. He wanted to write movies, and to be honest, he viewed the true *Happy Days* as too optimistic for him. His own humor skewed darker, more esoteric. When Penny bought a new house I said, "Isn't her house great?" And Jerry said without missing a beat, "It's a lovely house to live in if life were worth living." A ninety-three-year-old actress we both knew died, and when I asked how he said simply, "Skiing."

Funny things were always coming out of Jerry's mouth, and together we laughed all the time while working. The friendship and the laughter we shared would outlast even our writing partnership.

I wanted to continue to work in television because I thought it would allow me to be a better dad, too. Belson, though a good father, didn't have that same ideal. Jerry and I once took our kids to the zoo together and he was bored to death, while I loved it. I liked seeing things through children's eyes, especially those of little kids. And I loved television for the flexibility it offered me as a parent. If my son had a T-ball game on a Tuesday, I could be there. If my daughter Lori needed help with her tennis tryouts or her homework, I could be there. If my daughter Kathleen had a swim meet, I could be there, too. (To be honest, swim meets can be a little boring and long. You watch your kid swim the butterfly for five minutes and then wait another hour for the backstroke. I would sometimes bring my typewriter and write or read scripts in between races. Occasionally I talked to other dads. One said to me, "You think this is boring. My other daughter does twirling.") Being a dad meant showing up. I could be there for my kids and work on a hit TV series. I'd always dreamed of being the kind of hands-on dad my own dad had not been. *Happy Days* would allow me to do that.

Another difference between Belson and me was our attitude toward young actors and writers. Jerry knew his sense of humor was superior, while I was more interested in sharing my experience with the up-and-coming writers. Jerry thought they would steal material from him and eventually take his job.

One of the most influential men in my career was Tom Miller, the producer of *Happy Days*. Tom had grown up in Milwaukee, and that's one of the reasons the series was set there. His parents owned a dry cleaning business, and we figured we could get free dry cleaning when we shot on location. Tom was always promoting my career. He would say things in network meetings that I would never say myself, like "Garry is a major talent." Tom loved making entertainment, and before he went into television he had worked as director Billy Wilder's assistant. Tom wore the creative producer hat on *Happy Days,* and our other producer, Eddie Milkis, wore the technical one. Together the three of us made a great television producing team because we each brought our own talents to the table without too much ego to complicate things.

As with *The Odd Couple,* I put together a writers' table with faces new and old. Some got overwhelmed by the pace and we had to let them go. One writer locked himself in his office, started playing his guitar, and wouldn't come out. He didn't last long. But when writers left we replaced them the next day. When Lowell Ganz finished up on *The Odd Couple,* I moved him over to *Happy Days* to write and produce. Lowell broke up with writer Mark Rothman, and we brought in new writers such as Brian Levant and Babaloo Mandel. I also hired older writers, like Walter Kempley and Bob Howard, who had worked in New York with me on Jack Paar's *Tonight Show.* We even had a very young writer who had just gotten out of Chino State Prison for juveniles, and another one who lived out of his car until he saved enough money to rent an apartment. Again, you didn't need the perfect education to write for *Happy Days.* It didn't matter what background you had as a writer, you just needed to be funny and be able to stay up late. Stamina and quickness counted for a lot back then, and I was not afraid to fire those who didn't have both.

Happy Days will always be remembered most for the cast. Within the first season we all went from new friends to old friends. I didn't know Henry Winkler before he auditioned for the part of Fonzie. And I remember he was not at all the type of actor I was looking for. I thought I wanted a tall, handsome blond, and in walked a short, dark-haired actor from Emerson College and the Yale School of Drama. But before I could dismiss him, I hired him. His audition taught me something. Casting isn't always about what you're looking for. Sometimes it is about recognizing potential and what is standing in front of you. Henry wasn't Fonzie, but he could "act" like Fonzie.

We had no idea at the time that Henry's portrayal of Fonzie would become so popular with the television audience. In fact, Fonzie began as a secondary character with very few lines. When he started drawing so much focus, we had to adjust the scripts. Henry was very energetic and was becoming a more important force on the show. At one point Fonzie was so wildly popular that I got a call from ABC saying that they wanted to change the name of the show from *Happy Days* to *Fonzie*. Ron Howard, who played Richie Cunningham, and Henry both knew about this suggestion, but we didn't have to spend much time to decide what to do. Changing the name of the show would be insulting to Ron, our kind and steady star. Henry agreed with me and wouldn't support any change in the title. So Henry proved to be not only a talented actor but a sensitive gentleman as well. Another actor might have taken the new title and run with it, but that wasn't Henry's style, and it still isn't.

My relationship with Ron Howard began before *Happy Days*. I had known him since he was a little kid on *The Andy Griffith Show* at Desilu Studios. Sometimes I would throw a baseball with him during rehearsal breaks. From the time he first appeared on television, he had the dream temperament of an actor. His parents, Jean and Rance Howard, raised him far from a life of hysteria and drama. So his personality was on an even keel, and not subject to the slightest high or low. If I had to pick the perfect actor to work with on a sitcom, Ron was it. He reminded me of a professional basketball player. He had the ability to shoot the ball and score but also the strength and focus to pass the ball to others to let them score, too. Near the end of the show we would have quiet talks about directing, and I knew he would probably go on to another career. But to have him on *Happy Days* for as long as we did was a gift not only to the show but also to me and the other actors.

Before I met Tom Bosley, who played Howard Cunningham, he was a talented Broadway actor; Marion Ross, who played Marion Cunningham, was an eccentric actress, and a Scorpio, like me. On the show Tom and Marion could make scenes funny even when they weren't quite funny enough on the written page. Erin Moran graduated high school from the studio school while doing the series, and she was the only one in her class. She supported her entire family, and in exchange her *Happy Days* family tried to support her and watch over her on the lot. Anson Williams, Donny Most, Scott Baio, and other supporting cast members were as happy as the stars.

When some stars left we replaced them with others, for instance, when Al Molinaro took over Arnold's from Pat Morita. When we went to cast Ron Howard's onscreen girlfriend, we let his real-life girlfriend Cheryl approve the actress Lynda Goodfriend. Late in the run of the series we were still bringing in great additions, such as Cathy Silvers and Ted McGinley. To be on a hit show was something you always dreamed of as an up-and-coming actor, and these kids were living the dream, but they weren't destructive with their money or their talent. I can't say this for the sitcoms I would create later on, but the cast of *Happy Days* was as kind, nice, and humorous as the characters they played.

Despite the fact that our cast was nice, our scripts were not always simple. We could tackle complex subjects, like nuclear war. The first season we aired an episode called "Be the First on Your Block" about Howard's decision to buy a bomb shelter. For many families in America the first time their kids heard the term *bomb shelter* was on *Happy Days*. I remember receiving letters from college professors saying they mentioned the episode in their history classes because some students didn't know what a bomb shelter was. They watched the Cunningham family grapple with the dilemma of which of their friends to invite into the shelter should a nuclear attack happen. That episode made me realize something: Having a hit show was powerful, and we had to learn to wield that power wisely.

Some of our episodes reflected the direction of the show. For example, as Fonzie rose in popularity during the third season, we moved him into the spare room above the Cunningham garage in an episode called "Fonzie Moves In." Other episodes reflected my own life. I had gone through painful knee surgery, so I had Fonzie do the same in the two-part episode "Fearless Fonzarelli" when he crashed his motorcycle. There are a few episodes that I look back on as gold because they changed so many actors' lives forever and were remembered by audiences as being extraspecial. One of those was "A Date with the Fonz," when my sister and Cindy Williams first appeared as Laverne DeFazio and Shirley Feeney.

America loved the episodes with Pinky Tuscadero and Fonzie as well as Fonzie's special friendship with Mrs. Cunningham. When Pinky, a girlfriend from Fonzie's past, was reunited with Fonzie, it was talked about in the sports pages. Before a tennis match a reporter asked Arthur Ashe who was going to win and Arthur said, "I don't know but we are going to do it fast so we can go home and watch Pinky Tuscadero." With her pink leather outfit and matching motorcycle gear, Roz Kelly as Pinky was someone special to watch every time she appeared on *Happy Days*.

Another gold episode for me was in the fifth season, when Robin Williams first appeared as Mork in "My Favorite Orkan." When Robin walked into the Cunningham living room and launched into his Orkan voice, everyone on the set got goose bumps because we could see immediately that he had the potential to be a big star. The episode in which Fonzie got a library card made library card requests jump 500 percent in one month across the United States. Fonzie had a lonely Christmas. Joanie got kissed. Richie almost died. Marion went to jail. Fonzie lost his sight. We tackled every scenario we could think of in eleven seasons.

We constantly had to battle the network censors because they wanted a superclean show and took us to task if we tried anything they thought was too provocative. The coveted *Happy Days* time slot on Tuesdays at 8:00 P.M. was considered family hour. In an early episode the censors told us that we could not use the word *virgin* to describe a girl. Instead Fonzie had to use the line "she was pure as the driven snow but she drifted." There was no way for us to get around the censors, so we just had to please them as best we could. As a producer I had to make everyone happy, from the censors to the actors and the catering people. Some episodes were funnier than others, but I tried always to make sure they had heart. Families were inviting us into their living rooms every Tuesday, and I felt we had an obligation to be not only entertaining but also kind.

I was very clear, though, on what kind of help I could offer. I would stay up all night to fix a scene or a moment in a script. However, if someone wanted a better lamp in a dressing room or didn't have a ride to the studio, I would point toward someone else to help. I would be fibbing if I didn't say that some of the actors on *Happy Days* complained about things or made demands that were unreasonable. When that happened the person I pointed them toward was my levelheaded middle sister and associate producer, Ronny. In so many ways *Happy Days* was an easier show to produce than *The Odd Couple* because I had more experience managing television actors. *Happy Days* allowed me to take what I had learned from Tony and Jack and practice my skills on a new group of younger actors. Every single actor on *Happy Days* was easier to deal with than Tony and Jack. If actors came to me and whined, "I haven't been featured in an episode lately. I want a show all about my character," I would say, "Wait your turn," and they would. The supporting characters on *The Odd Couple* rarely asked for bigger parts because it was so clear Tony and Jack were the stars of the show. In fact, Tony and Jack were often the generous ones, saying, "Why don't you give Al Molinaro or Elinor Donahue a bigger part this week?"

The cast and crew of *Happy Days* were content most of the time because they were so grateful to be working. I was so thrilled to have a show on the air that was a success, and they were so happy to have jobs and paychecks. The biggest star we had was Ron Howard, and he was the most amiable one of the entire group. Ron's personality and upbeat nature set the example for the entire show. To have a temper tantrum when Ron was such an exemplary leader seemed crazy to the others, so they never acted up in front of Ron.

The first few seasons the cast was young and dating. The next few they were getting married and having babies. The last few they were having their second babies and settling into their lives as parents and grown-ups. These were not cocaine-snorting, Porsche-driving, wild nightclub-dancing people. Sure in the later years when Ted McGinley joined the cast and Scott Baio started dating Erin Moran and then Heather Locklear, we had our fair share of tabloid stories. But for the most part the press looked at our cast and said, "Those people are too happy." We didn't offer the dirt or the gossip they wanted to sell newspapers.

Part of the fun of *Happy Days* was that we were a hit show. We didn't have to think of new ways to save the show but rather ways to keep it fresh by bringing in new characters. I once auditioned Nathan Lane for a part and he wasn't quite right. Nathan went on to become a big star on Broadway. When I go to see him he will always

Left: My grandpa Willy Ward lived in the apartment next door to us. He used to make me laugh a lot, and he was the first person to ever tell me I was funny. He had a great sense of humor, so I believed him. *Right:* This is one of my first official baby pictures. Around this time, I won a contest in a local newspaper for being a cute child. My mother was very proud.

Left: My dad, Tony, taught me how to be a good boss. He invented his middle name, Wallace, because he thought it gave him more dignity. *Right:* My mother, Marjorie, thought the biggest sin in life was to bore people. She thought entertainers were the best kind of people on the planet.

Most of the men on my Falcon basketball team remain my closest friends and confidants to this day.

Above left: When I wasn't sneezing or wheezing in bed due to ailments or allergies, I loved to play sports of any kind. *Right:* I enjoyed growing up with two little sisters. My mom always said I was the sick kid. Ronny was the pretty child. And Penny was the one always getting into trouble.

I honed my writing skills as a soldier at the AFKN radio station in Korea in the 1950s.

Throughout college at Northwestern, I was always a drummer in a band of some kind to earn extra money so I wouldn't have to take out a student loan.

Danny Thomas and Joey Bishop were two of my earliest employers and mentors. One minute I was a struggling comic in New York, and almost overnight I was working in Hollywood as a comedy writer. These two men changed my life forever.

Producing *The Odd Couple* was my first chance to be a boss of a prime-time situation comedy. The experience was a dream come true for me, including the night we celebrated our 100th episode. *(Courtesy of CBS Television Studios)*

It seems almost a cliché to say that the cast of *Happy Days* was very happy, but they honestly were. They had careers, families, and children. They appreciated the fact they were on a top-rated sitcom surrounded by friends. *(Courtesy of CBS Television Studios)*

The hours spent on a movie set can be very long. You have to grab a nap where you can. My son, Scott, and I worked and napped together on the set of *Overboard,* which I shot in Mendocino and Los Angeles.

I don't like to dwell on success, but this picture made a lot of people successful. When Robin Williams appeared on *Happy Days* as Mork from Ork, we created a spinoff the same week. *(Courtesy of CBS Television Studios)*

Penny, Ronny, and I have taught our children and grandchildren that the only thing you can really count on is family.

The first time my wife ever appeared on the big screen was as a nurse in my first movie, *Young Doctors in Love*. For a hypochondriac to marry a nurse is like a marriage made in heaven. *(Courtesy of Paramount Pictures Corporation)*

Acting alongside Tom Hanks in my sister's movie *A League of Their Own* was a treat. We had not worked together since I directed him in *Nothing in Common.* *(A League of Their Own © 1992 Columbia Pictures Industries, Inc. All rights reserved)*

Directing Matt Dillon in *The Flamingo Kid* was like taking a trip down memory lane. Like Matt's character Jeffrey, I spent many summers working at resorts on the eastern seashore when I was growing up. *(Photo by Kevin O'Callaghan)*

When Bette Midler first sang the song "Wind Beneath My Wings" to me I literally got tears in my eyes. *(© Touchstone Pictures)*

Above: In *Mystic Pizza,* Julia wowed audiences with her wild mane of hair. In *Pretty Woman,* however, we purposely concealed her hair in the beginning of the film with a short, blonde wig. Then we revealed her beautiful hair to the audience and Richard Gere when they were finally alone in his hotel suite. *(Photo by Ron Batzdorff, © Touchstone Pictures)*

Right: I was so lucky to work with Michelle Pfeiffer not only once but twice: first in *Frankie and Johnny* and then again in *New Year's Eve.* *(Courtesy of Berliner)*

see me backstage and say with a smile, "There's Garry Marshall, who turned me down for a part on *Happy Days*."

While the *Happy Days* cast and crew became my family, I surrounded myself with my real family, too. My sister Ronny worked in the casting department as an associate producer, and my dad was on the producing staff. My mother and three kids acted in several episodes, my favorite being one in the second season called "Haunted," in which my kids each played a trick or treater. While my wife didn't appear on-screen until I directed movies a few years later, her job in the 1970s was to help me not forget I had a life off the lot. We continued to vacation in Carmel, California, every spring and go to Hawaii with the kids many Christmases. My wife remains one of the great road trip drivers of all time. On a dime she can be packed and ready to drive to San Francisco or Newport Beach for the weekend, even at midnight. So whenever there was a window, Barbara helped me make time for my kids and family. I was never a good driver, and in fact didn't get my license until I was twenty-eight years old. It took me three tries to get my license, and I rarely make left turns, even today.

The ratings triumph of *Happy Days* was great, but something was nagging inside me. As much as I loved television, I still longed to be a part of live theater. It might sound crazy, but the success of *Happy Days* spurred me to keep dreaming of other kinds of creative outlets. So twice during *Happy Days* I took theater breaks. The first time was in the winter of 1974 to work as a script doctor on a big Broadway musical called *Good News* starring the great Alice Faye. It was exciting to be in New York City in the winter and see my credit in the program, which read "written by Abe Burrows with additional dialogue by Garry Marshall." But the downside was that I had to be away from my family during Christmastime. For the first time in our marriage, my wife had to put up the Christmas tree and decorate it by herself.

The second time I left *Happy Days* was 1978, when I went to produce a play in Illinois called *Shelves*. It was the play I had written years earlier when my wife and Lori and I moved to Palm Springs for several months. I took it out of my drawer and cast the most likable mother I knew—Marion Ross from *Happy Days*—as the lead. We opened at a dinner theater called the Pheasant Run Playhouse in St. Charles, Illinois. The play was a tribute to my mother, who could have been a star but was born at a time when women were not encouraged to work.

My family and Marion's family had flown out for the opening, which would mark my debut as a playwright, something my mother had dreamed of since I was a boy. But this mood changed as my ten-year-old son, Scott, was rushed to the emergency room with pneumonia. They put him in an oxygen tent. On opening night I stood in the hospital room in my tuxedo with my two daughters wearing fancy new department store dresses. My wife said I had to attend opening night. I lifted up the plastic on the oxygen tent to kiss my son goodbye, but I was having trouble walking out the door. My wife encouraged me to go and take the girls to the theater. She would stay behind with Scott. So I went, weighed down by my own reluctance.

Over time my son got better, but I never forgot how conflicted I felt that night as a father and a playwright. When I should have been on top of the world about my play, I was worried sick about my son. I wanted to stay with him. I realized then how short and unpredictable life is. I had been a sick and fragile kid, and I had a sick and fragile kid that night. I realized you have to make the most of life while you can. So right after I returned home from Chicago, I went back to the safety of *Happy Days*. (Years later I did the play again at my Falcon Theatre and retitled it *Everybody Say "Cheese!"*)

When my writing partner Jerry Belson's dad died, Jerry wrote a beautiful letter saying how much his father had meant to him. But his father never had the chance to hear Jerry's thoughts because he was already gone. Around this time I decided to write letters to my parents while they were still alive. I wanted them to know how much I appreciated and loved them. I thanked my mother for always giving me aspirin, soaking my stitches, cooking for me, and bringing me sports magazines when I was sick. I thanked my father for taking me to professional football games. My dad also taught me how to be a boss, and took me to see live radio shows. In my neighborhood no other dads were taking their kids to radio shows, and that made me feel extraspecial. And finally, I thanked him for helping me get into Northwestern and carve out a new life for myself. Many years later I saw my dad still carried my letter in his wallet, and he would show it to bartenders whether he was drinking at a local bar or at his favorite golf club, Lakeside.

Back to the topic of *Happy Days*. People come up and ask me all the time about the phrase *jumping the shark* and if I find it offensive. The expression comes from a late episode of *Happy Days* in which Fonzie uses water skis to literally jump over a shark in the ocean. It was certainly not one of the shows I am most proud of. But I love the phrase *jumping the shark* and the way people use it today to signify a TV series nearing the end of its run. In 2009 I did a full stage tour of the *Happy Days* musical, which I wrote with Paul Williams and produced with *Happy Days* executive producers Bob Boyett and Tom Miller. One of the big jokes in the musical is when someone notices Fonzie is in a bad mood and says, "He hasn't been the same since he jumped the shark."

Happy Days was a hit television series for eleven seasons, and then we all knew it was time to say goodbye. The last season people were getting tired and wanted to move on to other things. We had gotten so efficient that sometimes we even shot the show in three or four days instead of five. We decided that to end the show we would do something we had never done before: Tom Bosley turned directly to the camera and thanked the audience for their support. Now that Tom has passed away, that decision seems even more appropriate. We were a family show, Tom was the dad, and it was his opportunity to say goodbye for all of us.

Knowing that *Happy Days* appealed to people from eight years old to eighty makes me smile even today. I always wanted to be remembered as the Norman Rockwell of television, and *Happy Days* represented the part of me that wanted to make mainstream America laugh. If television was the education of the American public, then *Happy Days* was recess. And I always loved recess best.

"Is it true that Fonzie's leather jacket is in a museum?" asked my grandson, Sam, one day.

"Yes. It is in the Smithsonian in Washington, D.C.," I said.

"But what good does it do there? Fonzie can't wear it and say 'Aaaay!'" he said.

"Fonzie has other jackets now," I said.

"But can he still say *'Aaaay'*"? he asked.

"Yes, sometimes on occasion, he still says it," I said with a smile.

Sam wasn't born when *Happy Days* went off the air, in 1984, and his parents, Elissa and Scott weren't married yet. But to think that Sam knows who Fonzie was and that he was a cool guy with a motorcycle makes me realize just how happy those days on the show were.

8. SCHLEMIEL! SCHLIMAZEL!

★

Laverne and Shirley Are Driving

the Writers Crazy

I LIKED TO BRING my three kids to Paramount Studios when they had days off from school during the mid-1970s. They were in elementary school at the time, and I wanted them to see where their dad's office was. When I said, "Dad's going to work," I wanted them to know what it meant. I was never really sure what it was my own father did day in and day out, so I was determined to show my children exactly what a television writer-producer did. For a while they thought I spent a lot of time sleeping because I would work late at night and still be in bed when they went to school in the morning. But eventually I brought them to the set and gave them a tour. They were rarely allowed to visit *The Odd Couple* because they were too young. But after I created *Happy Days,* cast and crew members brought their kids to work regularly.

One day I was walking along the lot with Lori (eleven), Kathleen (seven), and Scott (six), and I pointed out the *Happy Days* soundstage.

"*Happy Days* is one of my favorite shows," I said.

"Where do they do *Laverne & Shirley*?" asked Lori.

"Over there," I said and pointed to the soundstage adjacent to *Happy Days.*

"Let's go! Schlemiel! Schlimazel! Hasenpfeffer Incorporated!" said Kathleen, dancing the sequence from the show's opening credits.

"We can't," I said. "You don't want to go in there. It's not fun."

"Why not?" asked Scott. "It looks fun on TV."

"On the set they argue and fight a lot. Cursing happens," I explained.

"Does Aunt Penny curse, too?" asked Lori.

"I'm afraid so," I said.

"Lenny and Squiggy curse?" asked Scott.

"Yep," I said.

"Are you joking, Daddy? Is that true?" asked Kathleen.

"I'm serious. *Happy Days* is Daddy's happiest show, and *Laverne & Shirley* is Daddy's toughest show. So I don't take a lot of visitors to that set."

"I overheard someone say that the cast of *Happy Days* puts cups up to the wall so they can hear Penny and Cindy screaming at the writers. Is that true?" asked Lori.

"I wanna hear that!" said Scott.

"No. No. *Laverne & Shirley* is too chaotic. Let's go get some pizza."

"At the Pizza Bowl?" asked Kathleen.

"No. The commissary. Less cursing goes on there."

Laverne & Shirley did not begin as a tough show at all but rather a dream come true. I was attending a conference on Marco Island off the coast of Florida with the ABC brass, and executive Fred Silverman asked me to create more shows. *Happy Days* was a big hit, and he felt that to make ABC a powerhouse on Tuesday night, we needed another half-hour sitcom to pair with it. Every other word out of Fred's mouth seemed to be *spinoff.*

"So what else do you have?" asked Fred. "Any spinoffs?"

"Not a lot. I'm too busy working on *Happy Days,*" I said.

"Come on. You must have something else," he said. "A spinoff?"

The truth was I did have one idea I had been mulling over. My sister Penny and actress Cindy Williams had appeared a few months earlier on *Happy Days* playing romantic dates for Fonzie and Richie. Their characters were girls from the wrong side of the tracks set against the supersmart Richie and cooler-than-ice Fonzie. The studio audience seemed to love Penny and Cindy, and I wondered if I could build a new show around them. Cindy was an adorable, rubber-faced actress who could also sing. Together the girls were unpredictably funny. To create a popular show, however, I knew I needed to find a niche that wasn't currently being filled on television. So I brought up my idea with Fred.

"I was thinking that there are no blue-collar women on television," I said.

"What do you mean? Tell me more," he asked.

"There are all these middle-class or these fancy wealthy women on television like Lucy and Mary Tyler Moore—well-dressed women with perfect hair and good diction. But no women who do factory work or talk like regular working-class single people from the neighborhood," I said.

"I love the idea. Make it a show," he said. "I love a spinoff."

Affable Fred Silverman had written his college thesis on how to schedule network shows. He got an A.

And just like that I was handed the green light for another sitcom deal. Actually, Fred liked Penny when he was at CBS and Penny was on *Paul Sands in Lovers and Friends*. When that series was canceled, Penny and her friend Cindy were a struggling writing team. They were not really sure they wanted to be actresses.

Coincidentally, that same week my mother called and told me to get my little sister another acting job. Penny had done a great job on *The Odd Couple* as Oscar's secretary, Myrna Turner. But when *The Odd Couple* ended, Penny was out of work again. So I thought if I could create a blue-collar show starring Penny, then I could make Fred Silverman and my mother happy at the same time.

To create the characters of Laverne DeFazio and Shirley Feeney, I took pieces from their *Happy Days* appearance and then borrowed material from two characters I had once seen in Brooklyn. The year was around 1958, and we were all out of the army. My friend Jimmy, who had served in Korea with me, and I went out one night after playing in a nightclub. We met some girls and took them to a coffee shop around 2:00 A.M. Suddenly another girl said something rude to my date. My girl turned to me and said, "Garry, would you hold my coat?" And then my date beat up the other girl. I had never seen two girls fistfight before, and it fascinated me. The tough-as-nails quality of *Laverne & Shirley* was based on that single night fight in Brooklyn.

I cast Penny, and I was able to hire Cindy as the other lead. I knew Cindy well because she had once dated Fred Roos, who was now a producer for Francis Coppola. We also adopted our family dog from Cindy, and named her Cindy. I wanted the new show to involve a lot of physical comedy, and Penny and Cindy were both willing and able to tackle stunts. Penny was athletic and had once dreamed of being a stunt girl. Cindy was athletic as well and once told me, "I'm so little I better be brave." They also had the look that I wanted. I could put them in smocks and place them in a bottle-capping factory and they would be believable as regular, hard-working girls from Milwaukee. Casting for me is key, so to get one of my comic mentors, Phil Foster, to join the cast as Laverne's father made me secure, too. Penny and Phil had New York accents, and the show took place in Milwaukee, so we made believe they had moved back to Wisconsin from New York to explain their New York accents.

We shot the ten-minute pilot for *Laverne & Shirley* one night after *Happy Days* and paid that crew overtime. The studio and network liked the ten minutes so much they gave us money to make a full pilot that aired. Cindy Williams, however, decided after making the ten-minute segment that she didn't want to sign on for a sitcom. So we made another ten-minute presentation with Penny paired with an actress named Liberty Williams, who was no relation to Cindy. We gave both ten-minute segments to Michael Eisner. He decided he liked the one with Penny and Cindy best and said he would talk Cindy into signing a deal. And he did. Penny and Cindy went on to become television stars, and I don't know what ever became of Liberty. I always wondered how Michael talked Cindy into signing the contract if she didn't want to star in a sitcom. I imagine he probably told her it would run for one season, thirteen episodes, and then the show would be off the air. What happened, of course, is now television history, because *Laverne & Shirley* ran for eight years.

The day after *Laverne & Shirley* first aired I ran to check the ratings.

"Honey, I can't find it," I said to my wife at the breakfast table.

"What do you mean? It must be there," she said. "They list all the shows."

"No. Honestly. I don't see it. I'm going crazy," I said.

My wife took the ratings sheet, looked at it, and then smiled as she showed it to me.

"You weren't looking high enough," she said. "*Laverne & Shirley* debuted at number one!"

I couldn't believe it. I had never seen anything like it before. It was a miracle. Suddenly Penny and Cindy were in a hit television series, and I was my sister's new boss. My mom was happy, and Fred Silverman had his spinoff. We were all surprised at how quickly the show had found an audience.

Today, when I am feeling compassionate and kind, I think back sympathetically toward Penny and Cindy and how hard it must have been for them to suddenly be stars of a top-rated sitcom. A television show is so demanding that few can live up to the challenges. The job paid well, but the hours and pressures of performing in front of a live studio audience, and carrying an entire show on their backs, were an awesome responsibility for two actresses with hardly any experience who weren't even sure they wanted to become actresses. But when I'm not feeling compassionate toward them, I am saddened and disappointed that they were too immature to handle the job. If there was ever a show that was full of joy, it was *Happy Days*. If there was ever a show full of headaches and people taking aspirin, it was *Laverne & Shirley*.

Nobody knew exactly how big the show was until Penny and Cindy were in the Macy's Thanksgiving Day parade the first season. They were asked to ride on a float, and from the top of their float, they could see their success. Penny described the scene to me later. More than 100,000 fans were cheering their names. "Laverne and Shirley! Laverne and Shirley! Laverne and Shirley!" Not only were fans asking for their autographs, but most of the policemen running the parade asked for autographs, too. After that trip Penny and Cindy knew they were famous. What they did with that information and power became the problem. That moment made them feel in charge of the show. Fame can be a wonderful thing as well as a destructive force. It has ruined the lives of so many actors in Hollywood. Penny and Cindy weren't able to balance their lives with the notoriety. To me they both always seemed anxious, never settled or content. Also, despite their fame Penny and Cindy didn't think they deserved it. They thought it was a fluke and an accident, and in a few days or months it could all disappear.

It was the 1970s, so drugs and alcohol were prevalent on many television shows, except, I'm pleased to say, *Happy Days*. My challenge was to police the adversarial writers and cast and crew of *Laverne & Shirley*. Their meetings, whatever the reason, were bound to go off-track and I had to mediate. It drained me to the point that I started losing weight from stress and I had to drink high-calorie protein shakes to stay healthy. Penny and Cindy thought that they knew more than anyone else and that the writing staff was without talent. The writers, on the other hand, thought Penny and Cindy were mean, too young to be so bossy, and narcissistic. On a daily basis there was infighting, yelling, cursing, and so much more. My dad taught me that when other people are misbehaving around you, you need to find the strength to behave so you don't get caught in their drama. I tried to remind myself of that every day on *Laverne & Shirley,* but sometimes the stress got to me.

One day I got out of the shower at my house. I toweled off and reached for the blow-dryer. I stood there for several minutes until I suddenly realized something. There was no hot air coming out of the dryer. The reason was simple: I was holding the telephone receiver. The pulsating beep of a dial tone brought me back to reality. Another time I had lunch with an actress. While we were talking outside the restaurant, the valet brought my car around. I said goodbye to her as I opened the car door and stepped inside. It wasn't until I closed the door that I realized I was sitting in the backseat. These things could happen to anyone under stress, but they happened to me a little too often during the eight tumultuous years of *Laverne & Shirley*.

Penny and Cindy would plow through writers, leaving me constantly looking for replacements. Sometimes I would go over to *Happy Days* and entice a writer or two to come and take a spin on *Laverne & Shirley*. I pretended it was an easy, breezy show to write for, but most of the writers on *Happy Days* knew better. When you hire actors or actresses for a series, you look for people who have well-rounded lives with supportive friends and family. But when hiring writers, you look for people with no lives so they will be willing to stay as long as you want them to in order to get the script rewritten before the cameras roll. I searched in comedy clubs, workshops, and bars for writers with no lives who would work late on any episode, difficult or not.

When I see a problem, I don't like to let it sit there and get worse. I like to search for new ways to solve it. I thought if only I could give Penny and Cindy a writer they truly loved and bonded with, then everything would settle down. So one day I asked Arthur Silver to move from *Happy Days* to *Laverne & Shirley*. He agreed. Arthur is a man with a calm and quiet demeanor, and I thought he could bring serenity to the set of *Laverne & Shirley* just like he had to *Happy Days* when he produced it with Bob Brunner.

However, after only a few weeks in his new position, Arthur asked to have a private meeting with me.

"Garry, something happened last night," he said, looking ghostly white.

"What happened, Arthur?" I asked. "Please tell me. How can I help?"

"It was late and I had finished up on *Laverne & Shirley*. I got into my car, and as I was pulling out of the parking space, I saw Penny, Cindy, Lenny, and Squiggy up ahead. That is when I realized that my foot was on the gas pedal. I wanted to run them down. So I have to quit the show. It is too much stress for me."

"Ah, Arthur," I said with sympathy. "We can't have that."

"I know. I need off the show," he said. "Please can I go back to *Happy Days*?"

"Of course. I understand completely. I only wish I could go with you. Thank you for trying."

After Arthur I hired a very funny writer named Monica Johnson, who was the sister of my writing partner Jerry Belson. Shortly after Monica started I saw her walking across the lot on her way to the set. She was wearing pajamas, a fur coat, high heels, and curlers in her hair. That was how she would come to work. She didn't bother to take the time even to dress, and was clearly coming un-glued from the stress of her job. I hoped her quirky attire and abil-ity to call meetings at odd hours might be a good fit for Penny and Cindy. But Monica did not stay long at the *Laverne & Shirley* writers' table either.

We tried other solutions, including bringing on Paula Roth, a woman from the Bronx who had been friends with us growing up. Paula had no experience writing, but she seemed to get Penny's voice down right and the girls considered her a friend of the court instead of an enemy. Paula had tap-danced and performed with Penny, Ronny, and me in my mother's recitals. So what she lacked in experience she had in familiarity.

As the years went by, Penny's and Cindy's personal lives caused another layer of conflict. Penny got divorced and Cindy broke up with a boyfriend. Now they were still making a lot of money but were not happy because neither had a boyfriend or a husband to share it with.

The fact was my parents never accepted Penny's success. My mother had a linear mind. If you were good you should find success, and if you were bad you should find failure. In my mom's mind, Penny had been a bad kid, so her success as an adult didn't make sense. My mother couldn't get her brain around the fact that Penny was now more famous than all of us put together. Whenever I asked my mom if she liked the show, she would say, "Put more tap dancing in it." Mom was jealous. People would come up to my mom and say, "Wow, your daughter is famous," and Mom would remain unim-pressed. And Dad found it baffling that both Penny and I were mak-ing more money than he was.

One day Penny came to me and said she had not gotten her pay-check. I said I would find out where the problem was. After a quick trip to the payroll department, I found out my father was the prob-lem. Dad was now an executive producer on *Laverne & Shirley,* and that week he had not signed Penny's paycheck. He was withholding her wages for some reason. No one in the payroll department knew why, so I went to talk to my dad.

"Penny didn't get paid this week," I said.

"I know," said Dad.

"That's a seventy-five-thousand-dollar paycheck," I said.

"I know."

"So where is it?"

"In my desk drawer," he said. "Safe."

"Why?" I asked.

"She was fresh with me today. And I'm not giving her the check until she apologizes," he said.

"Dad, you can't treat Penny like a child. She is a grown-up with a mortgage."

"I don't care how old she is. She was fresh with her father and she needs to apologize," he said.

So eventually, Penny apologized and Dad gave her the paycheck. A small victory, but at least something on *Laverne & Shirley* was resolved. There were some good days on the show, but most were days filled with quarrels, fits, and fires I needed to put out. After a few years Cindy would listen to me when I said, "I have to go home to be with my family and rest. We will discuss the script tomorrow." But Penny wouldn't take no for an answer. If she had a complaint or concern, she would have her driver follow me home. I would be having a meatball supper at the dinner table and my wife would say, "There's Penny at the gate again. Now she is trying to climb over it." But she was my little sister, and she knew I would always answer the door and take her phone calls.

Penny and Cindy were not out of touch with reality. They knew they were tough on the writers and they knew they were driving me crazy. Animosity grew like mold in the walls of the *Laverne & Shirley* soundstage. However, it is customary for the stars of a television show to give the cast and crew Christmas gifts. One year Penny and Cindy gave out dartboards. The bull's-eye was a picture of the two of them dressed in costumes from an episode in which they played Santa's elves. It was the hands-down favorite gift of everyone who worked on the show. The writing staff, composed of some of the best in the business, couldn't wait to sharpen their darts and take aim at Penny and Cindy. Most of the writers I know from that show still have their dartboards in their garages and basements. I have to admit I still have my dartboard in my office.

I wished every night for eight years that Penny and Cindy could find happiness with the show. One night we were filming before our live audience and the show was just exceptional. It was so terrific that the studio audience gave Penny and Cindy a standing ovation. I have never seen anything like it before, not even on *The Odd Couple* or *Happy Days*. There was such appreciation in the room.

I turned to my sister, so proud of her.

"Penny, isn't this wonderful?" I said. "You are a gigantic success."

"Sure, but what am I going to do tonight? I have no boyfriend and bad hair," she said, and she meant it. One of Penny's first jobs in the business had been a Head & Shoulders shampoo commercial. A young Farrah Fawcett was cast, too. Penny was the girl with dandruff hair, and Farrah was the girl with clean hair. While Penny and Farrah were getting their makeup done, their stand-ins stood on their marks to light the shot. Farrah's stand-in wore a sign that said BEAUTIFUL GIRL, while Penny's stand-in wore a sign that read DANDRUFF GIRL. Farrah tried to cross out DANDRUFF, but the damage had been done. Penny always wanted to be the beautiful girl with the clean, fluffy hair, and she spent the rest of her life fighting to be her. Penny had been married to actor Rob Reiner, but as his show *All in the Family* was going off the air, *Laverne & Shirley* was becoming a hit. The incompatibility of their careers put too much pressure on their marriage. Penny was fine being the second banana to Rob early on in their marriage. But she had no tools to learn how to be more famous and powerful than he was. Her whole sense of self-worth appeared to be based on men rather than achievement.

Less than fulfilling home lives left both Penny and Cindy feeling that their television success didn't mean enough. They worried all the time about being pretty enough, about dating, and about girlie things that I had no experience with. They made Jack Klugman and Tony Randall look like perfectly behaved Prince Charmings. I thought if we worked hard, put in long hours, and made a decent salary, we would all find contentment on *Laverne & Shirley*. But they were never satisfied. Time and time again I would find myself drifting over to the set of *Happy Days* to hear about people getting married and having babies and being content. I was thankful to have at least one show where people were finding success on the set and off.

Laverne & Shirley was a television show that broke new ground, something I had never been accused of that often. Who would expect that a show about two female brewery bottle cappers would introduce the audience to a slapstick kind of humor that was designed as a tribute to Lucille Ball? I never had the chance to talk to Lucy about what she thought of *Laverne & Shirley,* but I think she would have been proud. I took the lessons she had taught me about comedy and taught them to my sister Penny and our friend Cindy. I was forever grateful for the time I spent writing for Lucy, because that training made me a stronger writer and producer for the rest of my career.

Like Lucy, Penny and Cindy were both fearless performers. To this day I admire them for that. They wanted to make *Laverne & Shirley* the very best sitcom it could be. They would be ranting and raving in the writers' meetings, but the moment the audience was there, they would rise to the occasion. They were both born to perform. They would never let the crew or the audience or the writers down in the final hour. They might drive us all crazy until the *final* hour, but they showed up when we needed them.

So as much as they frustrated me, I respected them both. Penny and Cindy were insecure and contrary but not without incredible talent and timing. That was the conflict: If they weren't talented, the series would have crashed and burned within the first few years. But they are two of the funniest comedians I have ever worked with in television. And I remember the day they both blew me away. It was an episode in which Laverne and Shirley worked as candy striper volunteers. In one scene I put a fat man in a hospital bed and told them they had to change the sheets with the man in the bed. I watched as they tackled the scene. Penny tried to pull the sheet out from under the patient and slipped halfway under the bed. We did the scene again, only this time I greased the floor so Penny slid all the way under the bed.

I think Cindy and I both knew that day what we could not say out loud: Penny's comic talents had surpassed us. Cindy would have to work hard to keep up with her, and I would have to work harder to find them both material to keep Penny on top and Cindy right on top with her. Penny had raised the bar of talent and timing for all of us. The episode remains my favorite one of *Laverne & Shirley*. My kid sister had surprised me and impressed me that day and earned new respect in my eyes forever.

Toward the end of the show's run, things got worse when Cindy's manager, Pat McQueeney, an old friend of mine, started making more demands. Eventually, Cindy left the show to have a baby. Penny went on for another season alone. Things ended with some hurt feelings, but now everyone seems to be friends again because most of us are too old to hang on to old anger. I think Cindy finally found happiness raising a family and Penny found her niche in directing movies. Penny became the first woman director ever to make a movie that earned more than $100 million, *Big*. She repeated that feat with *A League of Their Own*. But in my opinion her finest film did not make the most money. It was called *Awakenings* and starred Robin Williams and Robert De Niro. One day she called me and said she was very sad. Neither Robin nor Robert had noticed that she had gotten a cute bob haircut. She was still doing fine work while worrying too much about her hair.

Working with Penny and Cindy for eight years made me realize something else very important about myself: I was tough enough to work with any actress in the business. After I'd survived Penny and Cindy, no actress could bring me down, depress me, frustrate me, or make me yell at the top of my lungs. Bring me Bette Midler. Bring me Goldie Hawn. Bring me Lindsay Lohan. Bring me Jane Fonda. I was desensitized to every woman with a Screen Actors Guild card. I could handle them because Penny and Cindy made me tougher and better than I ever was before. I went forward into television producing and film directing with a new skill and a new label called women's director. From time to time people would say to me, "Oh, you don't want to work with that actress. She's too tough." And I would look them right in the eye and say, not with hubris but with pure confidence, "Sure I can." My wife said something good comes out of all bad things. She was right. I knew if I could survive *Laverne & Shirley* for eight solid years, I could get along with any actress in town. I still try so hard to make people happy, but I am always left with the knowledge that the one person I never made completely happy was my sister Penny.

9. MORK & MINDY

★

Managing a Martian and a New
Playwriting Career

EVERY FAMILY HAS its favorite stories, and one of our best is about how Mork from Ork was born.

I had noticed that my daughters, Lori and Kathleen, were just crazy about *Happy Days*. The girls couldn't wait for Tuesday night to come around so they could watch Henry Winkler and Scott Baio and the rest of the gang at Arnold's. The girls were always clamoring to bring their friends to the live filming Friday night on the Paramount lot. My son, Scott, however, was not interested in *Happy Days* at all. The year was 1977, and the first *Star Wars* movie had just come out. Scott was eight years old, and he walked around the house pretending to be R2-D2 or C-3PO during most of his waking hours. I found it unsettling that Scott was a fan of George Lucas but not a fan of mine. I had to find out why.

"Why don't you watch *Happy Days*?" I asked him one day while he was playing with some of his *Star Wars* action figures.

"There are no space aliens on *Happy Days*," he said very matter-of-factly.

"But it's the nineteen fifties. Kids are playing with hula hoops and wearing poodle skirts. Where does a space alien come from?"

He paused for a minute and then looked directly at me with the clarity and wisdom that seemed to belong more to a network executive than to an eight-year-old boy and said, "Fonzie could have a dream."

There are times when you are insanely grateful to have children, and this was one of them. I never would have thought of such a thing. On *Happy Days,* we were running out of adversaries or villains for Fonzie to fight with. I realized Fonzie could have a dream, and we could have a villain from outer space. We'd created Fonzie as a gangster with a heart of gold, and Mork was crafted as an alien with a heart of gold. I was big with hearts of gold.

Once the premise was constructed, we had one major hurdle left—to cast the right alien. I wanted the actor John Byner, who had a wild look in his eyes and the off-beat wit I thought would be good for the alien. With my funny co-producer/writers, Dale McRaven and Bruce Johnson, and my very calm and efficient sister Ronny (now my casting director), we arranged a meeting with Byner, and made a tentative deal for him to star in the series. Then an odd thing happened: Close to shooting, Byner decided he didn't want to play an alien on a television series. Then we were stuck with no alien and only a few days before shooting was set to start. Ronny contacted the William Morris Agency, who represented Byner, to see if they could suggest anyone else. A new agent named Alan Iezman tried to sell us Richard Lewis and Jeff Altman, but they were not quite right.

Iezman then asked Ronny to see a new comedian who he was representing named Robin Williams. When I asked Ronny what his credits were, she said he did street performing on corners and passed the hat for tips.

"You want me to build a major network sitcom around a man who passes the hat for tips?" I said.

"It is a VERY full hat," said Ronny.

Iezman started begging me to see him. It is not often you get an agent begging. So I sent Ronny and director Jerry Paris to check out this comedian. Ronny came back and told me Robin was indeed special, and now she begged me to see him, too. It is also hard to refuse a begging sister, so I said yes. The next week I walked into my office and the street performer was sitting on my couch upside down on his head. When he saw me, he stood straight up, and started pretending to drink a glass of water with his finger. That is how I first met Robin Williams. Ronny was right. Iezman was right. He was special.

Could I tell he was talented from the beginning? Yes. Did I know if he could carry an entire sitcom? No. But I knew I could build a show around him because he had the kind of talent that Danny Kaye and Jerry Lewis had. He would be the hip, modern, and zany centerpiece of the show, and we would surround him with calm, talented actors whom he could riff off of.

First, however, I wanted to put him to the test, so I put him on an episode of *Happy Days*. He guest-starred in an episode called "My Favorite Orkan," which ran in February 1978, during the fifth season of *Happy Days*. In the episode Robin plays an alien named Mork, who travels down from his planet, Ork, and wants to take Richie to his people to show them an example of a normal human. Fonzie stands in his way and protects Richie. Ron Howard and Henry Winkler were two of the more generous actors working in television, so when Robin guest-starred on the show, they gave him not only the support he needed but also the room to shine on his own. Robin's portrayal of the alien was so innovative and fresh, with his body language and quirky electronic noises, that it didn't take a genius to see this man needed his own sitcom. When Robin took his curtain call the audience gave him a standing ovation, giving even me the chills. Again, I was so happy to have a live audience, because they were the true arbiters of what was special. The Tuesday night the show aired on ABC, I got a call from my Paramount boss, Michael Eisner, who said, "Garry, I heard you have a Martian who got a standing ovation. Can you build a series around him? Do it fast." The impetus for the phone call was that it was pilot season. During that time the network executives review all of their choices for the coming season. It just so happened that this particular season, ABC and Paramount didn't have a lot of strong pilots to choose from. So when they came to us and said, "What do you have?" they were ready to buy something right away.

I wasn't thinking so much of the television show *My Favorite Martian* from the 1960s but more along the lines of a Martian from *Saturday Night Live*. So we threw together a pilot over the phone with ABC executive Marcy Carsey, who had seen Robin's first appearance on *Happy Days*. We needed a colead. Carsey and her partner,

Tom Werner, were instrumental in developing several of my TV shows. Tom then went on to own the Boston Red Sox. However, to play opposite Robin, I remembered an actress I had seen in a pilot that never sold, written by my friend Bob Brunner. The actress played a nun. But even with the nun's veil covering her head, I could tell she had a sweet face. So I told the network to get me that nun. Her name was Pam Dawber, and I hired her without ever meeting her. She had an honest, all-American girl face that I thought would provide a calming and steady counterbalance to Robin's zany, leaping, hair-flying demeanor. I think she was shocked to get a job without having to audition. We never even shot any new material. Marcy simply spliced footage from the nun pilot together with scenes from *Happy Days* and we sold the show off that assemblage. I was vacationing at a resort on the Caribbean island of St. John with my wife when a call came in on a phone that was attached to a tree. I stood under the tree, answered the call, and heard Paramount executive Gary Nardino say, "You just sold *Mork & Mindy*."

Another exciting casting detail about *Mork & Mindy* was the fact that I got to hire one of my idols, the jazz musician Conrad Janis. When I was in high school I would go downtown to the Child's Paramount Theatre to see Conrad Janis and the Tailgaters. They were a great Dixieland band, and Conrad was the best trombone player I had ever heard. When we were casting *Mork & Mindy*, I heard Conrad had moved out to Los Angeles, where he was playing music and going out for television auditions. We brought him in to read for the part of Mindy's dad, who owned a Boulder music store in the series. Hiring Conrad was a great casting choice and also allowed me to finally meet the idol whose music I had admired for so long.

Fonzie put his arms around Mork from Ork and introduced Robin Williams to America, a hit series was born, and we all ran with it. Robin burst on the scene and grabbed the audience's attention, whether they liked it or not. *Happy Days* was sweet and charming, and *Laverne & Shirley* was funny and slapstick; but Robin's humor was topical and edgy. And his quirky and charming Martian was irresistible—even to my son, Scott. He began to watch *Mork & Mindy* and walk around the house saying "Nanoo, nanoo" along with legions of other television viewers. Scott would also pretend to drink water with his finger and crack an egg on his head. Now my son was a fan of mine as well as Lucas, and I felt like a big success in one of the most important places: my own home.

During the first season we set up different situations to showcase Mork as a fish out of water (or an alien come to earth). For example, he went on a date with Laverne DeFazio (played by my sister Penny), fell in love with a mannequin, experienced snow for the first time, faced his first violent fight, learned the meaning of Christmas, and received his first human kiss. We were finding our way with new characters in new situations, and the audience seemed to love it. In the second season we got more complicated with our plots and invited more guest stars to join us. Roddy McDowall played the voice of a robot named Chuck, and Raquel Welch played another alien and romantic interest for Mork. When she arrived for work the first day, I asked Raquel if there was anything I could do for her. She startled me when she said, "Buy me a television." I, of course, wanted to make her as happy as possible, so I bought it for her. I thought she wanted it for her dressing room, but she took the TV right home.

Some of those episodes of *Mork & Mindy* were great, while others—when Mork became a Denver Broncos cheerleader—ventured too far into the land of zany and silly. Our ratings, however, stayed high, and we plowed ahead through the second season.

When *Mork & Mindy* went into production, in 1978, I was busier than I had ever been in television. I still had *Happy Days* and *Laverne & Shirley* on the air, and the network was pressuring me to create more shows. I read and approved the premises of all three shows. I would literally wake up in the morning and say, "Which show has the biggest problem to solve?" and then by the afternoon I was asking my secretary to close my door for thirty minutes so I could take a nap.

I was so busy that I couldn't have just one secretary. I needed to hire one secretary for each show, plus another secretary to oversee those three. The studio was very accommodating and paid for the extra help. They wanted to keep me as productive as possible so I would create more shows for them. I hired a supervising secretary named Diane Perkins Frazen, who had worked for the actor Jackie Cooper. Diane was then a single, peppy, very organized Boston woman who was my age. She grew to care about me, as well as about my wife and three kids. Over the next twenty-two years we could not get through a day without Diane. She was family.

The network was constantly pressuring me to make spinoffs of my successful series. Executive Fred Silverman had taught me about spinoffs, and we had big success with pairing *Happy Days* and *Laverne & Shirley* back-to-back on Tuesday nights. So immediately when *Mork & Mindy* went on the air the network wanted me to pair it with something else on Thursday nights.

To go with Mork, I created a show called *Angie* starring Donna Pescow. She played a poor girl who married a rich doctor, played by Robert Hays. Donna had been a big hit playing the part of Annette in the movie *Saturday Night Fever,* so casting her made good marketing sense. I also cast my good friend Doris Roberts as her mother; years later she was the mother in *Everybody Loves Raymond* and the grandmother in my son Scott's feature *Keeping Up with the Steins.* The show was sweet for a year and went well with *Mork* on Thursdays, but it didn't last beyond that. If I'm completely honest with myself, I have to say *Angie* as a sitcom just wasn't funny enough. We tried but just couldn't take it to a higher comedy level.

Mork & Mindy was the money show to watch. It had the talent of *Laverne & Shirley* without the stress. Robin knew we would protect him, so he felt free enough to push his own limits and those of the network censors. Very often the preshow live audience warm-up was funnier than the script because Robin could be more irreverent and use bad language, which can be very funny in the right hands. He would always try to make Pam Dawber laugh. Sometimes he would even walk out, offstage and then come back naked. He used any means he could to shock Pam and make her mouth literally fall open. Over time the on-screen relationship of Pam playing the straight woman to Robin's funny man became even better-defined and more reliable. The audience knew every time that if Robin did something crazy, Pam would react in a shocked and embarrassed way, like the proper character she was playing.

In the third season we tried to do things we hadn't seen on television before. For example, we aired an episode called "Mork Meets Robin Williams," in which Mindy tries to get an interview with the actor Robin Williams and Mork ends up meeting Robin and doing the interview himself. In the fourth season we tried to hold our audience with romance by having Mork ask Mindy to marry him. After their wedding and honeymoon on Ork, Mork got pregnant and gave birth to Jonathan Winters. We thought Jonathan was a good choice because he was one of Robin's comic heroes. These might seem like far-fetched plots, but it was obvious we were starting to struggle by the fourth season and would do anything to win our audience back.

When Robin and I were alone we would talk about his son Zak (he had only one child at the time), movies, and theater. During the show he was going through a bad divorce from his first wife but was always the hardest worker on set, in perpetual motion. I did get the feeling, however, that he was not 100 percent comfortable and happy unless he was on the nightclub stage, which to me looked like his home. Just give Robin a microphone and an audience, and he could entertain until the last person was ready to call it a night. Sometimes he would get through the filming of the show and then stay up all night at a comedy club. We couldn't control this. It was just the way he was wired. He'd be tired the next day, but he would always show up, ready to play Mork. Sometimes just the fact that he could shock Pam the actress as well as Mindy the character energized him.

Mork & Mindy ran for four years, but it was probably a great show for only the first two years. After that the network decided to put the show on Sunday night opposite *All in the Family*. The problem is that many kids don't watch a lot of television on Sunday nights, so we were basically sent to the wolves. We couldn't beat *All in the Family*. I think the time slot move was based more on greed than on intellect, and it ruined the show. Also, in the third and fourth seasons, I knew that Robin started dreaming of making movies. It is difficult to maintain the momentum on a sitcom when your star has one foot out the door and the rest of the cast and crew know it.

We will always have a lot to reminisce about from *Mork & Mindy*. David Letterman appeared in a small part during the first season, and my sister Ronny tried to recruit another funny comedian named Larry David early on, too. But when Larry came in for the audition, he penciled up the scene he was supposed to act in. Ronny asked him what he was doing, and he said punching up the script. He thought he was auditioning as a writer. He didn't think he was an actor at all. Years later, when he developed his series *Curb Your Enthusiasm,* he would think differently.

During *Mork & Mindy,* I decided to branch out from television again, this time to try my hand at a Broadway play called *The Roast.* I cowrote it with Jerry Belson, who was eager to write a play. *The Roast* was about a group of stand-up comedians who gathered to roast a philanthropic comedian about whom they had complicated feelings. While the comedian was in part based on Danny Thomas, whom we had worked for, we gave the character many traits and mannerisms from other comedians we had met over the years.

We did a reading of the play, and Carl Reiner loved it so much he agreed to direct it. Paramount, so pleased with the work I was doing for them in television, said they would put up the money for the play. However, their investment came with some strings attached: They would put up the $1 million if I would develop more television shows with Tom Miller, Bob Boyett, and Eddie Milkis, who had developed *Happy Days* with me. I agreed. I would have agreed to pretty much any deal in order to do a play again. While I was making my living in television, I still dreamed of finding success in theater.

We cast Rob Reiner as a younger comedian and Peter Boyle (*Everyone Loves Raymond*) to play the philanthropist. We relocated to Boston to launch the show before moving it to Broadway. It was a tricky time for me personally because Rob was in the middle of a divorce with my sister Penny. The headline in one of the local newspapers said LAVERNE & MEATHEAD SPLIT. Rob, normally gregarious and witty, was not that way in Boston. Penny had started dating musician Art Garfunkel, while her best friend Carrie Fisher was dating Paul Simon. All the while Rob was not happy in the lead of our play and was struggling emotionally.

I called up Penny and asked her to come and give me notes on the play. Penny, however, hesitated because she knew if Rob saw her it would upset him. I needed her notes regardless, so we ended up dressing Penny and Art Garfunkel in disguises and snuck them into the back of the theater so Rob wouldn't know they were in the building. Penny came, saw the rehearsal, gave me notes, and left without Rob ever knowing she was in town.

Playing the part seemed to be putting Rob under too much pressure. One day I looked out my hotel room window to see Rob sitting in one of Boston's famous swan boats with his head in his mother, Estelle's, lap. That same day we got word that Rob could not go on the first night in New York because he was clinically depressed. So we planned to put his understudy, Jeff Keller, in for him. I said to Jerry, "There's our star floating in a swan boat in his mom's lap and we are opening on Broadway with a competent but unknown actor named Jeff Keller. This is not a good sign."

Jerry and I flew in our friend Harvey Miller, the comedy writer, to help us punch up the script. Harvey didn't think he had the credentials to call himself a script doctor, so he ran around our hotel room calling himself a script nurse. Jerry and Harvey sometimes did drugs to help them stay awake, but my vices were now ice cream and cashew nuts, and a few strong cups of coffee one night. I hadn't had coffee in more than twenty years, since getting out of the army. But that night I was so desperate to stay awake that I drank coffee anyway, not realizing the jolt of caffeine might be too much for me to handle. I suddenly thought I was having a heart attack instead. I was rolling on the floor and I couldn't catch my breath. My secretary Diane helped get me into a cab at three in the morning and we went to the emergency room. It turned out it was an anxiety attack coupled with the effects of the strong coffee.

My anxiety attack was well-founded. When the play opened in Boston the reviews were bad. The premise lacked romance. We had fourteen men, two girls, and no romance. I would never make that mistake again. When Michael Eisner read the reviews of the play in Boston, however, he no longer wanted to offer his financial support. He wanted to get me back to producing television rather than give me the additional $250,000 to take the play to Broadway's Winter Garden Theatre. He did say he would consider giving me money for another play another time, but he didn't see the value of putting any more money into *The Roast*.

I had a dilemma: I wanted to go to Broadway, but I didn't have great faith in the play. Despite that fact, Jerry and I hadn't come this far and worked this hard just to see our play fall short of Broadway. I told Eisner to forget his money and I would find another way. Despite the headaches the cast of *Laverne & Shirley* gave me, Penny and I have always been very close. Whenever I have an ethical dilemma I ask for her advice. "Should I give up?" I asked. She said, "No. You've never been to Broadway. Go for it. We are people who learn from our experiences whether they turn out good or bad. So I would shoot for Broadway if I were you."

"But how am I going to raise the money?" I asked. "Paramount pulled out."

"I'll give you some, and then I'll raise the rest from friends. Give me a day or two," she said.

Penny wrote a check, and she got Cindy Williams and Jim Brooks to write checks, too. Cindy wrote me a note with the check that read something like, "I don't know what you are doing in Boston but without you I wouldn't have a career. So here is some money."

Jerry and I knew it was a long shot, but we went ahead and opened *The Roast* at the Winter Garden. Our friends, family, wives, and children flew in from Los Angeles to see us make our Broadway debut. Unfortunately, we lasted through only eleven previews and three nights; then we had to close the show. As we were leaving the theater we saw two men putting up a sign for a new show.

"*Cats*?" said Jerry as he read the sign.

"A show about pussycats?" I asked, mockingly.

"It will never last," said Jerry.

My friend Joel Sterns, always a great lawyer and adviser, said to me, "You helped *Cats*."

"How?" I asked.

"You lowered the bar," said Joel.

Cats went on to run for eighteen years on Broadway, making it one of the longest running shows ever. *The Roast* ran three nights. That's show business. But I don't regret it. I got to live my dream of seeing something I had written on Broadway, if only for eleven previews and three nights. And the three nights was even a stretch. We had to stay open those nights in order to collect the insurance money. However, Rob Reiner was able to come back and resumed his starring part for the last two nights, and he was terrific.

When we realized *The Roast* was a failure, we had to close it. Jerry took the first flight home to Los Angeles. I wanted to stay and throw a goodbye party, and his wife Joanne decided to stay with me and host it. I always feel you have to stay as a leader for better or worse. You can't leave the ship. We had a nice party, but the closing of the play still came as quite a blow to all of us. My eleven-year-old son, Scott, couldn't understand the injustice. "But they laughed, Dad. I heard the audience laugh." I learned that in theater, and later in movies, you need more than just "funny." You have to have a story with depth and emotion that people can follow. Unfortunately, while I was working on *The Roast,* ABC canceled *Mork & Mindy.* The show had a lot of problems, but one of them was that I was not there to produce, supervise, and spearhead as I had done during the first two seasons. I was too busy working on *The Roast* to give *Mork & Mindy* the time and attention it deserved.

Before *Mork & Mindy* was canceled in 1982, we had some wonderful acclaim. In 1978 I was named one of *People* magazine's most intriguing people. And in March 1979, Robin was on the cover of *Time* magazine. I had four of the five top programs—*Happy Days, Laverne & Shirley, Mork & Mindy,* and *Angie*—*Three's Company* was the only series I did not produce that was in the top five rated shows consistently. But even a great show can last only so long.

When I look back on *Mork & Mindy,* there is one story that epitomizes for me what the show was all about and why it was such a success. I directed one of the first episodes, and we had three cameras, which was typically the number used to shoot a half-hour sitcom.

One of the cameramen was an industry veteran name Sam Rosen, who was in his late seventies and had worked on all of my television shows. Sam was positioned at Camera A while other operators were at Cameras B and C. We filmed a scene of Robin entering his apartment in which he ran around the set performing dialogue from the script but also ad-libbing, as well as leaping and jumping, performing his heart out.

"Cut," I yelled when the scene was done. Then I turned to Sam. "Did you get that?" I asked him.

"He never came by here," said Sam, drily.

"Then you have to move the camera. Robin is such a genius!" I said, frustrated we had missed the magic.

"If he's such a genius, he should learn to hit his marks," said Sam.

Immediately, the other producers and I hired a fourth camera to follow Robin. It was clear our traditional camera model was not going to be enough to capture his brilliance, his ad-libs, and his physical humor. A fourth camera would be more expensive, but it was worth the money to capture all the different sides to Robin. We would save money on other things, but when Robin performed as Mork from Ork, you didn't want to miss a beat.

Nearly thirty years after *Mork & Mindy* went off the air, I went to see Robin in New York City, where he was starring in a play called *Bengal Tiger at the Baghdad Zoo*. After the show, in which he was terrific, my wife and I went backstage. When we entered his dressing room, Robin gestured toward me and announced to the others, "This is the man who gave me my first big job." Robin always knows how to make me smile.

10. YOUNG DOCTORS IN LOVE

★

Directing an Outrageous Hospital
Comedy as My First Movie

AT THE AGE of forty-eight I wanted to direct a movie. But you can't really wake up one day a television producer and become a movie director the next day—particularly when you are forty-eight years old. The truth was that nobody really wanted to give me a movie to direct. Most people in Hollywood wanted me to keep producing television shows. In Hollywood if you do something well that makes money, people say, "Do it again!" They don't say things like "experiment," "try something new," "see what else you are good at." These are things that would be considered risky, and in show business to take a risk could mean to lose money. While people in general don't want to lose money, in Hollywood that aversion is even greater because when people lose money, people lose jobs, too.

I, however, was ready to take a personal risk. Brandon Stoddard, an executive and a fan of my TV shows, had been doing Movies of the Week for ABC Television. The network asked him to start up a major motion picture division. He came to me with a complicated comedy script called *Young Doctors in Love,* written by two sitcom writers, Michael Elias and Rich Eustis. It was a satirical and romantic hospital comedy in the same vein as the movie *Airplane!* It wasn't great, but it was mine to direct. And it was the only script I had been offered, so I jumped at the chance. Without a studio or group of executives to come out in favor of my decision, only my agent, Joel Cohen, and my wife, Barbara, encouraged me. So to help support me during my adventure in directing, I gathered a group of aspiring directors to be my support system: Rob Reiner, my ex–brother-in-law; my sister Penny; and Jim Brooks, a television producer also trying to break into movie directing. I decided that we would look at each other's rough cuts, or rough drafts during the editing process, and offer critique and guidance.

Young Doctors in Love starred Sean Young and Michael McKean, with cameos from a bevy of ABC's most popular soap opera stars, including Demi Moore from *General Hospital*. Sean was an up-and-coming star who had made a name for herself in the hot movie *Blade Runner*. Michael I knew well from his years playing Lenny in *Laverne & Shirley*. As it was my first film, I was hoping to be paired with a veteran producer. However, the production company signed me with a brand-new producer named Jerry Bruckheimer. I didn't know it at first, but how lucky could I get? Jerry would go on to become one of the most successful blockbuster movie producers of all time. At the time all I knew was that he was there to support and protect me every step of the way, wearing his crisp blue jeans and tweed blazer. I also had an incredible cast of new and talented actors, many of whom went on to have big careers as well. Imagine directing your first movie with a supporting cast that included Harry Dean Stanton, Hector Elizondo, Pamela Reed, Crystal Bernard, and Michael Richards (later Kramer on *Seinfeld*).

I met Hector at my house, where I hosted a Saturday morning basketball game. I had also seen him in a play called *Sly Fox* opposite George C. Scott on Broadway. From the moment I met Hector I saw him as the world's most versatile actor because of his range as well as his wide and varied collection of toupees. Hector was an actor with the look of everyman. He stood tall and wise like a Spaniard but was really a Puerto Rican drummer and dancer from the streets of New York. In *Young Doctors in Love,* I cast Hector as a gangster on the run disguised in a dress through most of the movie. Some actors wouldn't touch a part in a dress, but Hector was fearless about his image. He would do whatever the acting job called for.

With my cast set I was excited to get behind the camera on my first feature. However, the first week of preproduction I was exhausted, and the reason was simple: I was smoking too many cigarettes and not eating enough. I had been trying to quit smoking for a long time, for my health and my family. Once a year I promised myself to stop smoking on my son's January 17 birthday, but by January 19, I was smoking again. So as I began my first movie at the age of forty-eight, I was also losing my battle to quit smoking.

I smoked around my kids. I smoked in the backyard. I smoked in my office. I smoked in the car. I smoked before, during, and after meals. At the height of my smoking I was up to four packs a day. I would light cigarettes and then smoke a few puffs and then snub them out when they got in the way of my writing or typing or eating. I didn't smoke them to the bone or save the butts because that was too much effort. I smoked Pall Malls and Larks with filters because they were supposed to be better for your health, as if there was such a thing. Even when I was sick I smoked, usually Newports or Kool menthols because they smelled more medicinal. I would drive my kids to school and light up at 7:30 in the morning. My five-year-old daughter Kathleen would say with a scolding tone, "Daddy, you are smoking again! You said you were going to stop!" Smoking was the bane of my existence. So after trying to quit on and off by myself, I decided to seek professional help.

The first place I went was the Schick Stop Smoking Program. I would stop smoking for a few days and then light up again. The Schick people wrote on my intake card that I was "incorrigible." I tried herbs. I tried chewing gum. I tried hypnotism. I tried patches. I tried everything under the sun, but nothing seemed to curb my desire to remain a devoted smoker. Then one day on the set of *Young Doctors in Love,* I met a young actress named Carol Williard, who played a nurse in the movie. We were talking while waiting for the cinematographer to set up a shot. She mentioned that she worked part-time as a smoking therapist. I asked if she could help me. She was also working at the time with Henry Winkler and Johnny Carson, and said she would take me on as a client, too.

The first thing she made me do was carry a pack of cigarettes in the front pocket of my button-down shirt every place I went. I could smoke a cigarette at any time I wanted to, but the point was that I was choosing *not* to smoke. The physical addiction eventually goes away, but the habit takes longer. When I was starting to direct my first movie seemed the worst time to quit smoking and I just couldn't do it. But Carol and I continued to talk on the phone about how to cut down my smoking during the movie. We talked about how much I didn't need the cigarettes and how much healthier I would be eventually without them. She acted pretty well in the movie, too.

The first location was a night shoot, and I was very nervous. We started at 10:00 P.M. and shot until 10:00 A.M. The first shot I had to complete was of a café awning held up by four posts. In the scene Sean Young is supposed to get dizzy, fall into the poles, and knock the awning to the ground, covering all of the customers. It was a tricky scene to direct and it took me a few tries, but I was able to get it right. If I had known, I never would have picked such a difficult scene to be my first, nor would I have chosen to do a night shoot on my first day. It was too grueling. But what kept me going was that my friends and family visited me throughout the night; they lifted my spirits and lowered the stress.

One of my favorite visitors that night was the director Francis Coppola. He came to the set and put his arm around me, which boosted my popularity with the cast and crew. I thought he was going to share some überintellectual, meaningful wisdom that only a seasoned director could give me. Instead he said these words: "Change your shoes a lot, Garry. Your feet are going to hurt. So bring a couple different pairs to the set and change them." So his advice had less to do with art and more to do with the comfort of standing on your feet all day long. He was right. He also gave me one other piece of valuable advice. He said if I ever found that I needed something essential to my story, like a piece of equipment or even the pivotal casting of an actor, and the studio wouldn't pay for it, then I should pay for it out of my own pocket. I honestly never heard that concept before. I never paid for anything on *Happy Days* out of my own pocket. I always asked Paramount, and they did it or not. I soon learned that movies were different and in many ways more personal statements than television. If you had a vision for your movie, Francis said, you had to be willing to defend it and possibly pay for it, too.

In my attempt to make everyone my friend on the set, I wore a different major league baseball jacket each day of the shoot, and then I rotated them back. I figured someone on the set would be a fan of the team each day, and I would have my secretary Diane or the set photographer take a photo of us together. I did make some new friends, but the working pace of my first movie blew me away. The crew lights a scene for an hour and then they want you to shoot it in five minutes. I didn't quite understand that the bottom line on a movie is to stay on schedule no matter what. One day I went into my trailer, shut the door, and couldn't come out. I wasn't trying to cause a fuss. I was simply paralyzed, unable to continue. My secretary called my wife, who rushed over to the set. Barbara entered my trailer and found me lying on the bed.

"What's wrong?" she said.

"I can't do it," I said. "I'm exhausted. I can't think."

"Fight through it. Do you want an ice cream sandwich or a Fudgsicle?"

Barbara knew that ice cream was and still remains my favorite treat and an easy distraction.

"I don't want anything," I said. "I'm too tired to even eat."

I knew I was sounding like a child, because that was how I felt, like an overly tired kid.

"You have to get through this movie," she said. "People are counting on you."

My wife, forever the clinical nurse, is not a person to dwell on anything. She is from the school of the stiff upper lip: Wash your face off and get a strong cup of coffee to fix any problem, night or day.

"I'm not in the right shape," I said. "I'm scared again all the time and I don't have the right energy. Maybe I'm not meant to be a movie director."

"We will decide that later, but right now get up, splash some water on your face, and get back out to your crew. They are waiting for you."

And I did. I muddled through the picture, each day trying to stay positive and figure out the job as I went along. I had directed episodes of *Happy Days* and *Laverne & Shirley,* but the length of the days on a movie set was nothing like in television. I could smoke and eat candy bars and produce television shows and then go to sleep. But you can't do that and direct a movie. You have to work harder and longer hours and spend all of your meals and waking moments on the set directing, thinking, making decisions that count and cost money. I realized very early on that in order to keep my head above water, I needed to find a mentor. I needed someone on the set I could turn to for guidance and support. I found that person in our production designer, Polly Platt, a pretty, petite woman who knew more about movies at the time than any man I had met.

Polly had been married for years to the director Peter Bogdanovich and had worked with Orson Welles. So she had career and life experience with crazy directors. She had worked on dozens of movies, including *The Last Picture Show, The Bad News Bears,* and *A Star Is Born.* She knew the movie business inside and out. She said when she met me that she thought I would make a good director because I was tall. A lot of directors are short, she said, and didn't date well in high school. They put all of their love fantasies on the screen, and do it badly. She thought because I was tall I must have dated well in high school, and therefore would direct more appealing mainstream love stories. This is the kind of wonderful logic Polly deals in. During the movie, I would turn to her whenever I was confused and needed advice from a person wiser than myself. We soon developed a not-so-subtle shorthand. Whenever I asked her if something was working and she made a loud gagging noise, I knew I was making a mistake.

One day I went in to pitch her a new idea. "So I think I will shoot this love scene on a lake. And while the lovers are talking, a beautiful sailboat will go by," I said.

Polly began to make the loud gagging noise. "No," she said. "No sailboats."

"Why not? Don't you think a sailboat will be pretty?" I asked.

"Who cares about pretty? It's not practical. A sailboat takes too much time to turn around for the next take. You have to shoot it a few times," she said very matter-of-factly.

"Then what should I do?"

"Get a motorboat," she said. "A motorboat turns around fast!"

Polly understood what I grew to understand, too: A director has to stay on schedule, and anything that costs too much time is not worth it. Even with the guidance I got from Polly, there was just so much for me to learn. I didn't know about rain or cover sets—backup sets to shoot a scene when another scene was compromised because of rain or illness or whatever. I didn't know when to use a crane shot. Jerry Paris, the longtime director on *Happy Days,* did give me another good piece of advice: "When in doubt, take a walk." He gave me permission to pause and leave the set whenever I needed a moment to think. He said that just a quick walk around the block could help me stop feeling overwhelmed.

One day I was feeling way out of my league. A scene was not working and I didn't know what to do. I told the crew that I was going for a quick walk. On that walk I realized something significant: I was not going to be able to show my cast and crew what a great director I was because the reality was that I was not a great director. I was a director with the best intentions, but I was not even a good director yet. The reason the producers had hired me to direct the script was that I could make it funny.

I went back, and I told the cameraman to get me the widest lens he had in his truck. I didn't even know the proper name of the lens yet. I just told him to get me the biggest one. Then we shot the scene I was having trouble with. Only this time I had actor Gary Friedkin, a little person who was playing a doctor, enter the scene and try to hang up a telephone bolted to the wall while regular dialogue was going on in the foreground. Gary was too short, so he had to jump and then slide a gurney along the wall to slam-dunk the phone. The scene proved to be one of the best comedy scenes in the whole movie. Taking my walk around the block definitely gave me time to pause and re-create this scene in order to make it work. After we filmed the scene the cast and crew seemed to look at me with a hint more respect in their eyes. Even our producer Jerry Bruckheimer patted me on the back and said, "That was funny!"

After we wrapped the shooting of *Young Doctors in Love,* I began editing my first feature film. It was then that my exhaustion really set in. I was almost taken to the hospital one day. Another day Bruckheimer came to me with a script for the next movie he was going to produce. It was called *Flashdance.* I couldn't even consider the script, however, because I was so tired. He wanted to shoot *Flashdance* right away, so he went with another director. (Was I sad later? Sure. Who wouldn't have wanted to direct a hit like *Flashdance?* However, at the time it would have been impossible for me to move immediately on to another movie. I didn't have the stamina or experience. That would come much later.) I returned to the editing room and started drinking nutrition shakes to try to give myself energy and boost my immune system, but nothing helped. I started to lose weight and looked thinner than I had ever been. I was basically working hours that were too long and smoking too many cigarettes. Chain smoking never gives a person the energy he needs or deserves.

To make matters worse, while I was editing *Young Doctors in Love,* a real-life situation came into play. My mother got sick and slipped into a coma. She had been suffering from Alzheimer's disease for many years, but things grew worse quickly during the end of my movie. I went to visit her in the hospital while she was in the coma. I had read in a magazine that when Dustin Hoffman's mother was in a coma, he squeezed her hand and she squeezed back, and that was how they communicated. But when I squeezed my mother's hand, she did not squeeze back. She died that Christmas while I was on a break from the movie celebrating the holidays with my family in Hawaii. I missed her, but her mind had slipped away from us many years earlier. I lost my mother, but I always knew she would leave me with her greatest assets: her biting sense of humor and superior comic timing. She was the Lucille Ball of the Grand Concourse, and to this day whenever I write a joke or punch up a scene, I know I'm using the humor tools my mother gave to me.

Young Doctors in Love did not, as they say, "do big box office" or "have legs" to become a runaway hit. It made money only in Spain, where there was a big rainstorm opening weekend and people decided to go to the movies in droves. It also did well in Sweden because socialized medicine was very popular there, so any film that made fun of Western medicine struck a chord with the Swedes. But you can't get a blockbuster from striking it rich only in Spain and Sweden. We had a big cast party, and I remember feeling tired beyond repair. I was doing interviews with the press and I could hardly form a complete intelligent sentence. When my wife finally dragged me home, I slept for three days.

I read some reviews of *Young Doctors in Love,* and they were all pretty bad. Although Janet Maslin, writing for *The New York Times,* didn't totally dismiss the film when she wrote: "Every imaginable kind of gag has been wedged into *Young Doctors in Love,* in hopes of getting another *Airplane!* off the ground. Not all of them are funny, and plenty of them fall flat. But there are enough bright moments to make this a passable hot-weather entertainment." So that pretty much summed it up for me—I was a director of "passable hot-weather entertainment." After reading the reviews I decided to make a deal with myself: If I ever directed another movie I would collect all of the reviews but not read them. I would put them in a file folder and wait a year from the release to allow myself some perspective. I then took some time to think about my future and what I wanted to do next. I remember calling Penny and saying, "I don't think I want to do another movie. Directing isn't for me."

I was, however, already signed up to direct another movie. My contract for *Young Doctors in Love* was a two-picture deal with ABC Motion Pictures. So while I'd passed on Bruckheimer's offer to direct *Flashdance,* I was faced with another decision: What script would I direct next for ABC? During one of my weekly Saturday morning basketball games, the answer arrived. Producer Michael Phillips showed up with a script called *Sweet Ginger Brown,* which he had won in a card game from the musician Mama Cass Elliot. It was a coming-of-age comedy about a teenager working one hot summer as a cabana boy at a beach club in New York, and it had a stronger and more believable story line than *Young Doctors in Love*. We rewrote the script, retitled it *The Flamingo Kid,* and started to work on casting.

I knew, however, that I had to do one thing before I directed another movie. I had to quit smoking. I went back to work with Carol Williard, who was now my smoking coach. I smoked my last cigarette before *The Flamingo Kid* started, and almost immediately I began to feel physically and emotionally better. Would my second movie be a hit? Would I find the process easier the second time? Would the pace be less stressful being in New York, away from Hollywood? I didn't know. I just knew that directing without a cigarette in my hand had to count for something good. Two hands free had to be better than one. And nobody was happier that I stopped smoking than my wife.

11. THE FLAMINGO KID

★

Going Back to My New York Roots

IN 1983 I GOT a star on the Hollywood Walk of Fame for my television work. I bought a piece of the Portland Beavers minor league baseball team with Ron Howard. I built a dance studio in memory of my mother at Northwestern University. I started playing more tennis and basketball because I had more energy since I'd stopped smoking. I produced a new spinoff from *Happy Days* called *Joanie Loves Chachi,* and Cindy Williams named me in a $20 million lawsuit because she said I made her work too hard on *Laverne & Shirley* while she was pregnant. A pretty busy year for a forty-nine-year-old married father of three. I liked getting my star. I owned the baseball team for three years. *Joanie Loves Chachi* was a big hit in Korea because the name Chachi sounds like their word for *penis.* And Cindy Williams eventually settled her lawsuit with me and we became friends forever. So I then had the time to focus on my next directing project: *The Flamingo Kid.*

I relocated to New York City for the summer to cast the movie and then stayed on throughout the shoot. I lived in midtown Manhattan at the Parker Meridien hotel, and most days we drove out to Far Rockaway, where the movie was shot at a beach club. I liked being in New York again. A few times since I left the Bronx I have gone back to visit my old apartment building, and taken my wife and children. I have always been nostalgic for the Grand Concourse. The time I spent shooting *The Flamingo Kid* was no different. How I went from a sick kid in bed to a movie director sometimes confounds even me. But as I started to direct my second feature film, a story about a gin rummy game at a beach club and a teenage boy on the cusp of becoming a man, I felt more grateful for my own career than I had ever been. I was still, of course, scared, in a new way, that if this movie wasn't a hit they would tell me to go back to television. But I would give it a shot. As Penny said, we are people who learn from our experiences. Samuel Beckett once wrote, "Ever tried. Ever failed. No matter. Try again. Fail again. Fail better." That's me.

Originally we cast Matthew Broderick in the lead, but then the deal fell apart and he took another movie. A nineteen-year-old Matt Dillon was hired by the studio and announced the first day we met that "I don't do comedy." I had seen his two recent movies *The Outsiders* and *Rumble Fish,* and he was right, they were not brimming with comedy. In fact, Matt spent a lot of time in those movies looking down and mumbling into his shoes. So I told him in this movie we would help him look up more. On the outside he was a tough and brooding movie star on the rise, but on the inside he was still a kid from New Rochelle. I knew that from a humor perspective, I had to find something that would work for the movie and for him. I took Matt to lunch at Wolf's, my favorite deli in Manhattan that is sadly now closed. I noticed that he made an unconscious little humming sound with his mouth as he ate the sandwich. I said, "Matt, that is funny! We'll put that right in the movie." I think I startled him by recognizing the comedy that was hiding inside of him. He didn't even seem to know it existed.

For the part of Matt's gin-rummy-playing mentor, our casting director, Margery Simkin, suggested Richard Crenna. I knew him casually and from seeing him from time to time at the girls' school where both our daughters went. But I didn't realize until we got on the set what a true godsend Richard would turn out to be. Steady and precise, his performance in *The Flamingo Kid,* in my opinion, is just brilliant. Richard, Jessica Walter, and Hector Elizondo, whom I cast as Matt's hardworking plumber father, were all pivotal to have on a movie set where most of the other actors were inexperienced and under twenty-five years old. I always find it helpful to surround young performers with adults like I did on *Happy Days* with Marion

Ross and Tom Bosley, and Phil Foster and Betty Garrett on *Laverne & Shirley*. Without the adults the kids don't have any role models to look up to.

I'm always casting people, even when I'm outside my office or on vacation. So it's no surprise that I found Matt's female romantic costar at a celebrity sports weekend in Southern California. I was down in La Costa with my wife at a tennis tournament hosted by Carl Reiner. I saw a young woman with long legs and strawberry blonde hair hitting the ball on a nearby court. I turned to Barbara and said, "If that girl can talk, I need her for *The Flamingo Kid*." I didn't need an experienced actress but I did need one who could deliver the dialogue in a convincing and charming way. Her name was Janet Jones, and she had played semiprofessional softball and was very athletic. She had exactly the peaches-and-cream look I needed to play opposite Matt. (Real-life hockey player Wayne Gretzky was also attracted to her athletic looks; he married her a few years after the movie came out.)

The Flamingo Kid was the first movie where I introduced pranks. I found you need something to think about other than the movie because the pace can drive you crazy. To lighten the atmosphere I introduced the concept of the last-day pie in the face. Whenever an actor was shooting his last scene of the movie, he would get hit in the face with a whipped cream pie when he least expected it. On his last day Hector thought he was safe because he was shooting a scene in a car alone. But I snuck someone with a pie into the backseat of the car and we got him anyway. The big stars didn't want a pie in the face, but they got hit anyway. There is no "star protection" from my list of pranks.

One of the things I learned early on to enjoy about directing is the unexpected. Studios make big deals, agents package famous movie stars together, and lots of money is made every day, but none of that excites me as much as when I get to discover a special person who has not been on the big screen before. That is what happened when I first saw little Peter Costa. His mother brought his sister in to audition, and she sang, danced, and did the hula hoop. When she was done they walked back out to the waiting room, and that is when I saw Peter, the little girl's brother, lying on the carpeting. He had a chubby face with freckles, white skin, and wise eyes that made him look older than he was.

"Who is that?" I asked the mother.

"My six-year-old, Peter," she said.

"What does he do?" I asked.

"Nothing. He doesn't do much of anything," she said. "He hardly talks."

"Are you sure?" I said excitedly.

She nodded.

I looked down at Peter and saw that he had perhaps the world's greatest deadpan expression. I hired him on the spot, confusing the mother to no end because she had brought her daughter in to audition. But sometimes you find your cast where you least expect them. I had to hire his sister, too, because I didn't want to cause any trouble at home for them. I used Peter throughout the movie at the cabana club as well as in our beach scenes. I wasn't the only one who recognized his talent. Later Peter became a regular on *The Cosby Show*.

The casting was more intense than usual on *The Flamingo Kid* because we had a lot of beach scenes and at one time more than five hundred extras. I tried to fill the crowd with interesting looking people I liked such as Jack Klugman's son Adam and a talented actor I knew would become big one day named John Turturro. I also remember sitting on the beach listening to two girls who were talking with the worst accents. One of them was named Marisa Tomei. I thought they were interesting girls—and not your usual actresses— so I put them right in the movie and gave them speaking roles. With the casting under control, I also was a happier director on *The Flamingo Kid* because it was a story I could relate to growing up with my own dad.

The original writer, Neal Marshall, no relationship to me, had written a solid script based on his youth spent in the Catskills. Neal and I rewrote the script with notes from the producers, then the screenwriter Bo Goldman took a pass at a rewrite but would not ask for screenwriting credit for it. Bo let Neal and me share credit because he said he didn't change enough to warrant credit. He did, however, tell me that while the dialogue was essential, the actors' reactions to things were even more important. So I never forgot that while directing the movie. Later, when I met director Blake Edwards, he said the same thing. "The reaction to the action is critical." To have a great line is nice, but to have a strong and memorable reaction is even better.

Directing a film *after* I quit smoking was a life-changing event for me. I had so much more energy and could come up with more material for the actors. In one of my favorite scenes, Matt Dillon visits the fancy home of Richard Crenna. Since moving to California in the 1960s, I have been to many people's fancy homes and have felt like a foreigner in a strange land myself. Just entering a home in Bel Air makes me feel like I'm going to knock something big and pricey over and break it. Once I went to the house of Doug Cramer, who was the head of Paramount at the time. I had to go to the bathroom, so I tried to pee in the fancy bathroom without making any noise so the people in the living room wouldn't hear me. I was able to remember my own nervous anxiety and put it into *The Flamingo Kid.* I also had Matt take some guest soap and put it in his pocket, and then had Richard voice-over the line, "What are you doing in there? Stealing the soap?" Matt might have been new to comedy, but he took what I gave him and made people laugh out loud.

As harrowing as the shoot on *Young Doctors* was, *The Flamingo Kid* was a delight. The cast and crew seemed to enjoy coming to work each day. I know I certainly did, especially working alongside cinematographer Jimmy Contner, who would go on to shoot the television series *Miami Vice.* Contner was an intense man with a great cinematic style. After I introduced pranks, the cast started making up some of their own. One day Richard and Matt were in a car set so long they made a cardboard sign that read, FREE THE CAR PEOPLE. Another day, after controlling five hundred extras all day long in a swimming pool scene with a giant bullhorn, the first assistant director, Stephen Lim, called it a wrap, then jumped into the pool fully clothed. These were not depressing movie days. They were truly happy ones. The hardest part of the movie was being away from my wife and kids, but they made several trips to New York to see me, which made me happy. With two kids still in high school and one in college, it was a tough time to be out of town. My wife had started to work again, too, as a nurse at the Los Angeles Free Clinic.

I shot the ending of the movie and headed back to Los Angeles. When I got home I realized I had shot the ending wrong. But I didn't have enough experience as a director to know how to fix my problem. Who should I talk to? How should I proceed? Was I overreacting? So I went to consult my producer Michael Phillips, who by then had produced three big films: *The Sting, Taxi Driver,* and *Close Encounters of the Third Kind*. He was a kind man who offered me nothing but patience and wisdom. If I didn't have the experience to know what to do about the ending, Michael certainly did. He told me if I thought that I really had the wrong ending, then I had to ask the studio for more money to reshoot it. So I did just that. But it was too expensive to fly the cast and crew back to New York, so we had to reshoot the ending in Los Angeles. Instead of building a set we decided to shoot at Alice's Restaurant in Malibu, because there we could have an inside-outside beach set to closely match the one we had shot in New York.

I thought a beach was a beach, but I turned out to be wrong. The sun on the West Coast sets on a different side than the sun on the East Coast. So we decided to shoot in Malibu at night. With the sunset problem addressed I had to deal with the thematic problem. In the original ending, the dad (Hector) and the son (Matt) never really made up. Their reconciliation was too casual and unsatisfying. So with the reshoot I had to bring the father and son back together with a more triumphant reunion. I did what I wished my own father had done more with me—I had them hug. I knew that the audience needed to see them hug. Even after a son "comes of age," he still can always use a hug from his dad to let him know he is on the right track.

When I was working in television I developed a crew who went with me from series to series, but in film I didn't have that yet. So I decided near the end of *The Flamingo Kid* that I had to start jotting down names of the people I might want to work with again. One day I was listening to the walkie-talkies, which the production assistants used to communicate with one another. Suddenly I overheard a thick, authoritative New York accent bellowing very intelligent commands from an outer parking lot. I went up to the first assistant director and said, "Who is that voice?" He said "Ellen Schwartz. She's great." So I made a note to hire her for my next picture and possibly promote her. When you see good people who do their jobs well and can make your life easier, you want to bring them onto your next picture, too. (Ellen later became a terrific producer and worked on several of my later movies.) The key for me is to make a cohesive team on my movies like I had done growing up with my Falcons sports teams.

The first editor who cut our dailies had to leave to do another movie, so for the major editing I hired Priscilla Nedd. She was a self-professed workaholic, and I liked her the moment I met her. She was unmarried, without kids, and could work as long as I needed her. (She would often say during our editing sessions that she worried she would never get married. But she was wrong: I later walked her down the aisle when she married producer David Friendly.) We edited the film at Raleigh Studios near Paramount, where I had done my television shows for so many years. I'm always one to appreciate good karma, and I liked being so close to Paramount and my old working neighborhood. Not only was Priscilla willing to work hard like me but she showed passion when necessary. Sometimes when we were arguing she would climb up on top of the editing machine and lay down and say things like "I can't do that edit. I won't do it. Please don't make me." She made me laugh, but I respected her, too. She had just worked as one of the editors on *An Officer and a Gentleman,* which I admired, so I trusted her taste. We literally had to work around the clock sometimes to get the job done on *The Flamingo Kid* because we always felt behind.

One day I went to the office to get something. I noticed a man in the office, wearing a wig, fixing our window shades. Suddenly the man turned around, and I saw it was Ron Howard and he said, "Garry, this is your life!" He quickly ushered me out of the building to a waiting limousine. Priscilla looked out the window from upstairs to see me leaving in the limousine with Ron Howard and she yelled down, "Garry, where the *fuck* are you going?" She was panicked because we were behind schedule again and had to screen a preview soon for test audiences. But I had no choice. Ron took me to a nearby soundstage, where they filmed my episode of *This Is Your Life* as a television special. My teacher Raphael Philipson from DeWitt Clinton High School was there, along with Pete Wagner, on whom I had based Fonzie. My family and other friends celebrated memories with me, too. Glory, however, passed quickly and later that night I went back to editing with Priscilla.

When I finished *The Flamingo Kid,* I hoped for bigger box office receipts than *Young Doctors* just so I could say that I had improved from my first picture to my second. I don't need a lot of praise, but I do always like to do better. But what I didn't expect was that there would actually be good reviews. They would prove to be some of the best reviews of my career. Critics were putting my picture in the same category as *Diner* and *Risky Business.* Audiences and critics were suddenly taking me seriously as a director and not telling me to go right back to television. Overall, reviewers thought Matt Dillon was great, Richard Crenna brilliant, and the story a strong, solid comedy.

A reviewer for the *Herald Tribune* said that the film was a "delightful surprise" and that Matt "looked like he enjoyed acting" again. Roger Ebert said it was one of the top ten summer movies and had a "surprising emotional impact." David Ansen, covering the film for *Newsweek,* wrote about my directing, "This big change of pace suddenly reveals a filmmaker to watch closely." *USA Today* called it the best movie about young people since *American Graffiti.* I was very excited when *The Hollywood Reporter* said that my movie was a winning version of *Goodbye, Columbus* because I loved that film. The bottom line was that *Young Doctors* showed I was funny and *The Flamingo Kid* showed I was a filmmaker to watch. All I had to figure out was what my third script would be. I felt like I had just been given a golden ticket that said: "Proceed with caution, you may now direct again."

12. NOTHING IN COMMON

★

Working with the Great Ones—

Hanks and Gleason

HAD A COMPLICATED relationship with my father. He taught me many things, including how to be in charge and a leader, but we did not have the same close relationship I saw other sons have with their dads growing up in the Bronx. He sometimes treated my sisters and me like business colleagues, as if we shared the cubicle next to him. There wasn't much I could do to repair the distance between me and my dad, even after he moved to Hollywood and worked with me at Paramount. I did, however, make a pledge to myself that if I ever had a son of my own I would hug him a lot, and tell him how much I loved him and was proud of him. I was able to do that when my son, Scott, was born.

I was thinking a lot about fathers and sons as I set out to direct my third movie, *Nothing in Common,* written by Rick Podell and Michael Preminger. The story of an adult son forming a relationship late in life with his dad was set to shoot in Chicago. That's when it became clear to me that a lot of the movie business is out of town. The problem with that is that I am a homebody. I love my San Fernando Valley house and my office, which are a five-minute drive apart. But the good news about *Nothing in Common* was that at the time my daughter Lori was going to Northwestern University, my alma mater, just outside of Chicago. So at least I would have family close by.

I had worked with producers Jerry Bruckheimer on *Young Doctors in Love* and Michael Phillips on *The Flamingo Kid,* and both ran in mainstream Hollywood studio circles. But *Nothing in Common* came to me from another direction. Alexandra Rose showed up at my office one day with the script. She said she was a big fan of *The Flamingo Kid* and had been one of the producers on both *Norma Rae* and *I Wanna Hold Your Hand*. Alex was bright, ambitious, and kind. She was a Phi Beta Kappa from Wisconsin who had the looks and brains to work with anyone. I'm glad she picked me. The moment I met Alex we got along, and I liked that she was a healthy person and took care of herself through yoga and a macrobiotic diet. After years of smoking and bad eating, I was trying to take care of myself, too, and she was a good example.

Tom Hanks was attached to the script for *Nothing in Common* from the beginning. It is the story of a hotshot advertising executive who must balance his demanding job with the unraveling of his parents' marriage and health. The movie centers on the relationship between the son and his father, a Willy Loman–style character whose professional and personal lives are falling apart. I knew Tom casually from passing him on the Paramount lot, where he filmed his series *Bosom Buddies* near our *Happy Days* soundstage. He had also done one episode of *Happy Days,* playing a bully who Fonzie beat up, and even played on the *Happy Days* traveling softball team a few times. I always thought Tom was a funny and talented comedian, but when we started *Nothing in Common* he was anything but funny. He was miserable, going through a bad breakup.

Initially Tom didn't tell me anything was wrong. This often happens with stars: You sense there is something wrong with their *private* lives but they are too *private* to share it with you. You have to do your homework and talk to their agents or managers or personal assistants to find out exactly what is eating at them. Another secret weapon I use to ferret out information is my wife, Barbara. One night we went to dinner with Tom and his wife, Samantha. After the dinner that I thought was great, my wife said, "They are going to get divorced."

"How can you tell?" I asked.

"They didn't look each other in the eye," she said.

A few days later Tom called to tell me he and Samantha were indeed getting divorced.

Another bump that occurred during preproduction on *Nothing in Common* was that I learned Tom didn't want to do the movie. He was locked into a deal with TriStar Pictures, the company that was bankrolling the film. Our producer, Ray Stark, told Tom that if he didn't do the picture TriStar would block him from working in Hollywood for two years. Even I knew it was not optimal to have a disgruntled star. I didn't want to walk on eggshells around anyone. I think the best way to confront a problem is to bring it up. So I asked to meet with Tom alone one day.

During our private talk I told him that I was sincerely sorry about his marital problems and I was sad he wasn't rushing to do this movie. But I said that the cast and crew and I had nothing to do with his divorce or his contract issues. We were all innocent bystanders, so he shouldn't take it out on us. After our talk I promised him that I would make a good picture, and that I would somehow find a way to make it fun for him. Shortly after that Tom made peace with the project, and he was a delight to work with for the entire shoot. First, we discussed the character fully, and then I asked him how he liked to be directed. He said, "Louder, softer, faster, slower." And I said, "Perfect!" Years later I ran into Tom, and he said a famous director once told him before a scene, "I see this scene as *chartreuse*. Act that way." Tom had no idea what that kind of direction meant. He was a meat-and-potatoes kind of actor and liked his directors that way, too.

What excited both Tom and me about the film was the chance to work with the man who had been cast to play his father: Jackie Gleason, otherwise known as the Great One. Jackie was on the fence about doing the film until we had a meeting with him. He was tired and not feeling well, and was hesitating about doing another movie at his age while his health wasn't good. However, Ray Stark crafted a very convincing argument. He reminded Jackie that his last film was *Smokey and the Bandit II*. Did he really want to go down in the history books with *that* being his last movie credit? When Ray framed the opportunity like that, Jackie smiled and said, "Where do I sign on the dotted line?" As I had with Tom, I promised Jackie that if he came onboard I would make a film that we could all be proud of and have fun making. Although it was only my third film, I had already learned that to make the time together work best, you had to have fun. A movie can take up to a year of your life to complete, and if things aren't going well, that time can seem like an eternity.

During the film Jackie's health was fragile on the screen and on the set. Every day he had to be wrapped by 5:00 P.M. So every day, shortly before the clock hit 5:00 P.M., I would have a production assistant play Jackie's exit music from his television show on a boom box, and he would smile and trot off the soundstage or location set. His wife, Marilyn, had been a good friend of my mother. Marilyn was the sister of June Taylor, who coordinated all the dancers on Jackie's show, and she knew my mother from her tap dancing days. My mother would have loved the fact that I was directing a movie starring the Great One. It was a little sad that she'd died the year before and was not around to see the movie.

As a relatively new director, I found it fascinating to direct a movie with one star on the rise and the other one a legend. Both men could not have been more generous or gracious with each other. One day Jackie's dressing room trailer broke down, and it would take some time to get him another one. Tom stepped up and said, "Give Jackie my trailer. I'll wait for the other one." The truth was that Tom didn't spend much time in his trailer. He preferred to hang outside and toss the softball with me and other actors and crew. Jackie, however, thought it was bad form to take Tom's trailer from him. "That's not necessary," he said. "Tom's the star. I'll wait for another trailer." But the Chicago heat was escalating, and we didn't want Jackie to be without air-conditioning. So we came up with a plan: Since most trailers look alike, I had a teamster take Tom's name off his trailer, drive the trailer around the block, and come back to meet Jackie. The teamster said, "Here's your replacement trailer, Mr. Gleason!" Jackie accepted the trailer, thinking it was new, and quickly ducked back in to enjoy the air-conditioning. I was learning that when directing a movie, diplomacy is as essential as a solid script.

Nothing in Common was my first film with drama in it. There were some emotional scenes when Jackie's character was in the hospital and his son had to leave his job to care for him. One day we shot a hospital scene and it didn't work. Jackie and I tried to figure out what was wrong with it. He came up with an idea: He felt there were too many opportunities for humor in a hospital room, and we needed to get rid of that humor. He suggested doing a "comedy exorcism" of the room. So Tom came in, and the three of us recited every bad hospital room joke we could think of until we were laughing so hard our sides hurt. We riffed on nurses, needles, bedpans, and more. After we were done we felt better and were able to go ahead with the dramatic scene between father and son. In one tender moment Tom even cried over his dad, which was new territory for Tom as an actor, because he had mostly done comedy before.

I never like the producers to talk to the actors. Francis Coppola taught me that. There can only be one director at a time, and if the producers start giving the actors notes on scenes, it undermines the strength and influence of the director. So I nearly flew off the handle one day when I saw my producer, Alex Rose, in a private, sidebar-style discussion with Tom Hanks. I was just about to intervene when Tom opened a door and revealed a large birthday cake for me. Birthdays are big deals on movie sets because often you can't be with your friends and family and have to celebrate with the cast and crew. I'm usually the one planning the birthday surprises. But on this day Alex and Tom fooled even me.

I think I'm a pretty easy director to get along with, but once in a while I meet someone on a movie set who just doesn't like my style. On *Nothing in Common* I was still developing my style of directing, but my cinematographer, John Alonzo, didn't like it one bit. He had worked on many movies before this one, and most notably shot *Scarface* and *Norma Rae*. John thought that he knew more about directing a movie than I did. The truth was that he probably did. But the reality was that he wasn't the director and I was. This didn't stop him from suggesting throughout the film that I would direct more effectively and command more authority if I stood on a ladder with a bullhorn. I didn't want to direct that way. I wanted to direct with a toothpick in my mouth and my feet firmly planted on the ground. It was just something we didn't see eye to eye on.

I worked well with Tom Hanks, and I worked hard to make him feel as comfortable as possible. I cast Hector Elizondo as his boss at the advertising agency, and they got along swimmingly. Tom, however, told me one thing he was not comfortable doing was sexy scenes. Maybe it was his divorce, or maybe it was just the way he felt in general about the big screen, but he was not comfortable doing love scenes at that time. We rewrote the script to make him feel more comfortable. While the film was a drama, the romantic part was mostly comedy, so it didn't call for any heavy love scenes anyway.

To play one of his love interests we cast a southern cheerleader and homecoming queen named Sela Ward. At the time she told me she wasn't even sure if she wanted to become an actress. She was mulling over a career as a stewardess, but this movie was a big break for her. I told her I would let her know after the movie was done whether she should head for the airport or stay in film, and I did. (She, of course, went on to work steadily in Hollywood for years and years.) The other love interest we had for Tom was Bess Armstrong, who had much more film experience than Sela.

I learned on *Nothing in Common* that as a director you not only have to work with the actors but also have to step back and look at all the other elements that come into play. How is the lighting? How is the wardrobe? Is the makeup subtle or too distracting? I was learning on the job, so I had to rely on the heads of all of those departments to bring me up to speed. In doing research for the movie I went to visit an advertising agency. On my tour I noticed that the ceiling was made of foam so the young copywriters would sometimes throw their pencils at the ceiling and the pencils would stick in the foam permanently. I came back and told my production designer to build that same ceiling so we could throw pencils up at it.

We shot a scene in which Jackie's character visits a house of prostitution, and we hired a number of actresses from Chicago to play the prostitutes. When I interviewed the local actresses, they all read well. But there was something missing. I wanted something, a sound or a look, to set them apart from the prostitutes we have seen time and again in the movies. So I said, "Do any of you ladies play a musical instrument?" One woman raised her hand and said, "I play the accordion." She then went to the trunk of her car, brought back her accordion, and played me a song. I put the girl and the accordion right into the movie. Her name was Isabella Hofmann, and she went on to work in television and many stage plays.

Nothing in Common represented a turning point for me as a director. I learned that I could get the actors to do what I wanted them to do if I could somehow make them think it was their idea. I discovered this method also works well with studio executives, and I have cultivated this skill throughout my life in film. There was a scene in which Jackie's character was riding on a ferryboat after being fired from his job as a clothing salesman. The scene was flat, and I knew I had to punch it up. Jackie's character had some pens with his name on them. So in the scene I wanted Jackie to take the pens out of his pocket and throw them into the water. But I thought Jackie would be able to bring more emotion to the scene if he came up with that idea himself. So I cajoled him down the right road.

"So you're sitting on the boat?" I said.

"Yes," said Jackie.

"And you have the pens with your name on them in your pocket?" I asked.

"Yes," said Jackie.

"What are you going to do with those pens? You probably wouldn't keep them now that you are out of work, right?"

"Maybe I could throw them overboard?" he asked.

"Perfect. Love it. What a great idea. Let's shoot it," I said.

"Garry?" said Jackie. "Tell me what great idea am I having tomorrow."

Jackie saw through my plan. He was just too smart, but he liked my idea and went with it anyway.

As the movie went along we all got happier. Eva Marie Saint, who played Tom's mother, was lovely and the consummate professional. Jackie was invigorated by life on the movie set. Tom Hanks started dating Rita Wilson. The happier people became, the more I felt my own creativity growing as a director and as a writer. I was eager to give everyone funny, touching, and interesting bits to do. I gathered material from everywhere, including my own life.

I remembered I had once seen a documentary on Italian conductor Arturo Toscanini. The film showed him going around the country, having dinner with different officials at each stop. At one point he was having dinner with a member of the chamber of commerce in a small town. The chamber member turned to Toscanini and said, "Sometimes I eat my whole meal with a salad fork." Toscanini's reaction was wonderful. He just stared at the man blankly and didn't know what to say in return. So I took that moment and put it right into *Nothing in Common*. Tom went a step further and added the response "Including your soup?" It was a great touch, and one of the funniest scenes in the film.

As a director you find success on a movie, and you inevitably make mistakes, too. There was a scene in which Tom needed to see Jackie's swollen and diseased foot in order to realize just how serious his dad's health issues were. I wanted to show the audience what an edgy filmmaker I was. So I had the prop department make this terribly ugly foot and then shot it up close. Sadly, Ray Stark later told me the scene with the foot cost us close to $10 million at the box office. The foot was too ugly and big, and it turned people off. I learned from my mistake. The first thing I did when the film was rereleased years later on video was cut out the foot. When I look back on it, I realize I should have let Tom "act" his reaction to the foot and put his face on-screen instead of showing the awful foot.

Nothing in Common did very well in the critics' corner. I, however, was not able to bask in the success because something distracted me. I learned that my business advisers had gotten me involved in an over-the-top real estate deal in Pasadena and money was being stolen from me. I have never had a head for numbers. To be told that my finances were a mess was overwhelming for me. I had to do something to calm myself down, so I signed up to direct another movie. I knew that if I lost a lot of money in the real estate deal, I would need to make another movie right away anyway. So I said a quick yes to a script called *Overboard,* and I headed to shoot in

Mendocino, California, a town known for its beautiful coastline, bed-and-breakfast inns, and the occasional smell of marijuana. I left my wife in Los Angeles to face the legal battles while I did the only thing I knew how to do at the moment: direct. Barbara and I were both stressed out at the same time, and we didn't have the leisure time to help each other through it. We both knew that in order to survive financially she had to face the legal challenges head-on with the help of our lawyer friend Marty Garbus, and I had to hustle up as much work as I could to pay the bills. For the first time in my life I took a movie not because I planned to take it but because I needed the paycheck.

13. OVERBOARD

★

Capturing Love on the Ocean with

Goldie Hawn and Kurt Russell

I REMEMBER SITTING beside a small harbor in Mendocino, California, trying to take stock of my life while the crew set up the next shot on *Overboard*. The reality was that *Nothing in Common* opened and even though critically it did well, financially it didn't do very much. Still, I considered it one of my best works despite the fact it did little for my career at the time. Big box office ruled.

I did know that getting my first chance to direct Goldie Hawn was a director's dream. Goldie represented that rare quality in an actress I have always found so alluring. She is not only funny but also beautiful. Some women who are great comedians are unfortunately not that attractive, so they can't play a romantic lead. They can make audiences laugh in nightclubs until tears are rolling down their faces, but we don't really want to see them kiss Brad Pitt on the big screen. Goldie, however, was and still is gorgeous and funny at the same time. She can get the laughs and win over the male lead. Plus, her training as a ballet dancer helped her have an elegance and grace that are rare for a comedian. I have heard it said before about Goldie that if you put a horizontal line across the center of her face, the top half is a glamorous movie star, while the bottom half is a quirky comedian. It is a winning combination.

Back in the 1960s, when I was producing my TV series *Hey Landlord!* Goldie worked on a series nearby called *Good Morning, World,* about early morning disc jockeys. I once acted in an episode of that show, so I knew her from that and seeing her around the studio lot. A few years later she won an Academy Award for her performance in the movie *Cactus Flower* and her career really took off. I was a big fan of her performances in *Foul Play* (which my friends Tom Miller and Bob Boyett produced) and *Private Benjamin,* which was written by my friends Nancy Meyers, Chuck Shyer, and Harvey Miller.

By the time *Overboard* was being discussed, Goldie was not just an actress but a powerful producer as well. The thought of working with her might intimidate some directors, but I was *Laverne & Shirley* strong. Working with strong, independent women has always appealed to me. The best news of all about the project was that she was in love with her costar, Kurt Russell. They had met on the film *Swing Shift* and had been together ever since. Unlike *Nothing in Common,* in which Tom Hanks was getting divorced, Goldie and Kurt were in the glow of falling in love.

When Goldie and I first met we talked about the things we valued most in life: our kids. Goldie had two little children at the time—Kate and Oliver. She had survived a bad divorce, and ironically her ex-husband eventually married my old friend Cindy Williams, who had starred in *Laverne & Shirley*. Goldie and I had a lot in common. I think I knew right from the start I was working with a woman who was not only talented and funny but a smart boss. There was no doubt she was a major motion picture star, but inside she was a decent human being.

Goldie was producing the movie with her business partner Anthea Sylbert and actor Roddy McDowall, who would play a small part as a butler. The only person in the equation who was totally new to me was Kurt. I knew that he had been working steadily since he was a child for Disney and other studios, but what I didn't know was what a professional he was. (I also heard he had once played baseball for the Portland Beavers, a minor league team I had once owned. So I almost owned Kurt.) I didn't know that Kurt would be one of the nicest actors I would ever work with because he was such a team player. He would turn in a beautiful performance in a scene. Yet a minute later if we started losing the light or the weather would turn on us, he would be the first one to pick up a light and help us move the entire set.

Kurt was always in a good mood and was great with the children. And it was fascinating to see him work so well side by side with Goldie. They have an amazing loving relationship despite the fact that she is a devout Democrat and he is a card-carrying Republican. I remember they would often fight openly on the set about their different political views. Kurt is, in every sense of the word, a regular guy, who told me he likes to go wild boar hunting without a gun. So basically he's running after crazy boar with just a knife in his hand. He is so rare in Hollywood because he doesn't have a neurotic bone in his body. He just exudes balance.

Before we began shooting *Overboard,* I had been waiting on another script called *Beaches,* which was the adaptation of a popular Iris Rainer Dart book with Bette Midler attached. As much as I wanted to direct *Beaches* and work with Bette Midler, I felt financially that I couldn't wait. I talked to my agent, Joel Cohen, and he said I could direct *Overboard* first, and by the time I was done the script for *Beaches* would be ready. Joel was always right.

I talked to Francis Coppola about my financial troubles because he had been in debt as well. I remember he said to me, "Garry, don't worry. You will make money again. Just get *even.*" He basically was saying do whatever you can to get out of debt and worry about making back your money later. He said a lot of people would be worried about starting from the ground up again, but he told me not to worry about that. "I have seen your work," he said. "You will make the money back." He seemed to have confidence that it would work out, and it did.

Overboard was a lonely picture for me because I felt so far away from my friends and family. My other movies had been shot in Los Angeles, New York, and Chicago, which are cities where I have many friends. But Mendocino, which is three hours north of San Francisco, seemed remote and isolated. My wife was able to visit the set, but her priority was getting us out of this real estate mess and making sure we had the financial security to survive and keep the kids in college.

With the exception of my family, we had hardly any visitors to the set. Our cast and crew, of course, fascinated the town's people, but we were basically a small band of film people on our own. Aside from wineries and plenty of marijuana farmers, there are few activities or businesses in Mendocino. On the flip side, there were no paparazzi around. So even Goldie and Kurt were able to move about without being bothered by the press or autograph seekers. Alexandra Rose, my producer from *Nothing in Common,* was on this film, too, and she met her future husband, Rob Meadows, while we were on location. So being at a remote location has its pros as well as its cons.

At the time Mendocino had one nightclub with a band. On every movie I have to get a physical for insurance reasons. Before the *Overboard* shoot my doctor worried that I might get too exhausted by directing another movie so soon. He told me one thing that might help was dancing. So I made a nightly pilgrimage to the only nightclub in Mendocino to dance away my stress.

Overboard was the story of a wealthy woman who falls overboard on her own yacht, gets amnesia, and is adopted by a local carpenter (played by Kurt Russell) and his family. Kurt tries to convince her that she is poor, married, and the mother of four children. I thought the script, written by Leslie Dixon, was funny, and I was able to put together a great supporting cast. Edward Herrmann played Goldie's husband and Katherine Helmond her mother. To play Kurt's four sons we cast Jeffrey Wiseman, Jamie Wild, Brian Price, and Jared Rushton, who would go on to star the following year in my sister Penny's movie *Big.*

I did not have a lot of experience working with young children. I had raised three children of my own and worked with the young cast on *Happy Days,* but directing four boys with relatively no experience was challenging. On purpose I cast the four kids out of Chicago because I didn't want them to look like Hollywood kids with blow-dried hair and dyed eyelashes. In one scene the youngest son, Jeffrey, had to cry, and we talked about the scene and how we would approach it together. He said he never got sad, but then I asked him if he had ever had a pet that died. He said, "A dog named Fluffy." So I said when we get ready to do the scene we will talk about Fluffy, and he agreed. Crying on-camera is not an easy thing, but six-year-old Jeffrey did a fine job, especially when we conjured up memories of Fluffy. But after we wrapped that scene, every once in a while he got a little paranoid and would say, "Are we going to talk about *Fluffy* again?" And I assured him no, we were done with Fluffy and the tears.

When you work with kids there is always the risk that one of them will get hurt, and that happened on *Overboard*. Jared twisted his ankle while he was riding on his skateboard between scenes one day. He couldn't walk, and we were about to shoot a big chase scene in which Goldie runs through the woods after the boys. The doctor who looked at his ankle said he could run in a day or two, but I didn't want to get behind schedule. It would have cost thousands of dollars to shut down for two days. So instead I improvised. I had the boys all put on Halloween masks. Then I could replace Jared just for that one scene with another young actor. Nobody knew the difference, and we were able to film the scene as written by purchasing some cheap Halloween masks. We didn't lose even a half day.

The best part of *Overboard* for me was watching Goldie in the scenes when Kurt tries to convince her that she is his wife. In one scene he tells her that she used to be chubby and quite promiscuous. Goldie, wearing a frumpy hand-me-down dress, turns to Kurt and deadpans, "I was a short, fat slut?" It is one of the funniest moments in the entire movie, and I still laugh when I see it. There was also a scene in which she cooks a chicken, and the physical comedy is quintessential Goldie. I gave her the idea of cooking a chicken in a small pot and she ran with it.

I loved working with Goldie and seeing her be sophisticated in the fancy scenes and do slapstick comedy in the others. On some days when Goldie was filming, her daughter, Kate, who was then nine years old, would come and sit in the director's chair with me. I would say, "Let's say 'Action, Mommy,' " and Kate would do the slate with me. Years later I would direct Kate in a movie of her own called *Raising Helen,* and we talked about our memories of filming *Overboard,* in Mendocino.

I cast a couple of friends in *Overboard,* too. My smoking coach

Carol Williard had a small part, as did Hector Elizondo. Hector couldn't have a big part in this picture because he was busy doing another project. But we did manage to squeeze him in as a Portuguese captain of a boat that finds Goldie after she has fallen overboard. Although I had a tough time working with him on *Nothing in Common,* I used cinematographer John Alonzo again because he does a fine job of shooting women. I needed him to capture Goldie. John and I were able to get along better on this picture. Sometimes knowing a person's baggage helps you both sort it out. He still didn't like my less than authoritative style, but we could work together to shoot a great scene with Goldie. One of the most memorable scenes with audiences is when Kurt reveals to Goldie her new walk-in closet that he has built especially for her. John shot a great sequence to reveal every girl's dream closet set to the beautiful musical score of Alan Silvestri.

I always try to put something in the actors' hands to make them appear more real. This worked well for Kurt because he likes to gesture and have something in his hands when he talks. I told him in one scene, "Your character likes walnuts. So sometimes we will have him cracking walnuts and eating them out of the shell." Kurt latched on to this immediately and sometimes would use it as a metaphor for needing something, anything, in his hands. He would look across the set to me and say, "Garry! I need walnuts." I knew that meant he wanted to have something in his hand or something physical to do while he was talking. At the end of the movie he sent me a silver walnut from Tiffany as a gift.

I have now watched *Overboard* dozens of times, often with my children and my grandchildren. One of my favorite scenes is the end of the picture—when Goldie, wearing a beautiful gold lamé dress, leaps off a fancy yacht and swims toward Kurt's waiting arms. The reason I like the scene so much is that we almost didn't get to put it in the picture.

In our story the Coast Guard gets an emergency call and has to rush away from Goldie's boat. This precipitates Goldie jumping off the boat and making a beeline for Kurt. Goldie's first jump was hard. We were shooting in the Long Beach harbor, and the water was freezing. After a few practice runs Goldie looked at me and said, "It's too cold. I don't want to jump in the water anymore." Kurt overheard this and walked over to talk to Goldie while the crew was drying her off. He said, "Honey, for the money they are paying you, you have to jump again." She looked back at her partner, knowingly, and prepared to shoot the scene again and again. She did a great job, and so did Kurt.

Over the several months of shooting *Overboard,* I was able to concentrate and even find my way out of my sadness, depression, and worry about going bankrupt. Working with Goldie was the perfect antidote for my mood. The picture, unfortunately, was not a big hit, but the problem was that the studio executives marketed it wrong. They thought it was an upscale comedy and they should target all of their marketing to rich people. They were wrong. It was a comedy that would appeal to families and children, even small children. *Overboard* didn't find that audience until it hit the video market, where it turned out to be a big hit. Sometimes you create a film you like yet the studio executives miss the whole point. *Overboard* is the perfect example of this. People with beluga caviar on their crackers didn't want to see it, while people with peanut butter and jelly on their crackers did.

So while I had fun making the movie, *Overboard* was a critical and box office disappointment. My finances were still up in the air, and again I wasn't sure what to do next. Should I do a comedy? Should I do a drama? Should I take a break and refocus my career? Some people even thought I should do a television show in order to make some fast money. Then I got the phone call that I had been waiting for. "The script for *Beaches* is done. Bette Midler is happy with it and ready to go," said my agent. So my decision was made: My next picture would be *Beaches,* starring Bette Midler. I packed my bags and headed back to the city of my own roots, New York.

14. BEACHES

★

Exploring Female Friendship with
Bette Midler and Barbara Hershey

W HEN THE SCRIPT for *Beaches* was ready, my agent, Joel Cohen, went to the powers that be at Disney and told them about my ongoing financial struggles in Pasadena. He was honest with them and told them I was deeply in debt. Executive Jeffrey Katzenberg made the decision to pay $500,000 of my salary up front, before even one scene of the movie was shot. I remember thinking the advance on my salary was unprecedented, and it still is. I asked Joel why they were being so kind to me. He said they knew my work and could count on me to turn in a movie on budget and on schedule. So as I began to direct *Beaches,* my fifth feature film, I felt grateful for the support from Katzenberg and Disney's head, Michael Eisner.

Both Katzenberg and Eisner are infamous in Hollywood for many things, but I will remember them most for what they taught me: Eisner taught me how to make the difficult phone call. He said every day when you are an executive or boss you will have to make at least one difficult phone call, whether it be to fire someone or to get mad at them for a job not well done. He told me to pick a time of day when you are most comfortable and confident to make that call. Katzenberg taught me that no phone call, no matter how important, should last more than *two* minutes. Both men taught me about the importance of an efficient telephone call.

Following a movie staring Goldie Hawn with a movie staring Bette Midler made me feel as if suddenly I was a hot movie director.

Back when I started directing I'd never dreamed that I would get to direct these famous women, or that I would find my calling as a director with a talent for directing women. I was raised in a house full of women, including my grandmother, mother, and two sisters. Then I became the father of two daughters and would eventually have four granddaughters. I felt by the time I did *Beaches* I had developed a sensitivity for figuring out how to make women happy. And perhaps most important, I understood that if they were upset, there were a number of avenues I could travel down to bring them back to happy. It goes without saying that when female stars are happy, they act better, too.

The script for *Beaches* was based on the wildly popular Iris Rainer Dart book of the same name. It was the story of two childhood girlfriends, CC Bloom and Hillary Whitney, who have a falling-out and lose touch, only to reunite after one is diagnosed with terminal cancer. So the premise was a heavy one: How do you help your best friend die with grace and dignity? Initially Disney didn't want to make the movie because they thought it was too dark. That's where I came in. I was often brought in to lighten up a script. I can just imagine the executives pitching the idea. "We'll get Garry Marshall to direct, and then we'll save money on the rewrite. Mr. *Happy Days* can lighten our dark script for less money than hiring another writer." So that was my assignment with *Beaches*. I was not to dwell on the death but instead to up the stakes on the comedy and the friendship between the two women from opposite sides of the track.

Beaches needed star power to work. It was not a small independent movie but a mainstream movie-star vehicle. The script came with Bette attached, so we had to find someone who not only could play the other part but also looked right side by side with Bette. We decided to screen-test five actresses. I watched each screen test on tape but still couldn't decide. So I watched them all again, only this time I turned off the sound. My decision became clear in an aha moment. It was Barbara Hershey who looked right with Bette. The two of them had the best chemistry. One of the other actresses was Sissy Spacek, whom I love, respect, and admire very much. But alongside Bette, Sissy looked like just another pretty, pale redhead. In a two-shot Bette and Barbara had a certain amount of class and elegance to them.

Barbara brought to the set her own experience as an actress and a bit of quirkiness as a person, too. You can ask around town and find out things about actresses, but you don't really know what they are like until you work with them for a year. Barbara, I knew, not only named her son Free but also once changed her own name to Barbara Seagull. When Barbara arrived on my set, she clearly was transitioning to more of an establishment person because she introduced her son to me and called him Tom. Nonetheless, she ran in a more spiritual crowd than either Bette or I did.

The two actresses' processes were completely opposite. Barbara was very sensitive and needed a lot of hugs. Bette, however, seemed to thrive on confrontation and resolution. Barbara would come onto the set a half hour before her call time, completely in character, and need to touch every piece of furniture to let it resonate with her. She would ask questions about the props and where they came from. Bette, on the other hand, would run in right before the cameras rolled and yell, "Let's go. I'm here. Where do I stand?"

The biggest problem we had was the day Barbara appeared with gigantic lips. Without giving us any warning, she had gotten a doctor to inject her lips with something to make them temporarily more plump and seductive. When we saw her arrive a cameraman turned to me with alarm in his eyes.

"What are you going to do with those *lips*?" he said.

I stared quizzically at her lips, too. I had never seen lips so large on such a petite face.

"We have to shoot them," I said. "We can't push them down."

I knew we couldn't stop production. The lips might take weeks to go down. So you will notice if you watch *Beaches* that Barbara's lips are larger in some scenes than in others.

Before we shot the lips, however, I had a private discussion with Barbara about her motivation for the cosmetic alteration in the middle of my movie. What was she thinking? She said she did it because she felt Bette was going to overpower her on-screen. She thought she needed an extra *something* to make her appear special in the role. I understood what she was saying. This is the reason many actresses and even ordinary people have cosmetic surgery. However, I was not beyond mocking the lips. Sometimes I would give Barbara a kiss and pretend to bounce off her lips. She and the crew always got a good laugh from that. Even with an actress as dedicated and serious as Barbara, humor was a good way to become good friends, which we remain to this day.

I worked well with Bette because she is a lot like my sister Penny. They are both creative, extremely opinionated, sometimes loud and sometimes bossy, but usually very smart and on the money. When I worked with Penny on *Laverne & Shirley,* I assigned her the extra job of policing the wardrobe. This gave her something to distract her. I knew Bette liked power and she liked flowers. So from the first day on *Beaches,* I told Bette she was in charge of all the floral arrangements. She could assign them, select them, and approve them. An outsider might think this was a strange task for an Academy Award nominee, but I knew that Bette had the energy not only to act and produce but to work with flowers as well. The flower assignment gave her something to think about in addition to the script, the movie, and her hair. So whenever I saw her getting anxious about some aspect of the movie, I would say, "Bette, could you go and check on the flowers?" This task helped her relax and regain her focus.

In addition to empowering Bette and Barbara, during *Beaches* I felt the range of my own power as director for the first time. I cast a little girl named Mayim Bialik to play the young Bette Midler. Unfortunately the casting was not picture perfect: Mayim has blue eyes, but Bette has brown eyes. So we knew we had to get brown contact lenses for Mayim, and we did. That was an easy fix. Except one Saturday we were shooting and Mayim lost one of her contacts. She was just an eleven-year-old, and like most kids she just lost one. So we had to get another pair, but the doctor's office wasn't open on Saturday, and to make things worse the doctor was on vacation in Lake Tahoe. The editing department said we could fix the mismatched eye color digitally in postproduction, but I didn't want to waste time or money on that. I had another idea.

We called the doctor and asked him where he kept the contact lenses in his office. So basically I was making the decision to break into the doctor's office. It was cheaper than losing a half day of shooting on the movie. A group of teamsters went over to the doctor's office, broke down the door like thieves, and got the replacement contact lens. I remember the day I said, "Knock down the door!" It was the first time I really understood how much power a director has. I had the power to authorize a burglary. Again it all came down to staying on schedule and doing whatever it took to spend the least amount of money. It worked. We got the right eye color and the scenes made sense. We did shoot one scene with the different color eyes, and it remains in the movie. The scene takes place in a hotel on the boardwalk where the two little girls sit in the hotel dining room to have a treat. In the background sits my father, who rarely acted in my movies but made it into *Beaches* as an extra.

One of the highlights of *Beaches* was that Bette got to sing. She was very influential in the selection of music for the film, and because she clearly had more experience at it than I did, I often deferred to her. But I tried my best to make her shine as an actress as well. Bette already had a successful career in music, and *Beaches* was a great vehicle to help broaden her appeal as an actress. She was eager to learn and improve as an actress, too. She had a habit of popping her eyes out during a scene, and I found it very unnatural. So when I would catch her doing it I would remind her to stop. One time I even told her, "I'm going to Scotch-tape your eyes shut if you pop them again!" She laughed and promised to do better on the next take.

One of the funniest lines in the movie had to be cut. There is a scene where the two girlfriends are fighting, and reveal some of their secret, longtime jealousies. Bette says to Barbara that she is so envious of Barbara and other actresses with "hair that moves." The line was so honest and heartfelt, I wish I could have left it in the film. But the truth was it broke the momentum of the scene; it was too funny for a serious fight. Bette really *is* jealous of Barbara and other actresses who have beautiful hair that moves. So ultimately I made the decision to cut the line from the movie, but it still appeared in the preview because I didn't cut it out until after the trailer was released.

We explored many aspects of female friendship in the course of *Beaches*. At one point Barbara's character is pregnant. I asked my wife for ideas on what would be a nice thing for a friend to do for another friend who is pregnant and uncomfortable. My wife suggested that Bette's character paint the toenails of the pregnant Barbara. I thought it was a great idea, so we set up that shot. The day we shot the scene Barbara, of course, was there early and Bette came rolling in just before I yelled "Action!" Bette took one look at Barbara's toenails and said, "Barb, what gnarly toes you have! Have you been working in the garden with those toes?" Barbara walked off the set crying.

"What happened?" asked Bette.

"You upset her," I said.

"But Garry, you saw those toes!" said Bette. "They *are* gnarly!"

"I know. But you should go and apologize," I said.

Watching the relationship between Bette and Barbara develop was similar to watching the ups and downs of their screen characters. The subject of female friendship was one of the reasons I wanted to direct *Beaches*. Women and men, for example, fight in completely different ways. Women can say terrible things to each other one day and then go out shopping the next, letting go of all of their differences. Men, on the other hand, look cross-eyed at each other and then don't speak to each other for the next ten years. So with Bette and Barbara, I tried to play referee when they needed me to.

Beaches was a transitional time for all of us. Barbara was coming out of her experimental period and looking forward to more mainstream moviemaking. Bette was settling into her domestic period—with her husband, Martin, and young daughter, Sophie. I was struggling with my financial problems, still on the brink of bankruptcy. I was trying to make as much money as I could to keep my house and my family afloat. I guess if I can give myself some credit for that period, it is that I was able to work at all. I found the strength to block out my financial stress and come to the set each day with a razor-sharp focus on the cast, crew, and plot. I lost myself in my movie. Creativity is a great place to hide out from the real world.

Humor always has been my lifesaver, too. In the later scenes of the movie I noticed that Barbara was spending more and more time in the makeup trailer applying white Pan-Cake makeup. She was starting to look very strange and almost scary. So I took her aside to discuss the situation.

"Barbara, what's going on with all the makeup? You're starting to look like death warmed over," I said.

"Good!" she said, proudly.

"Why is that good?" I asked.

"My character is dying. I want to look like death," she said.

"But you're not dead yet, so ease up on the makeup and steer clear of *ugly*. We don't want to scare away the audience before the ending." When your face is ten feet tall on a movie screen, you have to consider its impact on the audience.

There are problems on any movie, and as a director you just have to manage them as best you can. John Heard, for example, who played Bette's love interest in *Beaches,* was going through a real-life divorce during our shoot. So some of the scenes in which he and Bette had to fight were difficult for him. We helped him through it. Bette possesses the kind of professionalism that you hope for and count on in an actress. However, even the most experienced actors can lose their cool once in a while. There were a few times when Bette got fussy over something, and I cleared the set so I could talk to her privately. I told her that would be our arrangement. If she started yelling about the dialogue in a scene and I thought she was wrong, I would clear the set. It's not good to argue with the actors in front of the crew. I cleared the set a few times, and she understood the routine. However, one day she started to scream and I just sat in my director's chair and listened to her. My calm demeanor made her pause.

"Garry," she said. "Why aren't you clearing the set?"

"Because this time you are right to yell. We brought you in here at eight in the morning. It is nearly four and we still haven't filmed your scene. So I want the crew to hear me tell you how sorry I am for bringing you in so early and making you wait."

Bette smiled. We worked well together. One of my favorite moments with her was during the cast party. She sang "Wind Beneath My Wings" while I played the drums in the band behind her. At one point she came over to the drum set and sang directly to me. It was very moving. In fact the song was so moving that we couldn't have her sing it directly on the screen. We had to make a montage of it over a series of scenes.

When it came out the critics skewered *Beaches* for being too schmaltzy, but ultimately audiences enjoyed it. Girlfriends went together to see it in droves in the way they would go to see *Sex and the City* years later. When all was said and done, *Beaches* was a hit in my book. However, my financial problems were still not over. I believe in karma and spiritual signs, so I decided to seek out a psychic when I was back at home in Los Angeles. A man who played basketball at my house on Saturday mornings told me about a psychic who had a gold fang, which was the source of her power. She turned out to be a pleasant-looking, heavyset blonde who I might cast as a waitress in a diner, except for the gold tooth. I went to see her a number of times and she said that my life was going to turn around and there would be four people who would be influential in helping me: someone with the letter *M,* someone named Joyce, someone named Elizabeth, and finally someone with a *z* in his or her name.

When I told my wife, Barbara, what the psychic had said, she was doubtful. Firmly grounded in reality and the medical profession, my wife is not a fan of the occult. However, even she was amazed that everything the psychic said turned out to be true. Within weeks of my visit to her, I not only hired a new business manager named Marshall Gelfand, but had my friend Marty Garbus working on the case round the clock. So there was my *M.* Marshall introduced me to his head accountant, and her name was Joyce. Marshall's daughter's name was Elizabeth. Finally, a big real estate investor named Doug Stitzel (with a *z* in his name) helped me out by buying my remaining properties in Pasadena. Maybe it was a coincidence, or maybe I just wanted to believe I could find all the right letters, but the visit to the psychic gave me great comfort that someday I would have this financial crisis behind me. Marshall also introduced me to my head of business affairs Cathy Berry, whose loyalty and honesty have kept me financially safe ever since.

I have never been to a therapist. My wife has often said that if a therapist got ahold of me he would have a field day. Instead I like to rely on friends in the business to analyze my progress and advise me on career decisions. People told me never to feel trapped in my personal life or my profession. Barbara and I talked about the fact that we could lose our house and have to move into an apartment. We could borrow money from Penny, which in fact we did. I could make extra money producing television shows in addition to directing movies.

Sometimes the way out is to go back to where you started. I don't have a big ego, so even doing a television commercial was not out of the question. I ended up directing a Coca-Cola commercial with Art Carney, and it won an advertising award. I was fifty-four years old, and I decided I was not going to let stress or depression over money kill me just yet. I even created a few pilots for money—including one based on my movie *Nothing in Common*. The show ran for only six episodes. In my mind, it probably wasn't a success because my heart was not in it. I was just trying to get myself out of debt.

Shortly after my declaration to myself, the script for *Pretty Woman* came across my desk. If a movie can change a man's life, this would be that movie for me.

15. PRETTY WOMAN

★

Meeting a Hooker with a Heart of
Gold and a Girl Named Julia

IN THE MINDS of the executives of Disney, *Beaches* had been a hit in part because of me. I had taken a script with a serious story and dark ending and turned it into the feel-good girlfriend buddy picture with a great sound track. As a reward Disney gave me another dark script to lighten up. The script was originally titled *3000*, and it was the depressing story of an older, on-her-last-dime prostitute and a tough-as-nails businessman with the opulence of Beverly Hills as the backdrop. Disney asked me to "lighten it up" as I had done with *Beaches,* but with my own special blend of humor and romance. I decided to make the prostitute new to the profession so we could hire a younger actress. The title ultimately was changed to *Pretty Woman,* and the film starred a new actress named Julia Roberts and Hollywood's sexy bad boy Richard Gere. It remains the most famous movie I ever directed.

I'm getting ahead of myself because when we made *Pretty Woman* it was a low-budget picture without big stars that no one in Hollywood thought would become a hit. When you make a big-budget movie and it is a hit, you pat yourself on the back and say to your colleagues, "We did it. Aren't we smart?" But when a movie like *Pretty Woman* comes along and surprises everyone with its success, charm, and longevity, you can run into a production assistant or cameraman who worked on the movie years later and say to him, "How lucky we were to have been a part of that. How nice to see that magic still exists in Hollywood!"

J. F. Lawton wrote the original script on spec and had written eleven other scripts all on spec, or speculation, which means with no money up front. Lawton was a testament to the adage that good things come to those who are patient and persistent. He sold his twelfth script, *Pretty Woman*. Producer Steve Reuther got ahold of the script, and paired it with Julia Roberts, whom nobody had heard of before her debut in a small movie called *Mystic Pizza*. Reuther took the script to Disney, who then called me. The year was 1989, and at the time I worked out of a small suite of offices on Riverside Drive in Burbank two minutes from my house.

The studio arranged for Julia to meet me at my office. All I really knew about her was this: She was actor Eric Roberts's little sister. She had impressed audiences in *Mystic Pizza,* holding her own against Annabeth Gish and Lili Taylor. And she was dating the actor Liam Neeson. In walked a gangly girl, with schlumpy posture and hair all over the place. When she smiled, however, you just thought "wow!" The first thing she said was, "I won't be naked." She had read the script, knew it was about a hooker, and from the get-go she wanted me to know she was not comfortable doing nude scenes. I said fine. "You're only twenty years old. I'm going to do everything I can to make you feel comfortable on this movie, but I also want you to have fun." Once I had Julia locked in, I went after her costar.

We brought in a number of hot actors and put some on film with Julia to see how they looked beside her. Australian Sam Neil was a fine actor but wasn't right with Julia. Chemistry was key to this picture. Comedian Charles Grodin came in to read, too, and while very funny he wasn't quite right either. Richard Gere at the time had a shaky career and reputation. He had been hot after *American Gigolo* and *An Officer and a Gentleman,* but then after *Breathless* and *The Cotton Club* people weren't rushing to hire him. I knew Richard best from my daughter Lori's bathroom. She had every inch of her bathroom walls covered with framed photos of Richard taken from magazines or shot with her camera off the television screen. While I knew we didn't have any nude scenes, Richard Gere was an actor who could play sexy, and I needed that in the role of Edward. The first week of shooting there was a rumor that Richard was indeed going to do a nude scene. It wasn't true, but just to shock everyone one day he took off his clothing and did a quick walk around the set. He had energy and attitude, and I liked that about him immediately.

The first time Richard and Julia spent an evening out together was at my daughter's wedding that August at my house. They danced together and got the opportunity to know each other away from the set and the cameras. What made their chemistry eventually so powerful on the big screen mirrored some of their chemistry off-screen. Shortly after we started Julia broke up with Liam, and neither she nor Richard was dating anyone else. So they could hang out—unencumbered by outside relationships or paparazzi. We had a very quiet set. He taught her to play the guitar, for example. She bought a new dog. We played pranks on each other. Julia came to work tired one day, and Richard and I decided to keep her awake by having him snap a velvet jewelry box jokingly on her hand. It remains one of the hallmark moments in the film because Julia registers such true surprise with her smile and her laughter.

What people don't know about the movie is that some of it never made it to the big screen. We felt we would get such mileage out of showing Julia in Richard's fancy arena that we might get the same mileage from showing Richard in her dark and seedy world. So we shot a number of scenes in a club called the Blue Banana. I made up the name of the club because I love bananas and eat them often on a set. In our movie the Blue Banana was a place where Julia's character, Vivian, and her friend Kit, played by Laura San Giacomo, hung out. In one scene Edward almost gets beaten up in a back alley by a gang. My son, Scott, plays a knife-wielding, skateboard-riding drug dealer (which to be honest caused a slight rift between my wife and me, because she was against our son playing a drug dealer. But I needed a boy who could ride a good skateboard). Showing the characters in each other's worlds made sense mathematically but ultimately not emotionally. So most of that footage from Vivian's world got left on the cutting room floor.

One of the funny behind-the-scenes aspects of *Pretty Woman* was the merchandising that appeared in the movie. One of the ways a director gets extra money for his budget is by placing various products in the film. For example, I got a five-figure deal to mention a condom company. The fact that Julia was able to integrate the gold condom into the scene was funny and also talked about. In another sequence, involving a polo match, a car company gave me a big truck to use with money to match. I thought, rich people at polo matches don't drive this kind of truck. So instead of driving it I just had some attractive wealthy people lean against it, and I was still able to get the merchandising money.

Julia came to the set every day knowing her lines, but sometimes the tedious pace of the production would bore her. I think she started to do needlework on the set of *Pretty Woman,* a pastime she would continue on other movies. She had visitors to the set. Her mother came one day to watch when we were filming on Wilshire Boulevard. I always feel a certain responsibility when I am shooting other people's children, especially someone as young as Julia. I remember telling her mother that she was doing a wonderful job, and that I would do my best to watch over her. I think my experience as a camp counselor when I was in high school came in handy when I started directing young actresses. Often I got the best tips because I told the parents in detail how well their kids were doing at camp.

So you can imagine how worried I felt when Julia fainted in the middle of a night scene. On a movie shoot days are long, and nights can feel even longer. Emotions run high all the time, and people occasionally get sick and even faint. While the on-set nurse was tending to Julia, I went over to try to figure out what was wrong.

"What did you eat today?" I said.

"Half an avocado," she said.

"Maybe you should have gone for the *whole* avocado and then you wouldn't have fainted," I said. She said she would try to remember that. Then I shared my can of tuna fish with her. I always carry tuna fish with me on the sets of my movies in case I need a shot of protein. So Julia and I shared a little protein and conversation and then got back to work.

Working with an actress trying to stay thin is nothing new to me, but it's still worrisome. I made a point of seeing that Julia ate healthy food every day. Eating for me is one of the joys of filming a movie. At what other time in your life do you have complete access to a private chef and whatever food you want twenty-four hours a day? But for young actresses trying to stay thin, a movie set can present too much temptation and trouble.

While Julia was new to life on a movie set, Richard was a veteran by the time we shot *Pretty Woman*. I spent a lot of time with him talking about life and his career. He is a complicated person. He enjoys getting to know people, but at the same time he works hard to preserve his time alone. Comedy for him, as for Matt Dillon, does not come naturally. Matt and Richard love to play brooding, sexy characters, but sometimes they lack the confidence to reach for the big jokes. So as with Matt on *The Flamingo Kid,* I gave Richard comedy roads to venture down. He bravely took them, and did a wonderful job.

One of my favorite scenes in the movie takes place in an opera house. We were originally supposed to film inside the War Memorial Opera House in San Francisco, but the Loma Prieta Earthquake hit in October and the location was damaged. Instead, our brilliant production designer Albert Brenner built an opera set for us in Los Angeles. In this particular scene Richard delivers a beautiful speech about his love of opera. As a counterweight to his passionate words, I gave Julia some opera glasses to play around with. Richard knew that Julia was going to get the big laughs from flipping and flopping about with the opera glasses, and he wanted to exit the scene early. It was not always easy for him to be her straight man. To put a twist on the scene and make him happy, I gave him a new ending to the scene. When Julia turned to another patron and said she liked the evening so much she almost peed in her pants, I had Richard jump in to cover for her and say, "She said she liked it more than *The Pirates of Penzance.*" When Richard saw the final cut of the movie, he beamed with pleasure at his delivery of the joke because he got such a big laugh.

Some stars introduce you to their agents, but Richard introduced me to the Dalai Lama. I went to an event where His Holiness was speaking, and Richard and I stood in a receiving line to meet him. When we finally got to where the Dalai Lama was standing, Richard introduced me by saying, "Your Holiness, this is one of the funniest men you will ever meet." I was embarrassed, because that is an uncomfortable way to be introduced to the most famous living Buddhist. However, I quickly covered and said, "Your Holiness, I read that we are the same age." Showing his sense of humor, the Dalai Lama said, "And we both have done well." It was not like the Dalai Lama had met so many funny people in his life either. I couldn't imagine he had spent much time at the Improv in Mumbai or the Comedy Club in Delhi.

My love of playing pranks continued on *Pretty Woman,* and most of them involved trying to get Julia to laugh, because nobody laughs better than Julia. There is a scene when she takes a bubble bath in Richard's hotel room. She is listening to music on headphones, but at one point she takes off the headphones and goes under the water. During one take the minute she went under the bubbles, I had the whole cast and crew run off the set. When she came out of the bubbles, she was surprised to see that she was sitting on an empty set and broke into a full round of giggles and a couple of choice swearwords, too.

The reality is that young people get bored easily, even young people who are movie stars. So I like to keep my actors entertained and on their toes. When actors least expect it, I will pull a prank. I knew if I could keep Julia laughing, I could keep her interested in her job. That is important to me. I don't just want to make movies. I want to make actors enjoy the process. I don't want people to go away saying, "I just finished a Garry Marshall picture and it was hell." I want them to leave saying, "I had a lot of laughs with Garry on the set."

I always knew that a prostitute with a heart of gold falling in love with a wealthy businessman was a predictable story line; it was magical because of these two actors. But there was a glitch: Some of the other executives thought the manipulative business side of the movie was a stronger angle. So there is a scene in the Rex restaurant in which Richard discusses a big takeover deal with several other businessmen. I filled the scene with humor. Julia flips an escargot into the air and a waiter catches it. The line "slippery little suckers" was her own ad-lib. However, despite the fact that I thought the scene was working, I received some notes from the studio that the business deal was unclear and I should reshoot the scene. I knew that to rent the fancy Rex restaurant for another day would be ten thousand dollars, which would put my picture way over budget. I was not willing to do that.

My saving grace on nearly every movie I have directed is that I can pick up the phone and call the person in charge of it. I called Jeffrey Katzenberg to discuss the restaurant scene and we watched the footage together. I told him that in my opinion the scene was not about the hostile business takeover but instead about a young girl being in a fancy restaurant for the first time in her life. The business deal was merely background buzz for her humor. In fact, life was imitating the film, because Julia admitted that she had never been inside a restaurant as fancy as the Rex. Her honest and wide-eyed looks brought even more charm to the scene. Katzenberg agreed with me, and we left the scene alone and let Julia shine. When Julia saw the film for the first time, she laughed because she had no idea the waiter was going to catch her snail. She thought it just flew into the air off-camera.

Some directors have their entire plots mapped out, but on *Pretty Woman* I shot nearly the whole picture without knowing my real ending. My obligation was to have the lovers get back together somehow, but I wasn't sure how. I came up with a possible solution during an earlier scene in which Julia is eating a croissant in Richard's hotel room. She finally stands up and says to Richard's character in essence, "I want to be your girl, not just your beck and call girl." That's when it dawned on me that I was directing a fairy tale and I needed a fairy-tale ending. I had to find some kind of metaphorical way for Richard to ride up on a white horse and rescue her—in the most modern and feminist sense of the word.

In the film Edward is afraid of heights. This was in my opinion a brilliant character trait, and the credit for it goes to Barbara Benedict, the sole female writer on our rewrite team. How perfect to have a big corporate guy who does hostile takeovers without fear be afraid of tall buildings. To add to the character we had him book the penthouse in every hotel because that is usually the most expensive room. He pays for the high things in life but never allows himself to enjoy them. Despite the fact that he is in the penthouse, he never steps outside on the balcony because of his phobia.

So when I was thinking about the ending, I got the idea that it should somehow involve Edward overcoming his fear of heights in order to get the girl. We came up with the concept of his climbing up the fire escape of her building. A writer or director can spend all day trying to craft the perfect ending, but sometimes you show up at a location and things are not perfect. When we went to shoot the scene, we discovered, of course, you have to pull down the lowest set of stairs on a fire escape to make it work. At first glance it didn't seem like the most romantic ending to a movie ever shot. But then it struck me that one variable you can always change is weather. So I decided to make it rain, and then have Richard elegantly pull down the fire escape using the handle on his umbrella. Finally, the ending to *Pretty Woman* came together. Richard drove up not on a white horse but in a white limousine. He pulled down the fire escape with his umbrella handle, then climbed up with his umbrella in hand to rescue the girl. To make the story modern, our producer Laura Ziskin came up with the memorable line "She rescued him right back." Romantics rejoiced, and feminists weren't too pissed off either.

Janet Maslin of *The New York Times* was a big fan of the movie. She found Julia Roberts "so enchantingly beautiful, so funny, so natural and such an absolute delight." Maslin went on to call Richard Gere "dapper, amusing and the perfect foil."

The film turned out to be better than expected by me and everyone who worked on it. *Pretty Woman* made Julia Roberts a star. It put Richard Gere back on the top of everyone's casting lists. It introduced the fresh new face of Laura San Giacomo. It boosted room sales at the Regent Beverly Wilshire, where we shot some of the hotel scenes. It made me more in demand as a director than I had ever dreamed of. And finally, from a personal standpoint, it earned me enough money to get myself out of debt.

For a little picture, it had the greatest impact of any movie on my career and on the careers of many people associated with it. We made it for $14 million, and it grossed more than $178 million in the United States alone. Worldwide it has grossed more than $463 million, which is amazing any way you say it. The movie still makes money today. And it gave me the label of romantic comedy director.

People think Hollywood is about money, but to tell the truth, I have found again and again that it is about the friendships and lasting partnerships you form while working together. Julia, Richard, and I were an unlikely trio in terms of experience, personalities, and interests. There was just something about that time in history and about the movie itself that made the three of us friends forever. We made a pact: If two of us ever got a script they wanted to make, they would have to offer it to the third person first as a nod to the power of our friendship. It would be ten years before we would all come together again, on the set of *Runaway Bride,* but in the meantime we stayed in touch and always offered each other scripts when they arrived on our desks. That's just what friends do for each other, even in Hollywood.

One final funny memory about *Pretty Woman* concerns the hotel we shot it in. When we were scouting for the location, we went to a number of venues, and many of them said we could not shoot in their lobbies because "we do not allow prostitutes in our hotel." Big mistake for them. Only the Regent Beverly Wilshire (now the Beverly Wilshire) said yes. A few years after the movie was released, my wife and I went to stay at the hotel and bought the "Pretty Woman Package." It cost several thousand dollars and included a very large suite, champagne, and strawberries. Also available was a version of the red dress that Julia wore in the movie. My wife brought her own purple dress, so we didn't need a red one.

The night we stayed in the hotel Barbara and I laughed about the fact that *Pretty Woman* is the only one of my movies in which she was cut out. She appeared as a shopper in a scene we filmed in Gucci, but ultimately her dialogue had to be cut because of length

and pacing. But if you look closely in the scene with Elinor Donahue, from *Father Knows Best,* you can see my wife leaving the store
wearing a red blazer and carrying a shopping bag. Barbara understood that sometimes a director has to leave his family, even on
occasion his wife, on the cutting room floor.

16. FRANKIE AND JOHNNY

★

Pfeiffer, Pacino, the Clair de Lune,

and Me

AFTER THE SUCCESS of *Pretty Woman,* I could basically pick my next picture. I had to sit for a moment and think:
What do I want to direct? I was, of course, getting a lot of offers
for mainstream glitzy romantic comedies, but doing the same thing
right away didn't interest me. The truth was I wanted to challenge
myself and try directing a more serious movie. That's why I jumped
at the phone call from Paramount executive producer Scott Rudin,
who said he wanted me to consider directing the screen version of
Terrence McNally's hit play *Frankie and Johnny in the Clair de Lune.*
I had never seen the play, so Scott had me fly out to see a New York
City production. He promised the night after I saw the play that I
would have breakfast with Terrence.

So I flew to New York, went to the show, and phoned Scott later
that night.

"I love the play. I want to do it. I can't wait to meet Terrence tomorrow for breakfast to talk about it," I said.

There was a long pause on the other end of the line.

"Scott? Are you there? What's wrong?" I asked.

"Mike Nichols wants to direct the movie. He is in and you are
out," said Scott.

"So no breakfast with Terrence?" I asked.

"Mike Nichols is having breakfast with Terrence. Sorry," he said.

I hung up and then flew back to Los Angeles the next day.

I didn't direct another movie right away. Instead, I developed a stage play that I had written a few years earlier with Lowell Ganz called *Wrong Turn at Lungfish,* the story of a dying blind professor who bonds with a young woman who comes to read aloud to him in the hospital. It took a full year for Scott Rudin to call me again.

"Mike Nichols dropped out of *Frankie and Johnny.* Do you want to direct it?" he said.

"Yes, I do, but only if I get breakfast with Terrence McNally," I replied.

I flew to New York again and finally had my meal alone with the playwright. I had long admired his work, and meeting the man in person made me like him even more. Terrence is a bright, soft-spoken, frail-looking, sensitive gentleman and a true man of the theater. As a young writer he worked as a tutor for John Steinbeck's children. His life was dedicated to words and characters and creating and celebrating them. After our first breakfast we realized we would be not only friends but also partners and teachers. I wanted to learn to write and direct plays, and he wanted to learn to write screenplays. As Terrence began working on the screenplay for *Frankie and Johnny,* I started to direct a production of my play *Wrong Turn at Lungfish* at the Steppenwolf Theatre in Chicago. I helped Terrence write during the day, and he helped me direct at night. We continued to send notes to each other throughout the process.

One day Terrence sent me a note that said, "I'm including a speech about love for Johnny that I think is good for the quality of the character. I threw in a blow job for good measure." Later he wrote to me, "I'm very proud and happy you are directing this movie." For Terrence, *Frankie and Johnny* was not just a play or a movie but rather a labor of love. He was more of an intellectual than a show business writer, but he wanted to see what it felt like to work in the Hollywood mainstream. Together we knew we had to protect the characters he had written so well. We couldn't let Hollywood make them over to such an extent that they were unrecognizable.

One of the biggest hurdles we had to overcome at the beginning was casting. Kathy Bates had starred as Frankie in the stage version of the play in New York, and she was brilliant. But, obviously, the executives at Paramount wanted a bigger box office name for the movie. I couldn't argue with that logic. Kathy is a name today, but she was not back then. Luckily I later got to work with her when I cast her in my movie *Valentine's Day*. She is still brilliant.

They first sent the script to Al Pacino to see if he was interested in playing Johnny. He had not done many love stories because he was usually carrying a gun and yelling things like "Attica!" Al, however, was in the mood to do something new, too, so he agreed.

Once the studio signed Al they started interviewing actresses. Michelle Pfeiffer wanted the role badly. She drove to my office in Toluca Lake to try to convince me. She didn't come with an agent, manager, or entourage. She walked into my office alone. She knew that the problem was many people in Hollywood thought she was *too* beautiful to play Frankie. Who would believe that Michelle could play a lonely, regular girl who had given up on men? After talking with me for an hour, Michelle convinced me that she could play the part. She said the fact that she was pretty didn't mean she was a stranger to loneliness and heartache over men. I believed her. I read after the casting was announced that Kathy Bates laughed when she found out Michelle was taking over her role for the movie version and rightfully so. But the truth is that the studios think some actresses are better suited for the theater and others for film. In this case I agreed. I thought Michelle and Al were a great casting choice.

Terrence and I continued to work well together once the casting was done. He is a great storyteller and someone you always want to sit next to at a dinner party. He told me he once went to a production of *Frankie and Johnny* at a theater in New Orleans. He was shocked to see that the actors performed most of the play totally in the nude. When Terrence went backstage to talk to the director afterward he said, "Well, that was quite a version!" The director didn't understand. He thought he had directed the play exactly as it had been written in the Samuel French publication. Sure enough, the director was right. Terrence reviewed the stage directions, and after *Frankie and Johnny* took their robes off, there was no *written* direction for them to put them back on. In future publications of the play, Terrence corrected this to avoid any more unintentional all-nude productions.

I was finally ready to start filming *Frankie and Johnny*. As a director I had worked with so many up-and-coming actors, but these two were superstars. I couldn't deny that I was a little nervous, but most of all I was tickled and excited to be part of the project. Sometimes my wife and I would sit in bed and I would say, "Honey, I'm directing Al Pacino tomorrow. Can you believe it?" I also was thrilled because I was under the impression that Michelle and Al would come to the set with an acting shorthand in place because they had worked together on *Scarface*. I had seen *Scarface* and thought they had a nice chemistry together. You can imagine my surprise when I brought in Michelle and asked her about Al.

"I've never met him," she said.

"What are you talking about? I saw *Scarface*. You played the girl?"

"Yes, but he never talked to me off the set or out of character. Nobody ever introduced him to me," she said. In her defense she was only in her early twenties and didn't know very much about the movie business.

These are the kinds of stories that make you just shake your head and wonder.

"You did a whole movie with a man and never *met* him?"

"Yes," she said.

I had to fix this right away. So Michelle and Al officially met on *Frankie and Johnny*. They became very supportive of each other during the shoot. One day I remember her brother was in a car accident and she was upset about it. Al was particularly sensitive to her that day. Another day Al was on edge because he was going to the Academy Awards. (He wouldn't claim an Oscar until a year later, 1992, when he won for *Scent of a Woman*.) Michelle was very nice to him and kept him calm nearly all day long. They respected each other and protected each other as good stars should do.

Kissing was another matter. Michelle is gorgeous, but her skin is quite fragile and fair. Al, even after a shave, usually sports a five o'clock shadow because he is comfortable that way. So their kissing scenes were tricky to navigate. After three or four takes, Michelle would break out in a rash from his rough stubble. The makeup department would have to come in and put lotion on her to protect her face. So sometimes the kissing scenes took longer than others. However, I think one of the best kisses I ever shot was when we were on location at the New York flower mart. Associate producer Nick Abdo and I were pitching ideas about how to show their big on-screen kiss. I wanted flowers in the background, but I was having trouble getting the right angle. Nick suggested having a truck pull up behind them so a worker could open the door to the truck to reveal dozens of beautiful floral arrangements just as Frankie and Johnny came together to kiss. So that's what we shot. I think that is one of my talents as a director: When I hear a good idea I can recognize and appreciate it without getting my ego hurt that it wasn't my idea. When I see that scene now on television, it gives me goose bumps. As a director you are always looking for a new way to reveal a kiss, and this worked very well for me thanks to Nick's suggestion.

The play was intimate, and I wanted to maintain that feeling between Frankie and Johnny on the big screen. However, that was a lot to ask of Al and Michelle as actors. Many of the scenes had just the two of them and required multiple takes. One of the last scenes we shot was scene 105, in which Johnny calls up a classical radio station and asks them to repeat the song "Clair de lune." The scene ran about five minutes, and featured only Michelle and Al, so it was unusually intense to direct. It took five long days to shoot, so I made T-shirts for the crew that said "I survived scene 105." But Al and Michelle were professionals and never complained. They would stay as long as I needed them on the set.

I, however, lost my temper while filming the infamous scene. It was very important for me to get the scene right. As I was filming one of the producers' mobile phones went off. I walked over, picked up the phone, and threw it against the soundstage wall. It hit the wall and bounced off, breaking into many pieces. I am not normally a screamer or a man who loses his cool at work or at home, but in this case I just lost it. Later I apologized and we got her a new phone. But I remember being furious at the time that people's phones were ruining my picture.

The supporting cast included the very talented duo Nathan Lane and Kate Nelligan. Some people said Kate was going to be trouble, but she was not at all. My good luck charm Hector Elizondo played the manager of the diner where Al and Michelle worked. As always Hector was so consistently reliable and helpful that I was very happy he could be a part of the film. In the diner Al was a short-order cook and, although it was not essential, he wanted on-the-job cooking lessons. So I took him to Vitello's, my favorite neighborhood Italian restaurant in North Hollywood. My actor-friend Steve Restivo owned the restaurant at the time and let Al spend some time in the kitchen training with the other chefs. Al worked two or three nights. He became a master at chopping celery, and he came up with great ideas for other things, such as carving a flower from a potato and having Johnny give it to Frankie. The restaurant patrons at Vitello's could see into the kitchen as they were escorted to their tables. Some of them had to do a double take when they saw Al dressed in a chef's uniform behind the stove. "Since when does Al Pacino work at Vitello's?" one woman said.

I got to know both Michelle and Al pretty well on the picture, which was helpful in building their characters. Michelle has large, strong hands, and she doesn't think they are particularly pretty. In the film I had her co-workers at the diner coming up to her and without saying a word, just handing her a jar and watching her open it. Al and Michelle worked differently in terms of preparing and mastering a scene. Al liked to do a lot of takes, almost obsessively, without even pondering that a scene might require just a few. I had to learn to respect his process because that was just the way he did things, even if it took eighteen or nineteen takes to get a scene right.

Michelle, on the other hand, was usually happy with the fourth or fifth take of a scene. Sometimes Michelle would bring magazines so she could sit off-camera and have something to do while Al was doing his nineteenth take. We even joked with Al that members of the crew would bet on what take would be the one in which he felt he got it right. But the truth was we couldn't argue with him because on several occasions we saw him get it right on the twentieth take by delivering a moment that was absolutely brilliant. Then we would all look at each other and say, in happy disbelief, "Of course. He's Al Pacino!"

In my breeziest moments I felt like this was any other movie and I was just doing my job well. But the reality was that this was a tricky picture with two gigantic stars. People who come to see an Al Pacino or Michelle Pfeiffer movie expect the very best. Luckily I had Dante Spinotti as my cinematographer. He had worked with me on *Beaches* and knew how to light a scene beautifully. Dante spoke mostly in Italian and looked like a chef. He taught me about art and lighting, and he made me a better director. Albert Brenner, my innovative production designer, created a beautiful set. Transforming the two-person play into something like a hundred-person movie was challenging but creatively exciting for all of us. One day we were shooting on a soundstage and we opened up the big door and drove several cars by to create street traffic. It was just a simple thing, but it worked well in adding another layer of sound.

To do the music for the film I was lucky enough to get Marvin Hamlisch, whom I had met years earlier at summer camp. When I went to Camp Onibar, my two sisters went to Camp Geneva, the all-girls camp nearby. When my mother would talk about Camp Geneva, all she could do was rave about the impressive theater productions. My sister Ronny was the drama counselor, and she produced the shows. Penny was a bad waitress at the camp and was constantly dropping food on the heads of the campers she didn't like. But the real reason the shows were so good was that a sixteen-year-old counselor named Marvin Hamlisch wrote them. All summer camps should be so lucky as to have Hamlisch on the creative team for their musicals.

Marvin and I discussed what type of music would fit the plot of *Frankie and Johnny*. One of the studio executives cautioned me not to let Marvin put in "too many violins" and make the movie too upscale because, after all, it was a love story between a short-order cook and a waitress. But I disagreed. I said, "You mean poor people don't hear violins when they fall in love? What do they hear? Accordions? I don't think so. I think we all hear violins when we fall in love, no matter how much money is in our wallets." I enjoyed working with Marvin to find the right musical combination for a story about two lost souls who have given up on love until they find each other. We needed the music to suggest a feeling of hope.

For most actors, doing publicity is not a favorite thing. To say Michelle and Al would have preferred getting a root canal to doing publicity is pretty darn close. For me sports is a big touchstone, so sometimes I made Al and Michelle do a little ritual together before we shot a difficult scene. For good luck we would put our hands together, on top of one another and yell "Frankie and Johnny" before we broke our grips. I did it during the shoot to signify that we were a team no matter what, and we had to be there for each other. When it came time to do the publicity tour, I knew Al was a little nervous. He loves acting, but not talking about himself. Right before we did the first press conference, he came over to Michelle and me and said, "Can we do that hand-holding thing?" We did. The three of us stood in a circle, put our hands on top of one another, and yelled "Frankie and Johnny" before we broke to do the press conference. It was hokey, but it made us relax—and smile.

When we wrapped the film I think we were all happy. Unfortunately, life doesn't always line up perfectly to support you, and that is what happened with *Frankie and Johnny*. It came out the weekend of the Supreme Court hearings involving Clarence Thomas, Anita Hill, and a widely broadcast case of possible sexual harassment. Interest in Coke cans with pubic hair trumped the interest in my love story. The film's soft opening weekend was no one's fault, and nobody could have predicted it. All we could do was sit back and watch as people stayed home to view the scandalous hearing on television instead of going out to see *Frankie and Johnny*. Despite the low box office returns, we received some good reviews.

Terrence Rafferty of. *The New Yorker* wrote, "We understand why romance and comedy make an ideal inevitable couple." *Rolling Stone* called it a "perfect love story." Another reviewer said it was a romantic comedy for people who don't like romantic comedies. Yes, there were still a few reviewers who said Michelle was too pretty to play Frankie. However, I had tried something new. Even though the movie didn't make a ton of money, I was happy with the way it turned out.

When we finished I wondered what to do again. With a television series you can have a steady job for years. As a movie director you have to make a new choice every year or two. So when *Frankie and Johnny* came out, I was fifty-seven years old. I wondered exactly how many movies I would make before I should retire. Would someone tell me when it was time? Would I figure it out myself? I wasn't sure, but after *Frankie and Johnny* was completed, I knew I wanted to direct another picture. Someone gave me an erotic book by Anne Rice about an S and M island called *Exit to Eden*. I read the book and liked it. Suddenly I was about to enter my true experimental period as a director. My wife read the book, turned white, and said, "Are you kidding me?"

17. EXIT TO EDEN

★

Taking a Wrong Turn into
the Land of S and M

SO THERE I WAS, with a mask covering my face, standing
at an S and M party in Hollywood.

I was there doing research for my next movie, *Exit to Eden,* which
was based on the book written by Anne Rampling, otherwise known
as the queen of all vampire writers, Anne Rice. I didn't know much
about the underground S and M world, so I contacted a woman who
from time to time was my doubles tennis partner. I knew that in
addition to having excellent ground strokes, she worked as a professional dominatrix. When I told her I wanted to do research on
the subject, she offered to take me to a party. She said celebrities
and other people in show business didn't want to be recognized at
these kinds of parties, so they often wore masks. She gave me one to
wear to the party. That night as I was getting dressed and putting on
my mask, my wife peered up from bed over the pages of her latest
P. D. James novel.

"Where are you going again exactly?" she asked.

"It's an S and M party," I said.

"In a nightclub?" she asked.

"I think it's someone's house," I said.

"Do people spank each other there in full view? Like in the
living room?" she said.

"I'm not sure. I'll find out," I said.

"Why do you want to do this movie? It seems silly and unneces-
sary," she said. "And kind of strange. You are going to get killed by

the press when they find out Mr. *Happy Days* is doing a movie about bondage."

"I'm in the mood to do something different," I said. Alex Rose, who had produced *Nothing in Common, Overboard,* and *Frankie and Johnny* with me, had suggested *Exit to Eden* and said she would come onboard to produce it.

"Okay. Suit yourself. Have a good time and remember to turn on the burglar alarm when you get back," Barbara said, returning to her mystery book.

So that night I went to the party, thinking I was completely in disguise, on a secret mission to collect background information for my movie. I loved that I could go from room to room without anyone knowing who I was. At one point I went out on the patio where two women were smoking cigarettes.

"I'm ready to go home," said one woman. "How about you?"

"As soon as Garry Marshall comes. I hear he's coming to do research for a new movie about an S and M island, and I want to see him," she said. "Maybe we can be in it."

I ran over to my friend and said, "We're not so undercover! They know we're here."

The truth was that I was again in the mood for something different. I adore love stories, and I felt like I had done so many in a row in different settings: everything from love between a fry chef and a waitress to love between a prostitute and a corporate raider. I thought love on an S and M island seemed like a new direction. Initially I conceived *Exit to Eden* as a serious romance with some comedy moments. Its turn in a completely different direction is simply what happens sometimes in Hollywood. You can't predict all the twists and turns of making a movie. You just have to hold on tight during the ride.

Soon the announcement was in *Variety* and *The Hollywood Reporter* that Garry *Happy Days* Marshall would direct a new movie about an S and M island. An independent film company called Savoy was putting up the money. I was excited about the casting of Dana Delany in the starring role. Dana was best known for starring in the television series *China Beach*. She was now ready to shed her "good girl" image and take on a role that required full frontal nudity. Plus, she got to spank her costar. She hoped that this movie would do for her what the very sexy feature *Basic Instinct* had done for Sharon Stone.

When it came to casting an actor to play opposite Dana, I had a very tough time. I couldn't find a mainstream actor who wanted to get spanked by a woman on the big screen. So many actors who I thought would be good in the role flatly turned it down. I did get a meeting with one famous blond television actor who seemed very interested. We went to a bar to talk about the part. However, my interest in him began to wane when I realized that he was very drunk. He was so drunk in fact that at one point he fell off the bar stool. So I was back to the drawing board. When most American actors turned down the part, I decided to go to a different country: Australia. Up-and-coming Australian actor Paul Mercurio had starred in Baz Luhrmann's film *Strictly Ballroom*. In that movie he was nothing but delightful and charming. He read the script for *Exit to Eden* and wasn't afraid of taking on the part or the nudity that came with it. I finally had my match for Dana Delany.

I peppered the rest of the cast with some of my favorites, including Hector Elizondo, who explains some of the details of the S and M island. Through a series of flashbacks, he plays a therapist who initially trained Dana Delany's character to become a dominatrix. I also cast my daughter Kathleen as a flight attendant. I think nepotism is healthy. Unfortunately the script called for Kathleen's character to die in the opening minutes, thus setting off a mystery that would take several police officers to the S and M island. My wife, however, put her foot down. "You can't kill your own daughter! Even if it is in a movie. That's just not right!" Barbara is often the voice of reason in my life. So we rewrote the scene so Kathleen's character didn't die but instead got hit over the head and passed out for a few minutes. In the same scene my sister Ronny is an airport maid mopping the floor, and she finds Kathleen passed out.

Often I try to cast relatives or people I know because during the grueling pace on a movie it is nice to see people you like and know. To get up every morning and like my job and look forward to it is important to me. I remember the day I realized that. My friend the fast-talking writer, Sam Denoff, was working on *The Dick Van Dyke Show,* and I was writing for *The Danny Thomas Show.* We were talking one day about how much we liked going to work in the morning. He said, "Garry, that's what life is all about." I never forgot that. I am willing to work as hard and as long as anyone, but I have to like my job and look forward to it.

Back to the S and M island: I wanted *Exit to Eden* to have an air of authenticity as well, so I interviewed some real-life dominatrixes to cast in various scenes. My secretaries were all a-twitter the day I had my dominatrix casting call. One of the women seemed unusually bright. It's not as if a dominatrix should be a dummy, but you don't expect her to have a Ph.D. either. Anyway, this bright girl came into my office to read a scene, and when she got up to leave she looked a little funny.

"What's wrong?" I said.

"I need to tell you something," she said.

"Yes?" I asked.

"I knew your mother," she said timidly.

I was a little taken aback that my mother would have known someone in the sex trade, but it turned out the dominatrix's mother took dance lessons from my mother. When they knew each other my mom had shown her mother and the daughter pictures of me from when I was growing up. As the daughter was leaving she said, "Your mother was very proud of you." And that was a nice thing to hear, even from a woman who makes a living spanking men.

The premise of the movie interested me from the start. After *Beaches, Overboard,* and *Pretty Woman,* I felt a little as if I was running out of settings. So the idea of filming on a warm tropical island appealed to me. We found out we could shoot on the Hawaiian island of Lanai, which also sounded terrific. The setting, however, was never really the problem. The disagreement from the start was what the movie should be about. I thought I could make a serious love story with some sexy and lighter moments. But some of the other people involved in the project felt it should be a zanier comedy. That problem grew worse when we cast Rosie O'Donnell and

Dan Aykroyd as undercover police who travel to the island. The sex story line of Dana and Paul seemed to be in constant competition against the comedy story line that Rosie and Dan were starring in. We had one movie with two strong plots and we could never reconcile that problem to create one story.

I always loved the book the film was based on, and I was thrilled to get to meet Anne Rice when we filmed in her hometown of New Orleans after the island shoot wrapped. Anne is a fascinating woman and writer. She had a child who died and suffered from grief and writer's block for years before finding her voice again. When I met with Anne I was surprised to find that she was a tiny and soft-spoken woman. I somehow thought a woman who wrote about sex and vampires would be loud and tall instead. She read the script of *Exit to Eden* and liked it.

I wanted to stay true to her premise, but again the studio kept pushing me toward comedy because they were growing more afraid each day of having a purely erotic story line. Every time I got a note from an executive from Savoy, it told me I needed to "pump up" the comedy from Rosie and Dan. The executives seem to care less and less about the parts Dana and Paul were playing. I have to admit that seeing Rosie in a dominatrix outfit was funny, but we couldn't build an entire movie around that. Rosie later said on her talk show that *Exit to Eden* nearly ruined her career. We became better friends after the movie was behind us. A few years later she let me come on her show to promote my movie *Runaway Bride,* even after her producers had refused to book my appearance. She said, "Garry, you should have just called me directly. We are like family." She had worked with my sister Penny on *A League of Their Own.* Despite the fact that I knew there were problems on *Exit to Eden* during the filming, I didn't know what to do to fix them.

Dana was a brave and fearless actress when it came to shooting erotic scenes. Another actress might have been reluctant or anxious, but Dana was the opposite. She was wonderful to work with and had no problem doing as little or as much nudity as I thought suited the scene. We became friends during the movie and talked a

Al Pacino was an intense actor to direct, but after a few weeks on the set even he was game to play along with some of my gag-reel shots. *(Courtesy of Paramount Pictures Corporation)*

Reuniting with Julia Roberts and Richard Gere to shoot the film *Runaway Bride* was exciting. For years we tried to find a sequel script for *Pretty Woman II,* but nothing seemed like a good fit. *Runaway Bride* pleased all three of us. *(Photo by Ron Batzdorff, © 1999 Paramount Pictures Corporation and Touchstone Pictures)*

Julie Andrews, Hector Elizondo, and Anne Hathaway were a dream cast for *Princess Diaries I* and *II*. We loved seeing Anne mature from a young girl in the first film to a true movie star in the second movie. *(Photo by Ron Batzdorff, © Disney)*

Raising Helen was my chance to work with the lovely Kate Hudson, who, as a little girl, hung out with me on the set of her mother's film *Overboard*. *(Photo by Ron Batzdorff, courtesy of Holding Pictures)*

Georgia Rule brought together old Hollywood and new: Jane Fonda, Felicity Huffman, and Lindsay Lohan all turned in great performances in the movie, even if some audiences found it a difficult film. *(Photo by Ron Batzdorff, courtesy of Morgan Creek Productions, Inc.)*

Working with Jennifer Garner on *Valentine's Day* was a highlight for me.
Sometimes you meet an actress who you would be friends with if you
were working in another business, and Jennifer is that girl. A delight.

I had just finished seven
weeks of radiation treatment
before I directed *New Year's
Eve*. Coming to work
and getting to hug Halle
Berry is an excellent post-
radiation regimen.

When we can, my wife and I take our children and grandchildren to Hawaii for Christmas. We take a timer photo by the elevator each trip, and we are so grateful for the time we get to spend together as a family.

Playing softball is one of the joys of my life. The fact that I can still play ball at least once a week in my seventies helps keep me balanced.

My sister Penny is one of the most talented actresses I have ever known. She has a gift for physical comedy that I think is on par with Lucille Ball. *(Courtesy of © MLC)*

I have been married to Barbara Sue Wells for nearly five decades now. She makes me move into a hotel when I'm directing a movie, even when I shoot in Los Angeles. This is one of our many coping strategies and it works.

When I'm not directing movies, I'm at my Falcon Theatre in Burbank, California, where I produce a new season of plays each year alongside my daughter Kathleen Marshall LaGambina and Sherry Greczmiel. *(Photo by Ron Batzdorff)*

I call this picture from the set of *New Year's Eve* the Oscar winners shot. Hilary Swank, Robert De Niro, and Halle Berry all have gold statues at home.
(New Year's Eve photo by Andy Schwartz, © New Line Productions, Inc. All rights reserved)

I try to include at least one of my grandchildren in most of my movies because I think it brings me good luck. Spending time on the set or off with my grandkids is one of the things that makes me smile the most. Here I'm on the beach with my grandson Sam, an entertainer of the future. *(Photo by Scott Marshall)*

When someone comes in and interviews for a job with me, one of the first questions I ask them is, "Do you play softball?" It remains one of my passions. I have won three championships pitching for the Indians in the senior league. *(Photo by Heather Hall)*

Valentine's Day gave me the chance to work with some veteran actors like Shirley MacLaine and Hector Elizondo, as well as wonderful new actors like Taylor Lautner and Taylor Swift. (Valentine's Day *photo by Ron Batzdorff,* © *New Line Productions, Inc. All rights reserved*)

Here I am with the cast of *Keeping Up with the Steins,* which was directed by my son Scott. Pictured here are Jeremy Piven, Daryl Sabara, and Neil Diamond. *(Courtesy of Miramax)*

My daughter Lori and I had the pleasure of appearing on *The Oprah Winfrey Show* when we wrote our first book together. *(Courtesy of sgreenphoto.com)*

Working with the ensemble cast on *Valentine's Day* gave me the chance to work with so many different actors, including the versatile Jamie Foxx. *(*Valentine's Day *photo by Ron Batzdorff, © New Line Productions, Inc. All rights reserved)*

I like seeking new creative adventures even late in my life. I never directed an opera before Plácido Domingo asked me to direct the *Grand Duchess of Gerolstein*, which opened the Los Angeles Opera's 2005 season. *(Courtesy of Lee Salem Photography)*

lot about our families and dreams. Dana had found that, as is true for so many of the beautiful stars, dating was hard. Traveling to different television and movie locations was a way of life for Dana but not a very good way to keep a boyfriend. But by the time we did our movie together, she had made peace with the fact that acting would come first for a while and boyfriends would need to come second. This is a choice many actresses are afraid to make.

The only time we didn't get along was when she fooled me about her experience with horses. I wanted to film a scene in which Dana rode into the entrance of the island on a horse—like the world's sexiest army general reviewing the troops. I didn't think the horseback riding was a problem because I had seen Dana in the western movie *Tombstone,* in which she rode a horse. But when we started shooting our movie and I pitched the scene to her, she looked worried.

"What's the matter?" I asked.

"I'm sorry, but I don't ride horses," she said.

"But I saw that movie *Tombstone.* It was a western. Kurt Russell. Val Kilmer. You. Everyone rode a horse, and you even rode sidesaddle," I said.

"The crew made me a fake leg," she said.

They had built her a fake leg because she was not comfortable riding a horse sidesaddle. Luckily, one of my *Exit to Eden* actresses, Stephanie Niznik, a pretty blonde actress, was an excellent rider. She worked with Dana to help her feel more comfortable. At one point I put the two of them on the horse together, and if you look closely you can see Stephanie riding the horse triumphantly in while Dana has her arms around Stephanie's waist, holding on for dear life.

Paul Mercurio was also excited to try his best. He made up for not bringing the star power of the other actors by being more than amiable. He and his wife were former ballet dancers, and they brought their children from Australia to live with us on the island during the shoot. Life on the set was not stressful for them because they lived a bit like gypsies in Australia, too, always moving from one town to the next. His hobby was brewing beer, and he brought in many different beers for me to try.

Shooting on Lanai was a unique experience for all of us. Only Dan Aykroyd kept a little to himself. The rest of the cast and crew would hang out at night and sing songs in the hotel bar. The model-actress Iman, married to David Bowie, played a small part. Many nights Iman and Rosie O'Donnell would lead the cast in Broadway show tune sing-along sessions. Where could you see Iman and Rosie singing songs from *My Fair Lady* and *South Pacific* except on a quirky movie set in Hawaii?

One of the highlights of the editing process for me on *Exit to Eden* was the music. I got along well with the composer, a wonderful dapper Englishman named Patrick Doyle. In our first meeting I was kind of tired, so I talked shorthand. I said to him, "Put some harp shit into that scene to give it that celestial feel." He looked at me and said, "Let me write that down. 'Harp shit.' " To this day whenever I run into him he refers to my harp shit request and we share a laugh.

When the picture came out the critics were shocked that Mr. *Happy Days* could make an S and M movie. My joke was "I made a movie about S and M and the critics spanked me for it." My experiment with something new failed miserably. Instead of a sexy farce, audiences and critics declared it a smutty flop. Some people (mostly men) told me later what they hated most about the movie was the fact that Dana's character spanked the man she loved. After a few test screenings where the picture didn't go over well, we took out some sex and put in more comedy.

When all was said and done, however, *Exit to Eden* didn't turn out as I planned. One of the scenes that showcases the mix I was trying to achieve was a sex class my wife was in. A teacher walks over to Barbara, who was playing a very buttoned-up woman. The teacher tries to get her character to loosen up through erotic play. The teacher says to my wife, "Say something dirty." My wife says, "Soot!" It was a funny scene, but unfortunately the entire movie didn't strike that same chord.

Despite our best efforts to reconcile the plot, we got beat up by the critics for making two movies instead of one. When the film was received so badly I got a little blue, especially since it came on the heels of *Frankie and Johnny,* a film I was so proud to be a part of. Even though *Exit to Eden* didn't win any praise, I can say that we had a great time filming on Lanai, and the cast and crew felt like family to me. I don't normally like to shoot so far away from my own family, but this was a movie in which people really bonded.

After I directed *Pretty Woman* everyone was rushing to hire me. After *Exit to Eden* came out nobody came rushing. In fact, some were rushing away from me. I was no longer a hot director, however, I was not entirely unhappy because I was no longer in debt. The financial security that *Pretty Woman* brought stayed with me even beyond the failure of my adventure into S and M. Yet, I still needed and wanted to work. I could be choosy but not that choosy. So when Paramount sent me a script called *Dear God,* I didn't think too long before accepting the job. When you lose a lot of money and then earn it back, the goal remains just to keep working in case some bad financial thing ever happens again. The script for *Dear God* had no actor attached. Someone called me from the casting department to discuss some different choices.

"How about Greg Kinnear?" he said.

"Who is Greg Kinnear?" I asked.

"He starred in *Talk Soup*," he said.

"I don't know that either. But bring him in. I'll meet him," I said.

Before I started shooting *Dear God,* I went on a tour across the country to promote my book *Wake Me When It's Funny,* a how-to book about breaking into show business. At signings people would come up and whisper things in my ear about my movies. Time and time again women would lean across the table as I was signing their books and say, "I loved *Beaches,*" and then they would lean in closer and whisper more softly so no one could hear but me and say, "I liked *Exit to Eden,* too." That kind of comment always made me smile. At least some people understood that I was trying to achieve something different with my movie about the S and M island.

At the end of my book tour, my assistant of twenty-two years, Diane Perkins Frazen, retired. We interviewed several candidates and chose Heather Adams Hall, who worked at a law firm. Heather was a young, pretty, very strong Irish girl. She said she was single with no kids and no plans for either. Of course, she is married now and has two terrific girls. She remains my fiercely loyal executive assistant for the past seventeen years, and now co-produces my movies, too.

18. DEAR GOD

★

Building Stories in a Post Office
and a New Career as an Actor

AFTER THE DISAPPOINTMENT of *Exit to Eden,* I again wasn't sure what I wanted to do next. I turned sixty years old that November, and I took my whole family to Paris for Thanksgiving. It was an exciting time because we were all together as a family, but I still worried about my next movie. If a director is only as good as his last movie, I didn't want to be forever saddled with the less than memorable *Exit to Eden.* After all, I'd helped convince Jackie Gleason to do *Nothing in Common* so his last picture wouldn't be *Smokey and the Bandit II.* So I had to live by my own advice and look for another movie to direct, to redeem myself at least in the eyes of Hollywood, a very tough set of eyes.

While I was searching for another movie to direct, a funny thing happened. I got interested in acting. I have always liked acting because when I'm not in charge of a movie set I can relax, hang out, and eat at the craft service table. When you spend your life being a boss, it can be therapeutic to let someone else be in charge once in a while. I loved acting in my sister Penny's movie *A League of Their Own,* and before that in Albert Brooks's cult hit movie *Lost in America.* I acted from time to time in my own television shows and other people's movies, but I never wanted to become a regular in anyone else's television series. I changed my mind when I crossed paths with Candice Bergen when she was starring in her classic series *Murphy Brown.*

I had known Candice for many years and long admired her

famous ventriloquist father, Edgar Bergen, who went to my alma mater, Northwestern. When I was working with Debbie Reynolds in the 1960s on the movie *How Sweet It Is!* I would see Candice at Debbie's house. She and Debbie's daughter, Carrie Fisher, were childhood friends who had slumber parties together. They would be running around the house in their pajamas while I was working with Debbie. Flash forward to when the producers of *Murphy Brown* called and asked if I wanted to be in an episode with Candice. I jumped at the chance to work with her and the rest of the talented cast. As an adult actress Candice loved to laugh, but she also wanted to be dignified and not zany or crazy. She encouraged the other actors around her to be comic foils to protect her more formal, stoic, and very funny character.

Murphy Brown had started filming in 1988. When the producers called me it was already 1994, and the show was well-established with a loyal audience. They called me to assist with an episode featuring a cameo appearance by Candice's husband, Louis Malle, the famous French film director, whom she'd married in 1980. Candice felt he was a little nervous because he didn't really understand "television people." The writing staff discussed bringing me in, because I had worked in both television and movies. I was introduced as Stan Lansing, the head of the network that produced Murphy's news program. I came to the set, met Louis, and we got along great. It was a pleasure for me to work alongside him, and I learned something about his filmmaking, too. He was a lovely, talented artist.

A few weeks later the producers called and asked if I would come back and do another episode.

"Is Louis coming back, too?" I asked.

"Louis is not. Just you," they said.

Louis was returning to his day job as a French film director.

I was still trying to decide on my next movie, so I said sure as long as I could still make movies. For the next four years I appeared on and off as Stan Lansing and loved my work on the series. I think acting in a television series taught me how to be a better director and be more sensitive to the needs of actors. I came away from *Murphy Brown* with a greater appreciation of what it is like to be the person standing underneath the bright lights and in front of the camera vulnerable for all America to see. I admired actors more for the hard work they do, whereas in the past I think I gave more credit to the writers and directors.

Another thing I loved was seeing the writing staff of *Murphy Brown*. When I started writing for sitcoms, in the 1960s on *The Joey Bishop Show,* the writers were heavy drinkers, misfits, college dropouts, and people who wrote for nightclub comics who came up through the ranks like me. By the late 1980s and '90s, the staff writers on sitcoms were top-ranked students from Ivy League colleges. The 4.0 superstars had figured out for themselves how much money there was to be made as a staff writer on a weekly sitcom. Suddenly graduates from Yale, Brown, Harvard, Princeton, and Northwestern weren't going directly to medical or law school but instead were heading to Hollywood to start as entry-level sitcom writers at ABC, CBS, and NBC. I thought it was sad to have so many bright young people on staff as sitcom writers.

During *Murphy Brown* I had time to reflect on my television career. I've been on the comedy side of show business since the late 1950s and have tried to adjust to the changes. There were soft family comedies in the 1950s—and hipper and more sophisticated comedies in the 1960s. The 1970s took its cue from the rebellious 1960s and did social issue comedy, and then discovered the big-kid audience with *Happy Days, Three's Company,* and *The Partridge Family.* And the 1970s were the end of variety shows, to be replaced by late-night talk shows and *Saturday Night Live.* The 1980s became high-concept comedy and a stronger female comedy presence, such as *Murphy Brown.* Also, new outlets on cable started to take foothold—allowing comedy with less censorship.

The late 1990s made comedy and money bedfellows. It featured more costly special effects to make comedy moments. At the end of the 1990s, the Internet and cable came on strong, allowing many new outlets for entertainment. The 2000s saw so much new technology we now had to make people laugh in new ways. I dreamed of doing jokes on the big screen, only to realize that humor had to be scaled down to laughing at things on your computer or your tiny iPhone. With cable channels and Internet, there are many new outlets; comedy is more in demand than ever.

Some comedy devices, however, have suffered. Story is becoming more irrelevant. Simple stories, ensemble casts, fast-paced jokes, and the reality shows are in demand. Reality shows create comedy from laughing at your neighbors. They can be funny but often "mockery" has replaced "wit" and embarrassment or winning big has replaced "charming" and "delightful" humor. Who knows what the future will bring, but I hope to be a part of it.

Playing Stan Lansing on *Murphy Brown* gave a boost to my ego while I was still licking my wounds from the failure of *Exit to Eden.* It's hard to be too depressed when you are appearing on a national television series that is at the top of the ratings. The funny thing was that people would recognize me from *Murphy Brown* but they wouldn't immediately put two and two together. I would be in a restaurant and a guy would lean over to me and say, "Were you once my dentist?" Or "Did we go to college together?" And I would say, "I play Stan Lansing on *Murphy Brown.*" And he would say, "Aha! That's where I know you from!" Over time people began to stop me in the street and say, "Hey! Stan! How ya doin'?" For my wife and family this new notoriety was strange. After all of my work in television, people knew my name from my credits but very few people, except for those who had seen me in *Lost in America,* knew my face.

The experience on *Murphy Brown* also gave me the confidence to seek out other acting work, including the cable television film *The Twilight of the Golds,* starring Brendan Fraser and Faye Dunaway, in which I played the father. One entertainment magazine wrote, "Marshall continues to prove himself even more talented in front of the camera." I wasn't quite sure if I should feel flattered by that comment or take it as a slam against my directing skills. The film was rather controversial because it involved a family struggling with the ethical question, "What if you knew your fetus was going to be gay?" The story of love, acceptance, and struggle was topical at the time and I think broke some new ground. I was excited to be part of such a dramatic film, which was a departure from my own acting.

In one scene I had to cry, and I tried my best. It was not the greatest crying ever done on film, but I gave it a shot.

While I was carrying on with my acting, I got the phone call from Paramount's Sherry Lansing who said she was ready to make a movie called *Dear God*. She wanted me to direct, with Steve Tisch producing and Greg Kinnear set to star. The film was low budget, but now shooting a movie for me was about how much I liked the project, plus is the script ready to go and is the financing in place. In this case I was ready and the studio felt Greg was ripe to pop out as a star. He had appeared opposite Harrison Ford and Julia Ormond in Sydney Pollack's admirable remake of *Sabrina* and done a good job. After screening *Sabrina,* I had to agree that he could act. Besides, I met him, and I liked him.

The advantage of *Dear God* not being a big-budget picture was that I could hire some of my talented friends and give them a break. I hired the funny and intense Laurie Metcalf from the Steppenwolf Theatre Company and more recently the sitcom *Roseanne*. Laurie has always been one of my favorite actresses because she is like a chameleon, able to completely transform her body and look to adapt to a fictional character. She can bring an entire scene alive without saying a word because she uses her body to express emotions and is a master of guttural sounds. She has the best concentration while doing expressive acting that I have ever seen. (Years later I saw a play that starred a girl who demonstrated the exact same concentration, and it turned out she was Laurie's daughter Zoe Perry.) In other supporting roles for *Dear God,* we were able to get my friend Jack Klugman and comedian Tim Conway, whom I had admired since his days on *The Carol Burnett Show.*

Dear God was about a handsome and smart young man who also happens to be a con man. One day he begins answering people's letters to God and making their dreams come true with the help of a ragtag group of postal employees. Greg was well-suited for the role, but the problem from the beginning was that we didn't have any big-name stars. I guess our hope was that we would find an audience and turn our cast into big stars, but it didn't happen that way. Greg was up-and-coming, and very charming on-screen, but this was not destined to be his breakout movie. A year later, he was featured in *As Good as It Gets* and he was on his way. The rest of the *Dear God* supporting cast, while extremely talented, were not the kinds of actors who drove audiences into movie theaters.

Recently I had the opportunity to see *Dear God* again, and I recognized another problem with the movie—the music. When the studio saw our dailies, they decided that we lacked the story quality and star power to become successful. Based on that opinion, they held back on music financing. If we had had bigger stars and a more exciting story, Paramount probably would have spent more money buying songs and hiring a big orchestra. For a director it's frustrating not to get the proper studio support in any area.

Things also fell apart when we showed the picture to test audiences. When you have a movie that relies on the audience either believing or not believing in God, it is tricky. The religious people laughed at some jokes and not at others, and the atheists were a bit suspicious about the entire picture. So it was a tough audience to please. After Paramount saw our numerical results, they also cut our editing budget. Often I didn't have the budget to cut a joke out of the movie even when I had numbers that showed it wasn't working. Further, our title confused people. Audiences who had loved the movie *"Oh, God!"* wondered why George Burns, dead since 1996, was not in my picture, too.

A movie for me is never pure joy or pure hell. There are always highs and lows and many days in between. So when I look back on *Dear God,* I look at the positive aspects: The process had been fun and rewarding. Greg Kinnear was a delight and I had gotten to see my actress-daughter Kathleen almost every day. I'd been able to live in my house with my wife and work close to home part of the time when I wasn't staying in a nearby hotel. I'd enjoyed once again working with Hector Elizondo, who played one of the post office workers. And for the first time ever I'd put my twin granddaughters, Lily and Charlotte, into a movie. They played babies who were stressing their mother out so much that the postal workers granted the mother's wish to get a break from her kids. My granddaughters demonstrated excellent crying on command with chocolate pudding on their faces when I yelled "Action!" However, I didn't think they had a future in acting.

Finally, I stopped pondering the question, "Should I still be a film director?" I knew in my heart and at my age that film directing was the perfect job for me. But the fact that the profession was a good fit didn't mean that the projects I chose were always spot-on. After *Dear God* was released I continued to worry even though I had enough money to survive. I think my worry stemmed from some of the men I'd met at the beginning of my career. There was a chubby curmudgeon named Marvin Marx who wrote for *The Joey Bishop Show*. He was always worried about money. We would all go out to dinner and he would put the bill on his credit card and make us give him cash so he would have spending money. He also used to go to the Nabisco factory and wait at the side door, where they would hand out boxes of broken cookies for free. I didn't want to worry the rest of my life about money, and I didn't want to wait in line for broken cookie crumbs either.

Movie directing had not always been my only dream. I had another long-standing goal: to build a theater. On November 9, 1996, I signed the paperwork to build my Falcon Theatre on Riverside Drive in Burbank, California. Since moving to Hollywood I had wanted to build a space in my hometown of Toluca Lake to produce plays and musicals, partially in memory of my mother, who thought creating live theater was the most noble of all professions. My financial trouble in Pasadena had sidelined my dream for so long that I thought it might never happen. But now I finally had enough money to start construction. However, once we broke ground I began to worry about money again. You can't construct a building and not be constantly worried about how you are going to pay for it, especially if it is a 130-seat theater that's already $1 million over budget. I know how to bring a movie in under budget but not a building.

Building the theater was a highlight for me personally, but it did nothing for my movie career. I have often said that Hector Elizondo is my lucky charm, but if I had to name a female lucky charm for me, it would be Julia Roberts. She brought me creative and financial success on *Pretty Woman,* and I will always be grateful for her. What is lovely and amazing is that she brought me luck a second time when I needed it most. At home one night I was reading a play that we were considering producing at the Falcon when my wife came into the room. But I didn't want to be interrupted.

"Garry, you have a phone call," said Barbara.

"I'll call them back," I said.

"I think you will want to take it," she said.

"Why?" I asked.

"It's Julia Roberts," she said.

"Okay. Hand me the phone," I said.

"That's not all," she said.

"What else?" I asked.

"Richard Gere is on the line, too," she said.

"Richard and Julia are calling me together?" I asked.

"I know. The *National Enquirer* would have a field day. I'll go and get you a Fudgsicle while you start the call," she said.

The phone call was a big deal. It was about a script called *Runaway Bride.*

My life was about to change for the better again because of a lion-haired actress named Julia Roberts.

19. THE OTHER SISTER

★

Striving for a Different Kind of

Love Story

COMEDIAN JOE E. LEWIS once said, "You only live once, but if you work it right, once is enough." I have found that as you get older you naturally begin to question the choices you make. Why am I here? What do I want to be remembered for? What is my legacy to my children and my grandchildren? They are not lofty or egotistical questions but rather practical ones that go through most people's heads at some point. I never wanted to change the world. I wanted to entertain the world. I knew I would be remembered most for my television shows, but I wondered about my movies. Were *Exit to Eden* and *Dear God* the films I wanted people to base their impressions of my entire directing career on? My answer was no. I had talked to Julia Roberts and Richard Gere on the phone about doing *Runaway Bride* but the film was not ready to go into production. I could shoot another film before starting *Runaway Bride*. That's what I decided to do.

I knew that *Runaway Bride* had a good shot at becoming a hit, so I decided that for my other script I would look for something with depth on a subject that interested me: raising kids. In 1995 my daughter Lori gave birth in San Francisco to fraternal twin girls who arrived at twenty-seven weeks, or three months early. Lily and Charlotte lived in the newborn intensive care unit for eight weeks, and both were diagnosed with cerebral palsy at ages one and two respectively. I remember the first feelings I had upon hearing the news were fear and anger. I wanted to punch something. But the anger turned to love when I met these little beans, who came into the world weighing hardly more than two pounds apiece. I couldn't wait to kiss their faces and put them into my next movie. The subject of a family facing the challenges of raising disabled kids was on my mind in the mid-1990s as I watched my daughter begin to raise her daughters.

Stories about parents raising children had always fascinated me. Odd families. Quirky families. Not-your-average-run-of-the-mill families. Growing up in the Bronx, I always knew the family I came from wasn't perfect, and I saw how my parents struggled to keep us happy and healthy. I knew other families didn't drink Pepsi and milk to make the milk last longer. I knew most families didn't put ketchup on their noodles and call it spaghetti sauce. Many of the families I knew growing up and know today are dysfunctional in one way or another. I hoped I could find a script that addressed the struggles of parenthood rather than only the romantic and happy moments of being a mom and dad.

While I was looking for a good script about a family something else happened: I became a big hit on Nick at Nite. The cable channel bought many of my old television shows in a deal with Paramount. My wife and I would sit in bed at night, turn on the television, and literally watch my TV career pass before our eyes. I was happy to see my shows on television again. I wasn't proud of every single episode, and some even made me cringe. However, this was not the case with *The Odd Couple*. There is not one episode of *The Odd Couple* that makes me cringe. In my book Jack and Tony made each episode of that series special and above and beyond what we had set out to do.

To be able to laugh in the 1990s at jokes that were written in the 1970s made me feel good. I had created shows that lasted. Even if I had a shaky movie-directing career, on Nick at Nite I still had a very successful television career. It also made me happy that generations of kids, including my own grandchildren, who were not born when my shows were in prime time, could now get to know Fonzie, Richie, Laverne, and Shirley. The first time my granddaughter

Charlotte saw Lenny and Squiggy burst through a door in an episode of *Laverne & Shirley* she said, "Pop, those guys are *really* funny!"

When I wasn't watching Nick at Nite, I read scripts. Alex Rose, who had produced my movies *Nothing in Common* and *Overboard,* brought me a story that was loosely based on her own family. Growing up in Green Bay, Wisconsin, Alex had a sister who was mentally challenged. Her sister had moved out of the family house at a young age and into a home for children with disabilities. She was living in a group home in Chicago and was doing well when Alex pitched me the story idea. Alex and I decided to go to Chicago and meet her sister. I found her sister, and the way in which her family dealt with her disability, very compelling.

I decided to take Alex's sister's story and make it a screenplay with my friend Bob Brunner, who had started with me on the New York *Daily News* back in the late 1950s. We had come a long way together since our stint as copyboys. Bob had done some rewrite work on *Frankie and Johnny, Exit to Eden,* and *Dear God. The Other Sister* offered us the chance to write something from scratch. Nobody paid us to do this. We simply wrote it and hoped we could sell it. When we finished the script I took it to Disney. They had been so supportive during *Pretty Woman,* and I'd heard some of the executives in the land of Mickey Mouse had seen *Frankie and Johnny* and liked what I did on that film, too.

I met with Disney's Joe Roth, who said he liked the script. What clinched the deal, though, was that his wife read the script and liked it so much she said he had to produce it. He agreed to green-light the picture, but he said he had to be honest with me about it. This would not be a big hit picture, nor would it be a big-budget picture. But if we did it right, we could make a small picture about a special subject that might interest audiences, families, and also me. It was the right time in the history of their company for Disney to make a smaller picture. Roth suggested Diane Keaton to play the mother because Disney was looking for a suitable project for her. I had never worked with Diane, but my wife and I were big fans of her work in Woody Allen's movies.

I didn't even bother interviewing other actresses for the role of the mother. I always look for something quirky about an actress, and I remembered a story I had heard years ago about Diane. She was in the original Broadway production of *Hair,* and she was the only actress who would not take off her clothing for the big naked number "Where Do I Go?" She had a quirky side and a modest side that I thought was admirable. Also as we began production on *The Other Sister,* she had just adopted a daughter to raise as a single parent. Diane was developing a maternal side as well.

The thing I liked most about our script was that the mentally challenged daughter not only was from a wealthy family but also was beautiful. Too often this type of story would have depicted her character as an unattractive girl from a poor family. I thought our story was honest because not every family with a disabled child is living at the poverty level. In *The Other Sister,* Carla Tate is from a family that has money to fix most problems, but her disability is an issue that money can't fix. The other angle I liked was that when I went to meet Alex's sister, she had a boyfriend. So my script was going to have a love story angle, a portrait of what it is like for two mentally challenged people to date, fall in love, and try to build a relationship.

Many young actresses wanted the part of Carla. After holding auditions I decided the best actress for the part was someone I could not get easily. Her name was Juliette Lewis, and she had just gotten out of rehab. Disney doesn't love making pictures with actresses straight out of rehab, but I asked them to make an exception in this case. However, the executives at Disney knew they would have trouble getting insurance for her and they flatly turned her down.

Sometimes you have to think with your gut instead of your head. I was so convinced that Juliette would be perfect for the movie that I decided to put up the extra insurance money myself. Some friends and industry people tried to talk me out of it. We all knew one of the commonsense edicts of Hollywood is "never invest in your own movie." But I did it anyway. So if Juliette started using drugs again, or had to drop out of the movie for any reason, I would have been out of a lot of money. I didn't worry about that. I wanted the actress who was best for the movie. Casting is a little like magic, and when you find it, you don't want to see it walk out the door. I always joked that if you are having trouble casting a role, go and stand in the parking lot of a rehab center and grab some of the people coming out.

The most difficult decision of the entire picture was deciding not to hire my daughter Kathleen for the part of Carla's lesbian sister. Kathleen is an excellent actress and she would have done a great job. There were two other actresses, however, whom I thought made a better threesome with Juliette. So while I love the art of nepotism and I hated having to disappoint my daughter, sometimes you have to make a decision not to hire a family member. We hired Poppy Montgomery as Caroline and Sarah Paulson as Heather. For the father we needed a calm person who would play well opposite the more volatile and high-strung mother. I chose Tom Skerritt, who had been starring in television shows and movies for years. All I had left to cast was the part of Carla's love interest, a boy who also had mental challenges.

We found an up-and-coming actor named Giovanni Ribisi, who coincidentally belonged to the Church of Scientology, as Juliette did. I thought he might provide some added support for her if she needed some help with her drug addictions, or at least be a friend closer to her own age to talk to. Giovanni brought his young wife, Mariah, and baby, Lucia, to the set, which I thought offered some nice stability. From the moment I met him I could tell he had a talent well beyond his years. He was someone who would have a career as an actor for the rest of his life.

The Other Sister was not an easy film to shoot because it blended drama and emotion with lighter comedy and personality insights. Dante Spinotti, who had done *Beaches* and *Frankie and Johnny* with me, came onboard as my cinematographer, and that made me very happy. We shot part of the movie in Los Angeles, and I always like to work near my house. Some of the time, my wife makes me move into a hotel when I work in Los Angeles so I can order room service whenever I want and not subject her to our crazy work schedule. But I could still go home on the weekends and some early nights, sleep in my own bed, and play tennis or softball with my old friends. We shot the other half of the movie in San Francisco, where my daughter Lori lived, so I was able to get a home-cooked meal and visit my twin granddaughters while on location.

Directing *Frankie and Johnny* had taught me a lot about actors. Whereas Michelle Pfeiffer would do a scene in several takes, Al Pacino could take eighteen or nineteen. I knew that most everyone else would be in the range. Juliette fell into the quick category. She didn't need a lot of time to prepare and never stayed in her character. Giovanni, on the other hand, stayed in his character, with the same mannerisms and voice, even when the cameras weren't rolling. I learned to respect and admire the different ways they approached a scene.

As the movie veteran in the group, the eternally youthful-looking Diane had an opinion about everything, and I grew to depend on her experience and knowledge. She is one of the few people in the world who can say "Coppola did this" and "Woody would do that" and be telling the truth. The trick for her was finding a way to make Elizabeth Tate human. The mother was not written as a likable character. Many of the scenes showed her struggling to raise her disabled daughter, and being cold and even mean when others might have been warmer. Portraying an unlikable character, however, didn't scare Diane. She was excited to do something new and tried to infuse the mother with a level of humanity.

One of the things I liked most about working with Diane was watching her with the younger actors. She didn't have a big ego around them. In fact, it was the complete opposite. Diane believed that you stayed on the set to help other actors with their scenes no matter how big a star you were. (Two years later on *The Princess Diaries,* I noticed that Julie Andrews subscribed to this same philosophy.) If Diane had finished her scenes and Juliet still had closeups to do, Diane would stay to help. She never stayed in her trailer. She would change into her regular clothes and then recite lines to Juliette off-camera. This was incredibly helpful for me as a director and for the young actors, too.

There are some scenes in *The Other Sister* that I'm very proud of. There is a scene when Diane and Juliette fight on a golf course and in the middle of their fight, sprinklers go off. I thought it was an exciting and dynamic scene that they both did well soaking wet. There is a scene of my sister Ronny and me dancing at a wedding that always makes me smile. There are, of course, always things that make you squirm a little. When Juliette and Giovanni are talking one of them says, "Who invented sex anyway?" And the other says, "Madonna." I wish I had taken that line out of the movie. It was too big a joke for a quiet moment between a girl and a boy. But that is minor. I like what we were able to do with the movie.

On *The Other Sister* I started to learn some of the finer points of film, especially from cinematographer Dante Spinotti. In one scene with Diane we didn't have the right light. We also didn't have time to change the lights. So Dante came up with a trick. He told me to get the costume designer to dress three extras in white saris and have them stand near Diane. The wardrobe department just happened to have white sari-like shawls in the truck. We did that and presto! The white saris brightened the scene. It was not a surprise that Dante had been nominated for an Academy Award for *L.A. Confidential*. He has always been a brilliant cinematographer in my book.

The Other Sister received some very thoughtful and positive reviews. Stephen Holden wrote in *The New York Times* that the film was "a beautifully acted love story about two mentally challenged young people struggling for independence and self-respect." He attacked me a little for candy-coating some of the story line but ultimately praised the film for its "outstanding performances" by Juliette Lewis, Diane Keaton, and Giovanni Ribisi. At two hours and nine minutes, it was definitely one of my longer movies, but I felt I needed the length to tell my story. Some critics took me to task for the length, while others found the movie trite. Desson Thomson wrote in *The Washington Post* that "everything is reduced to a transparent formula. And everyone plays their schematic part." Everyone is entitled to his opinion. I didn't think the film was formulaic. I thought it was innovative.

I have always taken the critics' reviews with a grain of salt, often not reading them until a year later. What carried more weight with me were the letters I received from people who enjoyed the movie.

Some of them were from parents who were raising children with disabilities. Many of these letters thanked me for bringing their situations to light and showing their joys and struggles. I also received letters from people who said they showed the film to new employees in group homes and hospitals for clients with disabilities. The letters cheered me up and showed me that people had been inspired by the movie.

Whenever I get down or blue about a project, I remember a conversation I once had with my sister about art and creativity. Penny is one of the brightest and most creative people I know. So whenever I am considering a new project or having trouble with an existing one, I ask her advice. She once told me, "Garry, some people find success at making money out of money. Other people strike it rich by thinking of grand business ideas, or complicated schemes. Our family makes television shows and movies that last. So when trying to decide what to do next, think about whether it will last. That is our family business and our legacy—entertainment that has longevity." Writer Lowell Ganz once said that charm was our family business. I always think a lot about longevity and charm when considering my next project.

The next movie I would direct would turn out to be *Runaway Bride*. Julia Roberts was ready to go. Richard Gere had signed his deal, and I was ready to pack my bags and move to Baltimore. I needed a boost. I needed a hit. I needed a movie that would renew my status as a Hollywood director. I wasn't putting pressure on myself so much as I was renewing my focus and commitment to film and what I wanted to say. A love story. Four different weddings. Two of my favorite actors. I was ready to go. Bring on *Runaway Bride,* I thought, and let's hope it is a film that lasts.

20. RUNAWAY BRIDE

★

Walking Down the Aisle Again with
Roberts and Gere

WHEN YOU START to get older in Hollywood, people begin to give you lifetime achievement awards. When this happens you start to feel as if your life is over. The problem was that I was only sixty-four years old when this started, and I didn't feel like the end of my life was close at all. I felt fine and was doing a lot of acting. I was finishing up my stint as Stan Lansing on *Murphy Brown.* I had a nice size part in the Drew Barrymore movie *Never Been Kissed,* and I was preparing to direct *Runaway Bride* with Julia Roberts and Richard Gere in Baltimore.

Still, the invitations for lifetime achievement awards continued to roll in. I tried to appreciate the accolades without getting depressed that I would soon be living at the old folks' home. One of my favorite awards included my name on a street sign along the Bronx Walk of Fame. Although I had been in Hollywood for more than thirty years, I still felt like the stickball-playing kid from the Bronx, so a street named after me in my old neighborhood felt extraspecial.

Runaway Bride also felt like an extraspecial movie from the beginning, too. However, to shoot a film in Baltimore in the dead of winter was not on my bucket list. I also didn't want to be so far away from my family, but sometimes you have to sacrifice comfort for a good job. The producers of *Runaway Bride* got a great tax incentive to shoot in Baltimore, so we all packed up and moved there.

Early during the shoot a mugger held up some of our crew in the prop department. Two nights later we heard that some members of the cast of the *Riverdance,* who were performing nearby, were also mugged. Things got so bad that when my assistant and I would leave the hotel to go out to dinner we would *run* to the restaurant. I heard Barry Levinson, otherwise known as Baltimore's favorite movie director, was shooting close by. So I called and told him we liked everything about shooting in Baltimore except the crime wave we were experiencing. Immediately Barry made a few phone calls and had more police assigned to our set. We had no trouble after that, and I have always been grateful to Barry.

I had a lot riding on *Runaway Bride.* None of my last three pictures—*Exit to Eden, Dear God,* and *The Other Sister*—had been a hit, and I needed another hit. With a great script and two of my favorite stars, I thought the movie had a lot of potential. At the very least I knew we would have fun reuniting our *Pretty Woman* trio. For years we had been looking for a script but couldn't find the right one for a sequel. Richard said he was in a cave one day in Tibet and a monk came over to him and said, "When are you going to do *Pretty Woman Two*?" That's when Richard decided we should find a script, any script and not necessarily a sequel, so we could work together again. Julia agreed, and so did I. And Richard could then walk proudly in caves.

What I didn't anticipate was how cell phones would intrude on our production. When we filmed *Pretty Woman,* in 1989, nobody had cell phones. On the set of *Runaway Bride,* in 1999, everyone had a cell phone and some people had two. Julia and Richard always seemed to be on their cell phones. Richard was helping the Dalai Lama promote the cause of Tibet and Tibetan Buddhism, and Julia was saving orphans in Jamaica. I was afraid to shoot a scene because some orphans and the people of Tibet might suffer. I finally had to ask both Richard and Julia to put down their cell phones for a while so we could shoot the movie. I'm only thankful Facebook wasn't around back then.

As on the sets of my other movies, I liked to plan pranks, contests, and festivities that tied in to different holidays. One day in November the cast and crew decided to pull a prank on me. I was driving to work when a Baltimore policeman came up behind me with flashing lights on. Nervously I pulled over to the side of the road because I thought I was getting a ticket. I am notorious for being a driver so tentative that I make only right turns and rarely left ones. Suddenly the policeman handed me an envelope that contained a birthday card from the cast and crew. I had to laugh because this was the kind of stunt I usually think of.

We all liked to play pranks on Julia because we enjoyed seeing her laugh. Whereas the younger, inexperienced Julia was easy to make laugh out loud on the set of *Pretty Woman,* I was happy to see Julia the star was still an easy target for a giggle. Big stars like to laugh and experience surprise just like ordinary people. There was a scene in which Julia was going to marry a hippie. She was supposed to climb over a wall and jump onto a waiting motorcycle as her escape from the ceremony. On one of the takes, instead of the motorcycle waiting for her on the other side of the wall, we had a big cake in honor of her birthday. She gave us one of her best smiles.

Another time we were filming right before Christmas and I hosted a Christmas tree decorating contest. Richard won with a tree he decorated with different photos from his life and acting career. One of his favorite hobbies is photography, and each year he sends Christmas cards to his family and friends containing a picture he has taken during that year. My wife frames his Christmas photos and puts them in the now quiet, expensive guest bathroom where my daughter used to put up fan pictures of Richard back in the 1970s. So our tradition of having a Richard Gere–themed bathroom carries on.

It was reported that Julia and Richard got $20 million apiece to star in *Runaway Bride.* To say they were big stars was to make an understatement. Julia, in particular, was a powerhouse and being closely watched along with Benjamin Bratt, her boyfriend at the time. However, even on a major motion picture someone can pull the focus from the stars when bad behavior is involved. Our cinematographer got arrested for getting into a fight in a Baltimore bar. It was embarrassing, and we discussed what he should do to redeem himself at work. He decided to gather the cast and crew and apologize for bringing negative publicity to the production. While he was giving his speech, Julia was so excited that someone *else* was the center of attention that she could hardly stand still. For her, to be just a bystander felt like a day at the spa. She listened carefully to the apologetic cinematographer and looked just like a normal, everyday girl instead of an A-list movie star.

Even superstars being paid $20 million, however, have off days, and Richard and Julia certainly had one on *Runaway Bride*. The disagreement started over scheduling; to be honest, I'm not sure what the details were. I think one of them needed to go to a meeting in New York but the other one didn't want to change the shooting schedule. To me it didn't matter what they were fighting about. Directing a love story when the two stars are quarreling isn't easy. One day, they weren't speaking to each other. I knew them both well enough to talk to them individually, but I was unable to melt the frost between them. I couldn't rearrange the production schedule to make them both happy at once, so I had to come up with another plan. That night I was in bed pitching ideas with my wife who was in town visiting me.

"It has to be a love montage. Maybe they should eat something. Ice cream?"

"I think you can do better," said Barbara.

"They already ride horses at the end. What's better?"

"I've got it. They can fly kites. They can run and look romantic, but they both will have to look up. So they won't have to look at each other," said my wife.

The idea was perfect. And if you watch *Runaway Bride* today you can see the kite-flying scene and know that behind the scenes the two·stars were not speaking to each other off-camera. Flying a kite side by side, they look like any other happy couple falling in love. Despite the fact that my wife is a great nurse, I know in my heart she could have been one hell of a movie producer as well.

After that day things got better between Julia and Richard. When we moved on to the horse-riding scenes, they perked up because they are both excellent riders. However, when you work with animals something always goes wrong. We had a scene in which Richard is on a horse and Julia is seated behind him nuzzling his neck. Unfortunately, at that exact moment the horse bucked, and Richard raised his shoulders to control the horse, knocking Julia in the chin and jamming her teeth. So when I yelled, "Action!" all you could hear was Julia screaming "Ouch!" We had to shoot this beautiful and romantic shot many times to get it right without anyone getting hurt.

It rained a lot on our shoot, and we spent a lot of time discussing how cold we were. Yet on a positive note, I remember thinking more than anything else how strong we were as a team. I had Hector Elizondo, my lucky charm, playing the husband of Rita Wilson (Tom Hank's wife), who was Richard's boss. I had Paul Dooley playing Julia's dad, as well as the always dependable and brilliant Joan Cusack as Julia's best friend. I cast my daughter Kathleen as one of Julia's bridesmaids. At the same time Kathleen was appearing in an off Broadway play, so she flew back and forth between Baltimore and New York. Her play was so far off Broadway that it was in the basement of a supermarket. During scene changes you could hear shopping carts rolling overhead. But it was great experience for Kathleen to be in a $72 million movie at the same time she was in a minimum-budget subterranean play.

Among our *Runaway Bride* cast we didn't have a single weak link. Julia herself seemed physically and mentally strong. In one scene she even pulled an eight-year-old boy on the train of her wedding dress as she bolted out of a church. Some of the producers wanted to hire a little person, but I knew we would be fine with a little boy. I brought a group of boys out to a field to audition. I put my jacket on the ground and asked them to lay on their stomachs and let me pull them around. Some of them didn't hang on right, but I finally found a great little boy. I put him in a tuxedo and popped him right into the scene.

Richard was in a happy place in his life while we were filming. He was dating Carey Lowell, an actress who had appeared in my sister's television series spinoff of *A League of Their Own*. Richard's relationship with Carey, and the fact that she had a daughter, made him seem more settled than I had ever seen him before. I noticed he would fly back to New York on the weekends to be with Carey and her daughter. One day Richard was about to fly back and I asked him to stay to help me shoot some additional footage.

"Okay," he said. "Of course if you need me I will stay." I could tell he was disappointed, though, more than I'd thought he would be.

"Just for my own knowledge, were you flying back for something special this weekend?" I asked.

"Hannah, Carey's daughter, is in a horse show," he said.

"If that's the reason, then you can go. I'll shoot around you," I told him.

"You mean if there was another reason you would ask me to stay?" he said.

"Yes. To see a twelve-year-old who is expecting you to come to a horse show and watch her get a ribbon? This is a good reason. Always remember, life is more important than show business."

We both smiled as he headed to the airport.

I don't know if her daughter still rides horses, but Richard and Carey are definitely still a couple and even now have a son of their own, named Homer, who is one heck of a baseball player.

Richard and Julia were more mature on this picture because they had both loved and lost, and both understood sadness. Julia had several close calls at the altar, including her almost marriage to Kiefer Sutherland and her very short marriage to Lyle Lovett. Richard had been married to Cindy Crawford and was hurt when that marriage ended. So both Richard and Julia brought more wisdom to their characters in *Runaway Bride,* and more poignancy, too.

The funny thing about *Pretty Woman* was that Richard and Julia couldn't wait to do the kissing scenes because neither of them had a partner. In my opinion that is what made the kissing in *Pretty Woman* so sensational. During *Runaway Bride,* however, the kissing scenes were a little more challenging. Julia would say, "Make them shorter" or "Can we do it tomorrow?" I would say, "How about a little more passion, people! You're supposed to be falling in love." Eventually they did what they were supposed to do. Sometimes actors just need to act, and they both did a great job.

Despite the ups and downs of the movie, one thing remains for certain: Julia Roberts's smile is worth $20 million. Paparazzi were always swarming around our set. We were shooting in a church for one day, and I invited some of the reporters in to watch. Sometimes it is good to make your enemies your friends. We were all watching as Julia walked down the aisle to marry Richard. When she saw him she looked right at him and smiled, and everyone in the room melted. Then she bolted for the door. I have never worked with anyone else who could show so much love with her smile. I even joked with Julia that I could get piles of product placement money if we could figure out how to put a Nike swoosh on one of her two front teeth. She just laughed because she knew I always wanted to try something crazy.

On this picture I was the one who did something crazy, and it was all about music. By the time I did *Runaway Bride,* I knew that music is one of the keys to a picture. I knew that to open with a song by U2 would be a winner because U2 has the explosive kind of sound you want to open a movie with. The people in the music department, however, told me a U2 song would be too expensive. They were trying to convince me to use a Dixie Chicks song instead. I liked the Dixie Chicks and planned to use one of their songs in the movie, just not in the opening scene. The music people were making a record album, and I was making a movie. One music executive got ahold of a print of the film and edited in the Dixie Chicks song to open. He then sent it to me to demonstrate how right he was. I was livid.

I'm not the kind of guy who gets angry often, but this was too much. You can't just mess around and edit a director's movie without asking permission. So I first took a hammer and broke the plastic case of his CD. Then my editing assistant Robert Malina and I put it in the microwave until the CD was twisted and mangled. Then we sent it back to the music executive with a note that said, "Dear Sir, I don't think your song is the right one to open my movie. Yet you keep sending it to me again and again. Please don't send it to me anymore. You are making me crazy." Later that year someone went into the executive's office and saw that my charred CD was framed. The executive said it reminds him of the time he made a director very crazy. In the end we found the money to buy the U2 song to open the movie, and it fit perfectly. My son, who continues to shoot second unit for me on most of my movies, filmed the opening sequence of Julia racing through the woods on a horse, riding it superbly. It was exactly how I wanted to open my movie.

The reason this was such a big-budget picture was that Disney and Paramount combined forces to produce it. We shot for sixty-two days, much longer than my usual fifty-day shoot. But at the end of the picture I realized I had a problem: I had no ending. I knew the couple got together, but what were the last images I wanted to leave my audience with? A wedding ceremony in a quaint little church is not the way you end a big-budget picture. Paramount producer Sherry Lansing came to Baltimore to visit, and I explained to her that I needed another day of shooting. She agreed that the way I had planned to end the movie was not that exciting and said she would think about it. She looked toward a cornfield as we were talking.

"What is Scott shooting over there?" she asked.

My son was shooting some scenes in a cornfield, trying to come up with an ending for their story lines.

"Okay," she said. "You can have the extra day. And I like that cornfield. That's pretty."

That's when I realized I didn't need to have Julia and Richard get married in a church. They could get married in a cornfield. We filmed them with their horses and wedding attire, then had the rest of the cast running in their wedding outfits with bouquets. It was a wonderful, uplifting ending. The only trouble we had was the last shot. I wanted someone to throw a bouquet into the air and then have the flowers land and cover the camera lens with a freeze-frame to black. My son shot it. Family can come in handy in so many different ways. It took Scott something like forty-seven takes, but he finally got the perfect shot to end the movie on.

Critics knew that with this cast we were going to do well at the box office. I think because of this knowledge, the critics were out to get us from the beginning. One reviewer wrote, "Forget the bride . . . just run away." Women put it down. Men put it down.

Maureen Dowd wrote, "The woman treats the guy badly. So now women can be just as jerky and self-absorbed as men." Janet Maslin had some compliments, including praising a single joke. She said the movie contained "a FedEx joke so good it deserves a best place scenario for product placement." Hector Elizondo delivered that joke with excellent timing.

I knew *Runaway Bride* was not going to be praised by critics or win any awards. It was not that kind of movie. Instead it was a very commercial love story and a moneymaker. It cost $72 million to make, and opening weekend it earned $34.5 million. By the end of the year it had made more than $151 million. The sound track of *Runaway Bride* rose to the top ten. The film did great in Europe, too. My wife and I went on a press trip to Stockholm, Munich, Paris, Madrid, London, and Amsterdam to promote the movie. Europeans seemed to love Julia and Richard as a couple as much as or even more than American audiences did. They couldn't get enough of them on the big screen.

I was suddenly back in demand as a director. I was, however, a sixty-four-year-old director. And when you are that old, in addition to getting lifetime achievement awards, you start seeing your friends die. During the *Runaway Bride* shoot one of my best friends died. His name was Harvey Miller, and he suffered a drug overdose. Shortly before his death he did a one-man show, the first show ever staged at my Falcon Theatre. When he died I left the set to attend his funeral. It was hard because I was so excited for the new movie and working nonstop. When a friend dies, however, it puts everything in perspective.

It is interesting to note that two of the best speeches at Harvey's funeral were given by the dynamic director Nancy Meyers and Harvey's longtime masseuse.

Shortly after we wrapped production on *Runaway Bride,* I got a handwritten note from Julia. "Dearest Garry, well it is time again not to say goodbye but until we meet again. Director, teacher, father, brother and most of all special friend. Thank you is not enough. So . . . I will watch over you and make you smile and remind you I love you most. Love, . . . aka Maggie aka Julia. Don't wait another ten years to guide me."

We filmed *Pretty Woman* in 1989. We filmed *Runaway Bride* in 1999. Exactly ten years later I called and asked Julia to star in my new movie *Valentine's Day*. She checked to make sure it had been ten years, and said yes again.

21. THE PRINCESS DIARIES

★

Giving the Royal Treatment to

Andrews and Hathaway

"WHEN CAN I WATCH *Pretty Woman?*" asked Charlotte on one of our walks. Charlotte and her twin sister, Lily, were my first grandchildren, born in 1995.

"How old are you now?" I asked.

"Four years old and a half," she said.

"You're not old enough to see *Pretty Woman* yet," I said.

"But *why?* How old do you have to be?" she asked.

"Definitely older than four and a half," I said.

"Well, I already know it's about a hooker," she said.

"Who told you that?" I asked.

"I heard my mom talking about it with her friends," she said.

"You have good hearing," I said.

"Thanks," she said. "So what exactly is a hooker?"

"When you know the answer to that question, you will be ready to see *Pretty Woman*," I said. "Deal?"

"Deal!" she said and smiled.

Later that night it bothered me that Charlotte and Lily were both too young to see most of my movies. The preschool set wasn't rushing to rent *Beaches, Frankie and Johnny,* or *The Flamingo Kid.* I remembered feeling the same way when my three children were small and weren't interested in *The Odd Couple.* They rejected the sophisticated humor of Oscar and Felix and instead couldn't get enough of *The Brady Bunch* and *The Partridge Family.* That was one of the reasons I created *Happy Days,* so my kids would tune in to me. Now I felt compelled to make a movie that Lily and Charlotte would want to go see with their friends. Everybody says career decisions are based on where you are in your life, and at that moment I was a grandpa.

"If Pop made a movie you could see, what would it be about?" I asked.

"I want you to make a movie about a girl named Belle who wears a yellow dress and gets chased by a big scary Beast and then they get married," Charlotte said, as if giving a studio executive her one-line pitch.

"I'm afraid that has already been done, and done well I might add. What else?" I asked.

"What about a story about a Chinese girl. You can call it *Mulan*!" chimed in Lily.

"That's already been done, too. And don't even try to pitch me anything about a girl with a mermaid fin and a good voice. Been there and done that."

"Well, it has to have a princess in it," said Charlotte.

"Why?" I asked.

"Because all kids want to see a movie with a princess because there's always a big castle and a happy ending!" said Charlotte.

The next day I called Disney and told them to find me a script with a princess and a happy ending. *Runaway Bride,* a collaboration between Disney and Paramount, had been designed to become a hit, and it did even better than expected. So the powers that be at Disney were eager to sign me for another picture. I felt excited about finding something that would be a good fit for Lily and Charlotte as well as me.

I soon found out that Disney owned *The Princess Diaries,* based on the Meg Cabot book with a script by Gina Wendkos. The movie was about a San Francisco teenager who discovers she is a princess, the granddaughter of the queen of a country called Genovia. Whitney Houston owned the rights to the movie and was set to produce it. Several years earlier Whitney had starred in my sister Penny's film *The Preacher's Wife.* Penny had gotten along well with Whitney, and I thought that was a good sign. Also, this movie was small and had no stars attached. There was no pressure to make it a big studio film, and that's just the kind of movie I like. When people give me room to create amid low expectations, I like to surprise them. Now I just had to find my princess and my queen of Genovia.

When I was an enlisted soldier, before I shipped off for active duty in Korea, I knew I could get into Broadway shows for free if I was wearing my army dress uniform. So one night in 1956, I went in my uniform to see *My Fair Lady*. I missed the beginning because they let you in after the paying customers, but once I was inside I took my place in the standing room section. I watched as Julie Andrews played the part of Eliza Doolittle, a Cockney flower girl who takes speech lessons so she can pass for a lady. I remember standing in the dark, in my khaki army uniform, and just smiling from ear to ear. I had never seen a performance as impressive or delightful. She just exuded a type of charm and grace that, having grown up in the Bronx, I had never seen before. I was blown away, and it's pretty hard to be blown away when you are standing for a two-hour show. But Julie Andrews was perfection onstage in my book, and I never forgot her performance.

On paper Julie and I couldn't be more different. She is an elegant dame from England who drinks tea and wears silk suits without wrinkles. I'm a guy from the Bronx who grew up playing street games, reading superhero comics, and wearing torn corduroy pants that made a noise when I walked. She speaks with perfect diction. And I mumble with a New York accent. She likes rose gardens and writing books for children. I like playing softball and started my career writing humorous riffs for comedians in dirty nightclubs. But that's one of the things I like best about making movies: You meet people who aren't from your neighborhood. While I had worked with Goldie Hawn, Michelle Pfeiffer, Bette Midler, and Julia Roberts, working with Julie Andrews was not something I'd ever thought I would get the opportunity to do back when I was a kid wearing army dog tags. But after I read the script for *The Princess Diaries,* I thought of her immediately.

"How about Julie Andrews?" I said in a script meeting with some Disney executives.

"Julie Andrews? Isn't she dead?" said one very young Disney executive.

"No," I said, amazed by the ignorance in the room. "I just saw her in the newspaper. She's still around. Still lovely as ever."

"But I read someplace she can't speak anymore," said another young executive.

"No, she can speak fine. She just can't sing the way she used to," I said.

From my director's standpoint, the best queen for the job in my movie was Julie Andrews and I didn't need her to sing. Other names, such as Helen Mirren and Glenn Close, were pitched that day. But Julie Andrews was the perfect casting for me. Also, timing was on my side. I knew that Julie had recently settled a lawsuit over a tragic throat surgery that had left her barely able to sing. And I'd heard she was eager to get back to acting.

While we were waiting for Julie Andrews to read the script, I started to work on casting the part of Princess Mia. I talked to the extremely tall movie star Liv Tyler and the very funny television actress Amanda Bynes. While I found them both incredibly talented, their scheduling conflicts were too complicated and I had to rule them out. I decided to find my princess another way—discover her. The casting department interviewed more than nine hundred actresses, because any Disney project with the word *princess* in the title attracts the masses. Then they put close to sixty girls on tape, and they screen-tested about half of those for me to see. I then brought the best eight screen tests back to my secret producers, my four-and-a-half-year-old granddaughters.

"Pop, why do we have to cast today? Why can't we just eat ice cream?" begged Charlotte.

"We need to find a princess for Pop's movie," I said. "This is very important work. I'll pay you a dollar."

"I'll do it," said Lily, always one to want to make a dollar.

"Okay. Me, too," agreed Charlotte.

Out of the eight tapes I showed them, they liked Anne Hathaway's best. When I asked why, Charlotte said, without hesitation, "Because she has princess hair." Anne had dark black hair, dark makeup, and looked almost gothic. I had only one other piece of film on Anne, from a television show called *Get Real* in which she cried the whole time. I certainly didn't need crying in my movie. But when we did the screen test, she showed two sides to her character. First, when she came in to read for us, she dropped her purse, tripped on her chair, and showed a clumsy side of herself. Then, during the screen test, she was the only actress who picked up a scepter and crown we'd provided. With those props she recited Mia's pivotal speech with outstanding dignity. She had beautiful skin, and I could see in her eyes that somebody was home.

We were still waiting for Julie to decide about the queen role, so I called her manager, Steve Sauer, and asked him if Julie could come to my house for a visit. When he asked why I was so insistent that the meeting take place at my house, I explained the reason was karma. Julie had once lived in my house. It seemed like we were predestined to do a movie together. When Julie starred in *Mary Poppins,* Disney had rented her a house in Toluca Lake, the small suburb near the studio that was put on the map by its local residents Bob Hope and Bing Crosby. My wife and I bought that house in 1975 and have lived in it ever since. We raised three children in that house, sent them all off to college in the Midwest, and hoped to live there forever. Steve said Julie would love to meet with me and see her old house.

I very casually mentioned the visit to my wife one night at dinner.

"Julie Andrews is gonna swing by next week for some tea," I said.

"*The* Julie Andrews?" said Barbara. "She's going to swing by for some tea at our house? Here? With us? When? What will I *serve?*"

"Tea would be good," I mumbled.

My wife is usually cool as a cucumber, but she is also one of the world's biggest Anglophiles and biggest Julie Andrews fans. The thought of having Julie under our roof put fear into her heart. She searched the house for our finest china and chose some tea she had just brought back from Fortnum & Mason in London. I worried my wife was making too big a deal. I didn't want to make a big fuss and scare Julie away.

"A fuss?!" Barbara said. "You can't just serve Julie Andrews Lipton tea!"

The day Julie arrived there was no entourage or pomp and circumstance. She drove herself in her own car through our gate and was wearing a simple T-shirt and baseball cap. We were a little surprised by the baseball cap because you don't think of Julie as sporty, but she is. We half expected trumpets to announce her entrance, but she simply stepped through our front door like a regular person. There was no fanfare, just a warm and elegant new friend who happened to have starred in everybody's favorite movie, *The Sound of Music*. Meeting Julie Andrews instantly improves one's posture because her own is so exemplary. To hunch in front of her would seem rude.

Her visit went off without a hitch. She loved seeing the house again and told us stories about when she lived there.

"The pool was over there," she said, pointing to the backyard. "And we had that Jacuzzi back then, too. Plus an organic garden back there."

"There was also a bad half-basketball court. But we put in a new one, and Garry and his friends play every Saturday," added my wife.

Julie had brought with her a picture of her two-year-old daughter, Emma, taken years earlier in front of our fireplace. Barbara showed Julie her "Queen's Collection," two large glass armoires filled with plates, teacups, and other memorabilia from the reign of Queen Elizabeth II. The two women admired several items in the cases, including a dried flower bouquet that had been given to my wife by Sarah Ferguson, the Duchess of York. The resemblance between my wife and Julie Andrews is startling when you see them side by side. Although one grew up in England and the other in a poor suburb of Cincinnati, there is something about both of them that is refined, almost as if they are distant cousins.

That day we talked about our families and children, and another good sign emerged: Julie's mother's name was Barbara Wells, which was my wife's maiden name. When it came time for the fancy tea, however, it was too hot outside, so Julie opted for a bottle of Perrier. But otherwise it was a perfect afternoon and a perfect way to kick off our time together on *The Princess Diaries*. Shortly after our visit Julie sent word through Steve that she had finished the script and would love to star in the movie. I told my wife the good news and said we could buy more Fortnum & Mason tea.

What I loved about Anne Hathaway was what I loved about Julia Roberts: Each has the ability to be clumsy and beautiful in the same movie. Anne made us laugh in her screen test and moved us with her words as well. I was confident that I could capture that on-screen and make a great film. I also liked her youth and enthusiasm. Her mother had been a stage actress and toured with *Les Misérables* and Anne had worked at the Paper Mill Playhouse in New Jersey. If anything, Anne had more experience in the theater than movies. The first time I took her out to lunch, we went to my father's country club, the Lakeside Golf Club in Toluca Lake. The club has a beautiful dining room that is rarely crowded. But I think the silence, and probably me, scared her. Anne would later refer to our lunch at "that scary place" and ask never to go back there. However, a year later we went back to the club and she loved it and confessed that she was, at first, a little intimidated by me.

Once I chose Anne as my princess, I had another odd problem: I had to win over her parents, who weren't sure they wanted her to do the film. They were both concerned about the idea of their daughter becoming an overnight movie star. They worried, as most parents would, that she would become a drug addict or a crazy show business girl. I did some research and discovered her dad was a big lawyer in New York. So I called up my big lawyer friend Joel Sterns, who'd been one of my best friends at Northwestern, and asked him for a favor. "Joel, will you call up this girl's father, lawyer to lawyer, and tell her that I'm not going to give her cocaine? Fig Newtons maybe. But no drugs."

Joel made the phone call, and then I met with Anne's parents. I introduced myself as the man who created *Happy Days* to demonstrate my proclivity for family entertainment. I told them we weren't a crazy group in general; after all, we were from the studio of Mickey Mouse, not Mickey Rourke. Winning Anne's parents' support was important to me, and to the success of our movie. Two of the best parents I have ever seen were those of Ron Howard, and look what a sane and successful person he turned out to be. So once Anne's parents signed on, I had my princess and my queen of Genovia.

I expected Julie to be quite formal on the set, but she was not at all. She was professional yet warm and friendly to the cast and crew and got along well with Anne and with Hector Elizondo. Hector has appeared in each one of my seventeen films because I enjoy him so much personally and professionally. The first time I worked with him he starred in *Young Doctors in Love* as a gangster wearing a dress. It was not a role about which you say, "Let's do that every time." But I enjoyed working with Hector so much that I found a part for him to play every time I signed a new deal. He was the father in *The Flamingo Kid* and, of course, the wise hotel manager in *Pretty Woman*. In *The Princess Diaries* he played Joe, the chauffeur and queen's head of security.

On each film we do together Hector not only turns in a solid performance himself but makes the other actors' performances better, too. He commands the big screen and inspires the cast to rise to the occasion. Hector Elizondo and Julie Andrews are exemplary to work with in terms of timing, acting, temperament, and everything in between. They build their characters based on behavior. To watch them is to watch two perfectionists in action. And they both learned that the youthful Anne Hathaway was talented and certainly not a brat.

Hector even threw in several ad-libs to Julie, and she easily kept up with him. A little known fact about Julie is that when she lets down her guard she can swear with the best of them. What is odd is that she swears with impeccable diction. I have never heard someone curse so distinctly. She enunciated every syllable of every curse word. She is also a romantic and requested a relationship for her character in the movie. So we layered in a subtle friendship-with-potential between Queen Clarisse and Joe.

You might think that an actress of her caliber would be quite needy, but Julie was the complete opposite. Once she was wrapped for the day but I saw she was still on the set at two in the morning, and I wondered why. Anne was still shooting, trying to tackle a tough scene, and we were using a day player to stand in for Julie's character off-camera. Suddenly Julie said she wanted to read the scene off-camera with Anne. Like I told Diane Keaton, I told Julie she didn't need to do that. Her day had been long and it wasn't essential.

"I want to stay," said Julie in her proper, no-nonsense voice. "The young people must learn the proper way to be an actress. You must read off-camera for the other person's close-up."

Julie wanted to protect Anne, a trait I have seen in her many times since. I think as a director you have to know when to step back. If actors say something negative to each other or begin to fight or in rare cases hit each other, you jump in. I have never had hitting on any of my movies. But otherwise you allow them to build a relationship on their own. These two women bonded well. Anne had two minutes of experience, and Julie had decades of experience. Together, they made a lovely duo. Chuck Minsky, a wiry, youthful man, was my cinematographer on the movie. I have worked with Chuck many times before and chose him for this film because he has a gift for making women look beautiful on film.

Julie had played royalty in other movies, and her pet peeve was the obligatory queen crown. Crowns are tricky to get on and off without messing up your hair. In movies it often comes down to what will make the hair look best. So Julie never wanted to be seen putting the crown on or taking it off on-camera. The hair and makeup department built an ingenious little device that would help the crown sit more smoothly on her head. Other than the crown, she hardly fussed about anything. She always came to the set ready, willing, and prepared to assume the role of our queen and said, "Let's deal with that damn crown!"

After months of editing with Bruce Green, the movie's promotion went into high gear. The press junket for *The Princess Diaries* was exciting because our little film became the sleeper hit of the summer of 2001. We thought we were making a kids' movie, but it turned out mothers and daughters wanted to share the joy of watching

Anne and Julie. So our popularity spanned two age groups. When it came to handling the press, however, Julie knew the ropes, but the younger girls needed some guidance.

By the time the movie was released, Anne had been accepted at Vassar and was reading more intellectual works. And so, she took her first press junket a little too seriously. When the press asked her questions, she started quoting Nietzsche, Kafka, and Schopenhauer. Heather Matarazzo, whom I'd cast as Anne's best friend, Lilly, after she impressed me in the independent film *Welcome to the Dollhouse,* also did not want to talk about being the friend of a princess. She wanted to talk about gay rights and being a smart lesbian in Hollywood. This combo gave the Disney publicity people heart attacks. "Garry, do something," they begged me. To round out our press tour we had Mandy Moore, the singer, a pretty, blonde newcomer, who played a popular yet mean girl to Anne's nerdy girl. After watching Anne and Heather on the first round of interviews, I decided to jump in with a little avuncular advice.

"Ladies! Ladies! You are talking about existentialists and homosexuality. Schopenhauer and sex are not going to get you a feature story in *Teen Vogue.* Look at Mandy Moore. She's talking to the reporters about her hair and makeup. The reporters are eating it up, and she'll get good press in all the teen magazines. So please, do me a favor and perform breezy chitchat about what kind of shampoo and conditioner you use. Just talk about it today. Tomorrow you can talk about whatever you want." They both immediately lightened up and dazzled the reporters.

Why did my talk with them help? I knew it would because we all fall under the sign of Scorpio. I was born November 13, Anne's birthday is November 12, and Heather celebrates on November 10. I know from experience that most Scorpios have the same personality. They are very ambitious, and while they might argue and complain to try to get their way, they will always deliver the goods in the end.

Disney had signed Anne to a two-picture deal, which is typical in the industry. What is also typical is that for a twenty-year-old like Anne, trying to work out a career path is quite overwhelming. I heard she didn't want to do the second *Princess* movie. In between *The Princess Diaries* and *The Princess Diaries 2: Royal Engagement,* Anne had attracted an entourage—including agents, managers, publicists, and makeup artists, none of whom wanted her to make the second movie either. They were pressuring her to hang up her tiara because she and they thought she'd be typecast. Having been through versions of this before with the kids on my TV shows, I had empathy for the complicated insecurity of youth. Salad days often include drizzles of balsamic vinegar. I invited her to dinner to talk about our movie. Her people suggested Spago, so we went there.

She was locked into the contract; there was no way around it. So we discussed ways to make the film fun for her, including working with Julie Andrews again. While at dinner we were visited by a parade of big agents who smiled a lot and other industry insiders who were eager to be seen with Anne. But what I noticed was that two busboys came up to her sheepishly and asked Anne for autographs for their daughters. I knew at that dinner there was no question that *Princess Diaries 2* would be a big hit, and Anne Hathaway was on her way to becoming a star and my close friend ever since.

Anne was more grown up in the sequel and portrayed Princess Mia that way. Wiser, more mature, and seasoned for sure. On the first picture she was quiet and listened a lot. On the second one she had stronger opinions on plot points and dialogue. I'm fine with that as long as the star is collaborative, which Anne was. She wanted to talk a lot about her acting process and to make sure her character was not portrayed as a victim in any way.

I listened to her, and we pitched ideas around. I wanted to do a big scene that would be popular with kids. We talked about new trends like salsa dancing, which we both agreed was fun but too adult. I needed something else kid-friendly. Anne came up with a wonderful concept based on an experience from her own childhood. She'd had a girlfriend who lived in an elegant New Jersey house. When Anne would sleep over with her friends there, they would body surf down the staircases on their pillows. I changed the pillow idea to mattresses because it sounded safer. I wrote that scene right into *Princess Diaries 2,* and it proved to be one of the most memorable in the movie.

I was grateful enough to get the chance to direct Julie Andrews the first time, but I had no idea I would get to direct her singing on-camera in *Princess Diaries 2.* This is how it happened: One night my wife and I went to dinner with Julie and her husband, Blake Edwards. Blake directed *The Pink Panther, Victor/Victoria,* and *10* among many other films, and he is someone I have admired and stolen comedy ideas from for years. We were preparing to shoot our sequel, and that night, as the four of us sat down to dinner, Blake leaned over and whispered in my ear.

"I have heard her singing in the *shower,*" he said.

"What?" I asked, not quite sure what I had heard.

"Julie," he said. "I have heard her *singing in the shower.*"

"Oh, Blake, stop it," she said.

But we did discuss her singing voice that night. I said if Julie did want to sing on-camera again, I would make her feel as comfortable as possible. She said if I kept the song in her range she would consider it. I also promised that if she didn't like the way the scene turned out, we would cut it. No questions asked. I would protect her no matter what.

I went right to the music department and asked them to get to work on a song that would be well-suited for Julie's midlevel range. We also decided to write the scene so Julie would sing a duet with the supporting actress Raven-Symoné as a birthday present for Queen Clarisse's granddaughter, Mia. To have Julie and Anne sing on-camera would have been too much pressure.

We had to be sensitive to Julie, her voice and her legacy. People just look at her and hear the voice of Maria in *The Sound of Music* wafting into their ears. In order to please everyone and protect Julie's voice, we had the song crafted to include many lines that were spoken to the music rather than sung. I wasn't sure we could pull it off, but I knew it was worth a try. I wanted Julie to sing on-camera not only to make the movie better but for her own sake as well. I can only imagine what it was like for her to lose her singing voice, and I wanted somehow to be a part of giving it back.

Julie's singing took place during a slumber party scene featuring my granddaughters, Lily and Charlotte, as extras. The day we shot I sat behind the camera and couldn't believe my good luck. Raven and Julie came out in silk pajama sets and prepared to sing "Your Crowning Glory," written by Lorraine Feather and Larry Grossman.

I had cleared the set, as a director might when shooting a nude scene. Only the essential crew and cast were present. The day Julie sang was a very emotional day. I looked over my shoulder and saw that members of my crew—tattooed teamsters who drove big-rig trucks for a living—had tears in their eyes. Even with all the cables, lights, and cameras, we knew we were capturing magic on film as we watched Dame Julie Andrews sing once more.

For me it was like being twenty-one years old again, standing in the dark in my khaki army dress uniform, just smiling from ear to ear as Julie brought Eliza Doolittle to life. Watching her now I thought the same thing that I thought back in 1956: Her performance is so impressive, delightful, and rejuvenating. To see her act and sing reminds you that magic still happens. As a director you can't hope for anything better than that.

22. RAISING HELEN

★

Directing Kate Hudson and the
Next Generation

RUNAWAY BRIDE DID more for my career than I ever could have hoped for, and then *The Princess Diaries* knocked me over the top as a major league comedy director. Back-to-back hits meant that I could choose my next picture slowly and pace myself. I wanted to pace myself, like the Pro Football Hall of Fame player Jim Brown. I used to watch the way he would use all of his energy to run through another player with power and speed. Then, when he got up, he would move slowly, shuffling like an aging cat. He was conserving his energy so he would have it when he needed it the most. I wanted to direct movies and pace myself in the same way.

Disney sent me a script called *Raising Helen.* I found it interesting, although a little predictable until they said something that turned my head around: Kate Hudson would star. That sealed the deal for me. The last time I had seen Kate she was nine years old, sitting on my lap on the set of *Overboard* while I was directing her mother, Goldie Hawn. I loved working with Goldie, and I was excited at the prospect of directing Kate, a slender blonde with tousled hair and a great giggle, who was one of Hollywood's hot new actresses. My lucky number is 13, and *Raising Helen* would be the thirteenth movie I would direct.

For the male lead, Disney wanted John Corbett, a big, calm West Virginian. I went to meet him in Hollywood at a bar he owned called, coincidentally, The Falcon, the same name of my theater in Burbank, which was named after the athletic group I played with while growing up in the Bronx. I thought it was a good omen that John and I both had Falcons in our lives. We sat and talked at his bar, and he mentioned his longtime girlfriend, Bo Derek, with whom he lived in Santa Barbara. I thought he was a stable, fun, and extremely easygoing guy who had good buzz from his great turns in *Sex and the City* and *My Big Fat Greek Wedding.* I knew I had made a good casting choice when both of my daughters screamed with excitement when I told them John would be in my film. Big fans of *Sex and the City,* my daughters couldn't wait to visit the set and meet him. I also liked the fact that he would play against his usual type. In *Raising Helen* I had him play Pastor Dan, a man of the cloth who also happened to be quite sexy.

We started filming at the end of January and shot straight through until June, doing many locations in New York City. *Raising Helen* is the story of a young woman faced with raising her older sister's children after her sister and brother-in-law die in a car accident. But it's the kids who end up helping her become more mature. Key to the casting were the young people. I wanted them to look real, not too Hollywood-like. Luckily I found two of my kids in the same family. Spencer Breslin was a hot young actor who was coming out in a new version of *The Cat and the Hat.* He had a little sister named Abbie who had just been in the Mel Gibson movie *Signs.* From the moment I met both of them I knew they would be terrific. Just as important, I liked their mother, Kim, who traveled with the kids and managed their careers. It's always helpful when kids have a strong support system.

After I auditioned Spencer and Abbie, I called Kim and offered them the parts. Initially she said, "No, they are tired. I'm tired. We're not going to do any more movies for a while." But I talked to her some more and said, "Look, wouldn't it be nice for you to drive both the kids to the same location every morning? Think how pleasant it will be for them and for you if you all work on the same movie together." She finally agreed with my logic, and I signed both Breslin kids to play Kate's niece and nephew in the movie.

I also needed to cast the oldest child—a sixteen-year-old girl. I found Hayden Panettiere, who later became a star of the television series *Heroes*. When I cast her Hayden was only thirteen, but she delivered an audition that seemed to demonstrate more experience than was on her résumé. After you've directed many movies in a row, discovering a great new actress can invigorate you. I knew Hayden was going to become a star. However, the script described the character as a sixteen-year-old. I decided that if the wardrobe department dressed her in more sophisticated clothing, she could act older.

Sometimes casting is all about people's schedules and smaller parts. This is one of the reasons I lucked out and got one of my favorite actresses, Helen Mirren, to play Kate's boss. Helen would win an Academy Award a couple of years later for her work in *The Queen*. I had never worked with her before *Raising Helen*, but I knew her for years socially as the wife of my friend and colleague, director Taylor Hackford. My son, Scott, is also one of Taylor's son's best friends. Helen is a petite, down-to-earth lady who can create the illusion of a tall actress with the demeanor of royalty. Normally Helen wouldn't take on a small supporting part like this, but sometimes even a big actress likes to relax and play a small comedy part. Kate worked at a fashion magazine and Helen played her boss, a character not unlike Anna Wintour, the infamous editor of *Vogue* magazine.

My style of directing often involves giving actors things to hold in their hands or do with their bodies—as I had done when I gave Kurt Russell walnuts in *Overboard*. I decided to put a treadmill in Helen's office so she could look at files and have meetings with her staff while walking on her treadmill, still wearing a fancy designer suit. It was a difficult scene to shoot, but visually it was funny and Helen, as always, did a superb job. People are always surprised to hear that Helen is quite short. When acting she can appear to be almost six feet, but in reality she's petite. To play Kate's other sisters I cast Joan Cusack and Felicity Huffman, both incredible and versatile actresses. Joan had worked with me on *Runaway Bride*, and I asked her to do *Raising Helen* as a favor. I knew she could do comedy, but I needed her in this movie for heavily dramatic scenes.

Kate is a California girl, so shooting in New York City was not her favorite thing to do, but we had a lot of fun. There is a certain energy that builds when you shoot in the city because people stop on the street and talk to you, and sometimes you run into people you know. One day we were filming in Tribeca and Robert De Niro walked up and said, "Hey, Garry! Thanks for shooting in my neighborhood!" Robert had originally been pegged to star in Penny's movie *Big* but ended up working with her in *Awakenings* instead. Another time a kid threw his résumé out the window from the fifth floor just to get my attention. I was so impressed with his ingenuity and assertiveness that I hired him to do two lines in a scene we shot in Central Park. Later I asked him, "Why didn't you just come and hand me your résumé?" He said he was too shy to meet me and thought throwing the résumé out the window was a better way to get my attention. In the end, I think he was right.

When we went back to film in Los Angeles, Kate was more comfortable and Goldie even came to visit the set. Mother and daughter took a picture together, and it was such a treat to see Kate introducing Goldie to the other members of our cast and crew. Like Goldie, Kate is smart and funny without being at all whiny or diva-like. Goldie doesn't like it when people swear. So on *Overboard* we had a Goldie Box on the set, and whenever someone cursed they had to put a dollar in the box. Kate isn't that keen on swearing either. So on *Raising Helen* we decided to introduce a similar box. Instead of calling it a Kate Box, though, we called it a Goldie Box as a tribute to Kate's mom. When the Goldie Box got too full, we used the money to buy pizza for the cast and crew.

I like to find out as much as I can about the actors I direct because it helps me connect with them. I found out that John Corbett was from West Virginia, and that his dad had been a rancher. I knew his father didn't know much about Hollywood, so I sat down and wrote him a letter, not a text. I am a big fan of writing and receiving nice letters. In my home I have files of nice letters people have sent me over the years. I've learned that one of the ways you reach out to stars is to be nice to their parents, especially if they are far removed from Hollywood and don't know what's going on day to day with their adult children. These days I'm usually the same age as or older than my actor's parents, so it's a good connection to make. I told John's dad what an excellent job his son was doing in my movie. It was a way to reach out to John and show how much I appreciated his work.

Many stars don't like the paparazzi that swirl around movie sets, but Kate loves them. She was nice to them and looked forward to seeing them each day when she arrived. Kate has spent her whole life watching her mom and partner, Kurt Russell, walk down the red carpet, and now it is her turn and she enjoys it. She likes being famous. She never yells at the press but rather waves hello and courts their lenses. While we were shooting *Raising Helen,* Kate was married to The Black Crowes front man Chris Robinson. He visited the set a lot. One week Kate got sick and I noticed that she appeared to be gaining a little weight. I remember thinking that if she was sick she should be losing weight and not gaining weight. What I didn't know at the time was that she was pregnant with her son Ryder. It was so early in the pregnancy that very few people knew about it.

The three kids on the set were great to work with. Smart-as-a-whip six-year-old Abbie knew everyone's lines. And if Abbie ever forgot a line, her brother, Spencer, would jump in to protect her. He liked to play football with my son, Scott, while Abbie took little catnaps in her trailer. Kate was great with the children, and I thought some of the best scenes were between Kate and Hayden, who had to tackle the role of a difficult teenager. Abbie went on to get an Oscar nomination for *Little Miss Sunshine,* and I tapped her again to be in *New Year's Eve.*

The funny thing about directing kids is that although they are professional most of the time, sometimes they start behaving like real kids. Hayden had a few days acting like a difficult teenager when the cameras were not rolling. She would be late to the set, or we couldn't find her between scenes, or she got distracted by boys. One day I had to sit down with her and talk about her behavior. "You have been given a gift and you are a very good actress," I said. "I would hate for you not to have a career because you are rebelling just to rebel." I think I got through to her, because for the rest of the movie she was on target, even during a difficult scene in which she had to kiss a twenty-six-year-old. She was only thirteen years old at the time.

There are some scenes that you think about in your mind but never have the right movie to put them in. I have always wanted to do a big scene with a Zamboni machine, which cleans ice-skating rinks. I was able to do that in *Raising Helen* with Kate and John, and it made me happy. It also made me happy to once again find a good spot to put my lucky charm, Hector Elizondo. Kate's character loses her job at the fashion magazine and then gets a lower-paying job selling cars. Hector plays her boss at the car dealership, and their relationship on-screen is very reminiscent of Hector and Julia in *Pretty Woman*. Again Hector stepped up to the plate, making another actress shine and making me very happy.

But allergies never make me happy. I have suffered from them for my entire life. On *Raising Helen* I had a particularly bad nose, so I started using a lot of Flonase nasal spray.

One day I was using it and one of the producers noticed. "I was in Cuba once and Castro leaned over to me and said one word: Flonase," said the producer.

That is where I learned that Fidel Castro and I both have bad noses and a love of Flonase. On nearly every movie I make I get a severe cold and have to carry a box of Kleenex as well as my shooting script under my arm.

Another thing I struggled with on this movie was my hip, which was starting to fail after years of playing sports. I knew that I would need a hip replacement, but in the meantime I learned to use a cane. One day we were shooting a very emotional scene, and in the middle of our take an ambulance drove by with its siren blaring. The scene was ruined. I was so frustrated that I threw my cane into the air and it hit one of the teamsters who was standing near me. The cane startled him but didn't hurt him. The next day all the teamsters came to work wearing helmets to make fun of me. It just went to show that on-set pranks were things I not only gave but also received.

I wanted *Raising Helen* to be a salute to single mothers everywhere. Raising kids is hard. Raising kids on your own is even more difficult. We made a movie that entertained people and spread that message, but unfortunately it didn't find its primary audience until it was released on DVD, a year later. Maybe most of the single mothers of the world are too busy to go out to the movies so they wait for the DVD to come out. I have always been very supportive of my movies when they come out on DVD. I believe it's part of the whole package: You do publicity when the movie comes out in the theaters, and then you make the time to do more publicity when the DVD is released. Some directors don't see the point of this extra work. But I put in the hours to add new material in order to make the DVDs more interesting. We now do Blu-Ray.

Raising Helen was a sweet romantic comedy that allowed me to work with a great cast. It was never going to be the kind of picture that made big money or took home prizes, but it would turn out to make people smile, and I like making audiences smile. At the same time I was continuing to build my reputation as a "woman's director," and that made sense since I was never any good at making movies with explosions and guns. What I like best is making movies that parents and children can go to together. When the script for *The Princess Diaries 2: Royal Engagement* came across my desk, I was eager to do it but still paused. I had never done sequels or movies with Roman numerals in their titles. However, there is an exception to every rule. Who would turn down the chance to direct Julie Andrews and Anne Hathaway in a second movie? Certainly not me. That's why I did it.

23. GEORGIA RULE

★

Jane Rules and Lindsay Misbehaves

IN MARCH 2004, I had finished directing both *Raising Helen* and *Princess Diaries 2,* and after that I didn't direct another movie for two years. It was harder to find financing for movies, and I was getting older. I had my hip replaced, and in a rare move for a medical doctor, mine told me the truth: He said I would be back pitching softball twelve weeks after my surgery, and he was absolutely correct. My wife, the nurse, did a stellar job at helping me recover. I was getting more involved in my Falcon Theatre, too. I liked the pace of play rehearsals and going to the theater to greet audience members as they arrived. I liked saying, "Hi, I'm Garry. Welcome to the Falcon." I thought about movies, but the scripts coming across my desk weren't that intriguing. I had directed fourteen pictures already, so I wasn't running just to direct another one. I didn't want to do a science fiction movie. I didn't want to do a horror movie. I liked romantic comedies, and Hollywood wasn't rushing to green-light another small romantic comedy. So I was content to play softball and oversee my theater, while still open to reading new movie scripts.

I had read a script years before by Mark Andrus called *Georgia Rule*. Mark went on to write *As Good as It Gets* and *Divine Secrets of the Ya-Ya Sisterhood*. I remember when I first read the script for *Georgia Rule* thinking that it struck a nice balance between the heavy subject of possible incest and some strong comedy moments. I also liked that it was a multigenerational film that followed the stories of a mother, daughter, and granddaughter. Flash forward years later and I heard through the grapevine that Lindsay Lohan wanted to star in *Georgia Rule*. I called Mark and talked to him about the script and the possible casting of Lindsay. I found out that this movie was being financed by an independent film production company called Morgan Creek. One man, James Robinson, was in charge of Morgan Creek.

At this point, because I had not directed a movie in two years, part of me wondered if I would ever do so again. I went to talk to James, and after meeting with him, I was sold. The idea of dealing with one man instead of a team of studio executives appealed to me. I also liked the script, and I liked Lindsay as an actress. In the beginning James and I talked about shooting the movie in Idaho, but we found it was cheaper to use a green-screen backdrop of Idaho and shoot everything in Los Angles. If you are from Idaho, you can probably tell where we shot, but most people couldn't tell the difference. I liked the idea of working near my home, too, so I ended up making a deal to direct the film and accepted about one third less than my usual salary. There was also another incentive to go ahead with the movie, and her name was Jane Fonda.

I had met Jane before. In a way our friendship was similar to my relationship with Candice Bergen. We knew each other, and talked politely when our paths crossed, but we had never worked together. There are many actresses I know like this. Whenever I see them at a party we say to each other, "When can we work together?" My relationship with Sally Field was like that until we finally worked together on the television series *Brothers & Sisters*. I had met Jane at political events with her then husband, Tom Hayden, and we'd talked about doing a movie together. There was a script we used to pitch around called *Mrs. California*. It took place in the 1940s and was about a beauty contest in which each housewife had to cook a meal, iron a shirt, and pack a suitcase for her husband's business trip. Jane and I never got the funding to make that movie. So *Georgia Rule* seemed like something that had been well worth the wait.

I had known other Fondas. My daughter Lori went to school with Jane's niece Bridget from kindergarten through twelfth grade. I never had the pleasure of meeting the great Henry Fonda, but I hung out with Bridget's dad, Peter, at school events and even before that in the early days of Hollywood, when he ran with Dennis Hopper and Harry Dean Stanton. I wasn't in the movie *Easy Rider*, but

I was in another movie around that time called *Psych-Out.* I played a plainclothes narcotics agent and won the role because I owned a dark suit. I got to arrest Jack Nicholson and Bruce Dern.

When we started production on *Georgia Rule,* Jane and I both had new hips. We talked about what it was like to go through hip replacement surgery and rehabilitation. This is what happens when you get older in Hollywood. You schmooze about the replacing of body parts and which doctors you liked best. My hip was replaced by the same doctor who replaced James Brolin's hip. My wife slept on a cot in the hospital room, and so did Barbra Streisand for James. While I was recovering at the hospital, James and my friend Jeff Wald, Streisand's manager, sent me a pair of tap shoes to inspire me to get back up on my hip soon. It used to be that you met people at parties, nightclubs, or fancy restaurants. When you get older you meet them in orthopedic offices and doctors' waiting rooms.

When we were filming *Georgia Rule,* Ted Turner came to visit Jane on the set. He was dapper and rich, just the type of man my dad wanted to be. Ted and Jane remained friends even though she'd divorced him in 2001. She liked to refer to him as her "favorite ex-husband." The day Ted came to visit we talked about his baseball team, the Atlanta Braves, and then we gave him a good seat to watch us film a scene. Jane came over to me afterward and said that Ted was a little bored just sitting on the set, and asked if one of my assistants could take him out to lunch. I assigned someone, and they went to a nearby deli. My assistant said later he sang to her during lunch, which I thought was funny. I invited Ted to join us on the set for lunch another day, but Jane said he didn't like craft service food. Whenever he visited, though, it put Jane in a good mood, and I liked that. Jane has had some highs and lows in her life and career, but smiling and happy is her best angle.

In terms of acting, Jane is like a pro from the early days of Hollywood. We had trouble finding footage to put in the gag reel because she never made any mistakes. She always knew her lines and exact motivation, for a scene from the script or for lines that I just wrote on the fly. She has such a strong, disciplined way of acting that nothing throws her off. The only thing that ever went wrong was that sometimes her dog, Tulea, would run onto the set and ruin a shot. So we got her in the gag reel that way, by featuring her runaway dog. To play Jane's daughter I cast Felicity Huffman, who'd also been in *Raising Helen*. I told Felicity, "I killed you off in the last movie. In this movie you get to live."

Lindsay Lohan was set to play Jane's granddaughter and Felicity's daughter. That was good news and that was bad news. I knew from the beginning that I would have my hands full with Lindsay, because the press was already floating reports about her being difficult. However, I felt confident that I could manage her, just as I had done with other young actors before and after rehab. Her casting was what got the movie financed, and we needed her. Her problems, however, ballooned slowly. In the beginning she would show up late so we would shoot around her until she arrived. Then she would be slow to come out of her trailer. I tried joking with her and said, "We are all taking bets on when you will come out. So if you want your friend to win the money, come out at ten fifteen A.M." She would smile and come running out of her trailer at that exact moment. But every time we figured out a way to help and support Lindsay, things grew worse: Some days she wouldn't show up for hours or would call in sick. The cast and crew knew that she wasn't sick at all because we'd seen her on the news at a nightclub the evening before.

She was young and vulnerable and reminded me so much of the other young actresses I had worked with. Like Julia Roberts in *Pretty Woman* and Juliette Lewis in *The Other Sister,* Lindsay was so talented. But unlike Julia and Juliette, Lindsay was still struggling inside to build a career and carve out her own identity. A few weeks into the movie I had to have a heart-to-heart with her.

"I see you on television sometimes and hear about you going to nightclubs," I said.

"Are you going to yell at me? Everybody yells at me," she said.

"No. I'm not going to yell at you. One night I'd like to go out with you and see what goes on," I said.

She thought that was funny, so she invited me to go out on the town with her girlfriends. All they talked about was boys. We went to a fancy restaurant called Koi, and I met lots of sons and daughters of Hollywood executives, fortunately not my own children. We went to nightclubs and hung out. I thought I was hip and happening until Lindsay said, "We don't wear Velcro shoes like you, so try to keep your feet under the table." So much for trying to fit in with the in-crowd.

Lindsay was able to balance her work on the set with her nightlife, until her nightlife began to affect her job and cause additional delays on the set. The pressure to stay within budget was even greater on this film because a small independent company was financing us. We tried to cover for Lindsay, but eventually James Robinson had had enough. He wrote Lindsay a personal letter, scolding her for her unprofessional behavior. The letter was leaked to the press, and our set was hounded by more media attention than we knew how to handle. Lindsay and I discussed what she should do to make peace again, and I suggested that she apologize to the crew for delaying production. She told everyone she was sorry, and we got back to work. After that she would still be late sometimes, but she didn't miss any full days of work.

The paparazzi, however, wouldn't leave us alone. This was the hardest picture I ever made in terms of press attention. Photographers would be literally hiding in the trees stalking Lindsay. I hired extra security, but still we got very little relief. Sometimes I had to whisper the word *action* because I didn't want them to know we were filming. Lindsay couldn't go anywhere without it being reported in the newspapers or online. The most down-to-earth I ever saw her was the day she got a new car and locked her keys inside. One of the production assistants helped her call the car's security support phone number and ask them to unlock the car. The technician asked to speak to the owner of the car. Lindsay said, "I'm Lindsay Lohan." The technician didn't believe she was the tabloids' own Lindsay Lohan. We went back and forth getting different people on the phone to support her claim. It was very funny, and while it was happening Lindsay looked just like a regular young girl who had locked her keys in her car.

Lindsay was insecure about her hair and freckles, so we used a tanning solution to at least cover the freckles. She ended up looking so suntanned that I had to add a line about that, to admit we knew she looked tanner than everybody else in town. Freckles weren't the only thing she was covering. The movie proved hard for her emotionally. She was trying to concentrate on her acting career while at the same time trying to live her life and be with her girlfriends. I worried that Lindsay had no support system to provide her with balance and guidance. She had a driver name Jazz who helped us keep track of her, but not much more support. On-screen her acting was wonderful. Inside I worried she was falling apart.

One day Jane tried to talk to her, actress to actress. Jane has had well-publicized struggles with eating disorders and self-esteem. She wrote about them beautifully in her memoir, *My Life So Far,* which my wife and I both loved. Jane warned Lindsay that if she continued on this road of late-night partying, she was going to get into trouble. Sometimes, however, you have to live and learn, and I think that's what Lindsay was doing. There was no amount of warning or wisdom that Jane could provide that would prevent the legal battles that lay ahead for Lindsay.

With the paparazzi present wherever we went, the crew and Lindsay bonded. We had someone make a different iPod playlist each day. Felicity like the Pointer Sisters, Jane the sound track from her movie *9 to 5,* and Lindsay was partial to a band called Fisherspooner. Despite all the Lindsay drama, I had to focus on directing the movie. I didn't have the right ending, so I had to shoot an extra scene after we had wrapped. Morgan Creek was very supportive and gave me money for the additional day. I shot a scene with Lindsay getting out of the shower with a towel around her head. Her hair was already a different color than it had been when we started the movie, but no one knew it because it was tucked under the towel. I often find towels very helpful in re-shoots.

Georgia Rule was probably the most emotional movie I ever directed, aside from *The Other Sister.* The problem was that moviegoers didn't like Lindsay's character, and worse, they didn't like seeing press coverage of her running around partying all the time. I would ask people if they had seen my new movie, and they would say, "I don't want to see that slutty Lindsay Lohan in anything."

That was hard for all of us to hear about a film we had worked so hard on, and about a girl we liked. We knew she had problems, but we also knew that her star power was what had gotten the movie made. It reminded me of audiences boycotting Jane Fonda's movies because of her position on the war in Vietnam. People were slamming Lindsay for her real life, rather than letting her film work stand on its own. The movie was also difficult to market. *Georgia Rule* was not for teenagers, yet teens liked Lohan from her other movies. To market a film about incest starring Lindsay to adult audiences was challenging, to say the least. Also critics don't like it when you take a risk with your career and status. I got slammed for making a movie about incest when I was famous for being Mr. *Happy Days*.

At the time Jane lived in both Santa Fe and Atlanta and worked on a number of charities for women's issues. We had a big premiere for the movie in Atlanta to help raise money for her charitable causes. Ted was there, and we hosted an auction. I flew in from Los Angeles but got a terrible case of sciatica on the airplane. At the premiere Jane had to help me get into the limousine. There I was standing in between the famous Jane Fonda and Felicity Huffman at the premiere, and I was in utter agony. Sometimes life just gets in the way of show business and you have to do the best you can to get through it. But I wouldn't have missed that premiere for anything. It was exciting to see our movie on the big screen in a room filled with the movers and shakers from Atlanta.

The New York Times never lets me forget that I come from television. In his review of *Georgia Rule*, A. O. Scott wrote, "The man who brought us *Laverne & Shirley* ventures into territory better suited to Todd Solondz or Lifetime and, as you might imagine, he has some trouble finding a consistent and appropriate tone." It had been more than twenty years since *Laverne & Shirley* went off the air, and I was still getting knocked around for its success. Ultimately, the reviewer recognized that the performances of Jane and Lindsay were the biggest takeaway from the movie. Scott wrote, "The movie really belongs to Ms. Fonda and Ms. Lohan, actresses whose formidable skill is often underestimated and overshadowed by off-screen notoriety. Ms. Lohan in particular has been subjected recently to the prurient, punitive gaze of an Internet gossip culture that takes special delight in the humiliation of young women with shaky discipline and an appetite for fun."

Lindsay has been in the press pretty much nonstop since we wrapped *Georgia Rule*. People say to me, "Why did you do a movie with Lindsay Lohan?" The truth is that without her there would have been no movie. Lindsay might be insecure about her hair and her freckles, but she is not one bit insecure about her acting. She knows she has talent, and she knows how to use it. I think figuring out how to live and keep herself safe is a much harder project for her.

Georgia Rule was released in 2007. Over the next few years I would act more, write more, and spend more time producing theater at the Falcon, including plays for children with my daughter, Lori, and her writing/directing partner Joseph Leo Bwarie. (Joe went on to great success starring as Frankie Valli in the touring production of *Jersey Boys*.) I also spent several years developing a *Happy Days* musical with composer Paul Williams, a show that eventually toured nationally and in Italy. I still read movie scripts and considered them, but I wasn't rushing to do another one until the day I got a script called *Valentine's Day* by Katherine Fugate, a writer known for her success on the television series *Army Wives*. When all is said and done, I am a man who believes in romance, happy endings, and people falling in love. So after I read *Valentine's Day* I turned to my wife.

"Okay. I think I found my next movie," I said.

"Does it have anything to do with an S and M island or possible incest?" Barbara asked.

"No," I said.

"Good," she said. "Then I think you should do it."

24. VALENTINE'S DAY

★

Turning the Camera on Love and
My Favorite Day of the Year

I HAVE WORKED IN Hollywood for so many years that many things don't surprise me. I try to go with the flow. Maybe it's experience. Maybe it's wisdom. Maybe it's just the fact that I'm old. So when I was about to direct a movie called *Valentine's Day,* and I read in the paper that our production company, New Line, had gone bankrupt, I thought, okay, here's a new twist. It wasn't, however, the end of the world. What happened was that half of the New Line people went to New York and the other half stayed in Los Angeles and merged under the Warner Bros. umbrella. New Line, led by Toby Emmerich, had just made a very popular picture called *He's Just Not That into You,* so there was a good vibe about the company. The format of a romantic comedy with many stars featured in cameo parts seemed appealing to audiences. *Valentine's Day* would be crafted in that vein, and I was tapped to direct. It would turn out to be one of the most memorable movie experiences of my career.

Ken Kwapis, a talented Ivy League type who happened to go to my alma mater, Northwestern, directed *He's Just Not That into You.* I called Ken up and talked to him about what it was like to work with New Line. He was very positive about his production and gave me tips on juggling so many actors on the set every day. I always love connecting to a fellow Northwestern alum. Even though Ken went to Northwestern years after I did, we shared the camaraderie of people who can survive the ice-cold wind along Evanston's lakeshore.

The New Line group was made up of young modern executives,

none of whom were fat, short, or wore suits. They wore T-shirts and blue jeans and were a pleasure to work with. However, once I signed my deal I saw something odd about the list of producers and executives: There were no women. I said, "Not one female in the whole bunch? How can this be? It's a romantic comedy. We need both sexes represented." My regular line producer, Mario Iscovich, was busy doing another movie. Line producers are in charge of creating and maintaining the schedule and budget on a movie. New Line gave me a list of line producers, and I immediately chose Diana Pokorny.

"Have you worked with her before?" said one of the producers.

"No," I said.

"Do you know her?" asked another male producer.

"Never heard of her. But she's the only woman on the list, so I'm going with her," I said.

"How can you hire someone you don't know?" asked a producer.

"It doesn't matter. I just need a woman in the mix," I said.

Diana, a striking, no-nonsense single mom with two kids, turned out to be a great producer. I worked so well with her that I hired her to produce my next movie, *New Year's Eve*. Also, my own executive assistant, Heather Hall, another top-notch lady, got her first associate producing credit on *Valentine's Day,* and was a great help to me on the film.

Valentine's Day, a romantic patchwork of stories about singles and couples all seeking love on Cupid's holiday, came along at the time I was considering a movie called *Senior Class* with Bette Midler. *Senior Class* was about a couple who meet and fall in love while residing in an assisted living facility. We were trying to pair Bette with Richard Dreyfuss, Anthony Hopkins, or Jack Nicholson. I liked the script because I thought I could weave in a scene that would feature a senior softball league, like the one I play in in Los Angeles. However, the deal for the film was moving along too slowly for the high-energy Bette. She got bored and decided to do her act in Las Vegas instead. With *Senior Class* on hold, I jumped at the script for *Valentine's Day* because it was a done deal, ready to go with financing in place.

In my opinion the multistar movie concept did not start with

He's Just Not That Into You. The movie *Love Actually* was the first and most famous example of what you could achieve if you asked a bunch of big stars to work only a few days on a major motion picture. Movies can take weeks to film, so from an actor's perspective shooting only a few days is appealing. I knew that the key to the ensemble cast was to get a few big names to commit early; then others would follow. I picked up the phone and called the biggest movie star I knew.

"Julia, will you be in *Valentine's Day*? It would really help me, and it's only for three days," I said.

Yes was her answer. It had been ten years since our last film. She talked to her agent who later told me she had put it this way: "For someone who gave me my career, I can give him three days." That made me smile. Before we signed Julia, many of the actors we liked turned us down. When word got out that Julia was in, suddenly actors were reconsidering their decisions. In fact, it was raining famous actors and actresses.

Another personal phone call I made was to Anne Hathaway, whose career had skyrocketed after our time together on *The Princess Diaries 1* and *2*. Anne wanted to meet about the script because in the first draft her character was not as well-defined as some of the others. This is often the problem with ensemble scripts. Some of the characters are better-written than others. Anne and I met at Spago. She recalled that the first time we met when she wasn't even twenty years old I had taken her to the Lakeside Country Club, but now Spago was much more show business, and more her style, too.

During our lunch we decided that her character's secret would be that she moonlighted as a phone sex girl. Anne suggested that she do the calls with different accents, and I liked that idea. Anne always comes up with great details to further develop characters. A more difficult decision was what male to cast as her costar.

She'd had to kiss more than six actors before we chose Chris Pine for *The Princess Diaries 2*. I didn't want her to have to go through all that random kissing again, so I cut to the chase for *Valentine's Day*. "So in this picture who do you want to kiss?" I asked.

Anne came up with an inspired choice: Topher Grace, who had

starred in *That '70s Show*. Anne said she had once had a crush on him and she thought he would be good for the part. I met with Topher and thought he made a nice match with Anne, too. After Anne said yes, we also got Academy Award winner Jamie Foxx. I had never met Jamie, so I came right out and asked him how he preferred to be directed. He said that he had done a lot of jobs, including acting, singing, and playing the piano in rich people's houses. But he said in his heart he was, and always would be, a stand-up comic. So I treated him like all the other comics I had met while I was working my way up through the nightclubs of New York. He didn't need a lot of preparation or direction; he just needed me to say "action."

Another actor I met for the first time on *Valentine's Day* was Ashton Kutcher. Our producers arranged for me to talk to him while he was in France.

"Thank you, Ashton, for calling from France," I said.

"France?" he asked.

"Yes. Paris, I assume?" I said.

"I'm not in France," he said. "I'm on Highland Avenue in Hollywood."

"Really?" I replied. "My office is nearby. Let's meet in person."

We hung up the phone and met nearby. That's typical show business logistics.

There are some actors you just click with immediately, and that's the way I felt with Ashton and his costar in the film, George Lopez. The two worked as colleagues in a flower shop owned by Ashton's character. The shop was called Siena Bouquet, after my granddaughter Siena LaGambina, which made her father, Doug, laugh. The scenes with Ashton and George were easy to direct because there was natural rapport between them. It was a relief for me as a director that working with them came so easily. The rest of the time I was introducing myself to a new and different actor every other day.

In *Valentine's Day* we also had a senior romantic story line, and for it we cast Academy Award winner Shirley MacLaine and, of course, Hector Elizondo. For many years I have been carrying around a script I wrote called *Time Step*, which is the story of my mother's life. I have always thought that Shirley MacLaine would be perfect to star in the movie. We were never able to make a deal and get a studio interested, but I still carry around the script. So I looked forward to working with her in *Valentine's Day*. Directing Shirley is a unique experience. She operates on a more spiritual level than most people. One day I got a call from the studio to say that Shirley wasn't happy with her paycheck. I called her up and said, "What's wrong? You don't like your deal?" And she said, "Those are not lucky numbers for me. The money is fine. I just need the numbers at the end of the check to be 131." It wasn't about financial compensation but about lucky numbers. We changed the numbers and Shirley was happy.

Shirley also loved working with Hector, as do most actresses because he is such a generous acting partner. One night we shot until 4:00 A.M. in a cemetery in Hollywood that projects movies on a big screen. As we were walking through the cemetery rehearsing the scene, Shirley suddenly turned to me and said, "Is there anyone you want me to contact?" gesturing at the rows of grave sites. "I don't think so," I said. "They all look pretty busy." You never know what Shirley is going to say next.

In one scene Shirley had to confess to her husband that she had had an affair. The scene was stalled because Shirley was having trouble with her motivation. Why would a woman confess such a thing on Valentine's Day? Hector agreed with Shirley, but I didn't have an answer for either of them. Shirley was a pro, however, and found her way through the scene. Several days later Hector called me up and said he had a reason for us: He said the wife confessed because the couple was going to renew their vows. She felt compelled to confess so she could celebrate her vows with a clear heart and conscience. Shirley and I liked that reasoning. We didn't have money to do a reshoot, so instead we added some voice-over material that explained their plans to renew their vows. Shirley, Hector, and I were all happy with the way the story line turned out. Hector's perseverance is another reason I value his friendship so much.

Sometimes you meet an actor on a movie that you just know you are going to be lifelong friends with. As with Hector Elizondo and Julia Roberts, I knew it when I met Jennifer Garner on *Valentine's Day*. I knew her work and had read about her marriage to Ben

Affleck, but I had never met her in person. She was beautiful, but you could tell that inside she was a regular girl from West Virginia, where she was raised. She became one of my closest friends on the set. We talked a lot about marriage, kids, and divorce. There was nothing fake or pretentious about her. The first day we met she blurted out, "Garry, look at my boobs! I'm still breast-feeding, so you probably don't want me to take my clothes off in the movie."

Jennifer has told me many funny stories, including one about her daughter Violet. Since birth her daughter knew her only as Jennifer Affleck, which is Violet's last name. One day Violet came home from a playdate and said to her mom, "My friend said there is a girl named Jennifer Garner living here with us. Do you know *her*?" She said, "My name is Jennifer Garner when I act. That's me." She said when Violet was very small she thought Jennifer worked in a trailer because she spent so much time in the makeup trailer on the set!

In *Valentine's Day* Jennifer was cast as a woman who was unknowingly having an affair with a married man. She had to play a sweet and likable schoolteacher who eventually falls in love with her best friend and owner of the flower shop, Ashton Kutcher. When Jennifer started the movie she was indeed still breast-feeding her newest daughter, Seraphina, so we had to take breaks for breast pumping. Sometimes the baby would visit the set, too. We just decided from the get-go to make room and time for the baby. I know some directors who take themselves too seriously and would find a baby on the set a problem. But I love babies on the set and wish there were more of them. Jennifer is one of the most likable actresses I have ever worked with. In my mind she is the female version of Kurt Russell. She is a movie star but also a regular girl and a team player.

To play opposite Julia, we cast Bradley Cooper. I thought I had never met him before either, until I remembered that Julia introduced us. I went to see them when they were starring in a Broadway production of *Three Days of Rain*. Julia and Bradley got along very well on the set of *Valentine's Day,* and I even made reference to their play in the movie. I had a voice-over in which the pilot of the plane they were flying in said they would be landing in Los Angeles after "three days of rain." I didn't tell Julia and Bradley I was going to put the voice-over in, and they were surprised and tickled when they saw the final version of the movie.

The *Valentine's Day* cast also included Queen Latifah, Jessica Biel, Jessica Alba, Eric Dane, and Patrick Dempsey. I had heard that Patrick had applied to clown school in Florida. He also liked race-car driving but never had time to do it because of his busy schedule on *Grey's Anatomy*. One of the rewrite guys on the movie, Matt Walker, had been valedictorian of a clown school. So I introduced Matt to Patrick on the set. After tossing around some ideas we decided to have Patrick's character juggle as a nervous habit. It was a good activity for a character, and it let him do something that he enjoyed. I always tell actors to put their hobbies down on their résumés because you never know when a director will want to use them.

While we were shooting the movie in Los Angeles, we got a lot of press interest from our pairing of two Taylors: Taylor Swift with Taylor Lautner. When New Line first said they signed Taylor Swift, I was confused. I flipped through the script and didn't see a part for her. They said, "Come up with something." So I did. Another person we found a good part for was Julia's niece Emma Roberts. The only problem was that she didn't have a driver's license and her part called for her to drive. We rigged up a car and pulled it off-camera so she appeared to be driving herself. It was a little harrowing because she didn't always hit the mark, but we made it work.

I joked on the movie that we had a lot of Js. Everyone seemed to be named Jennifer, Jessica, or Julia. Jessica Biel was a new, fresh face for me. What excited me about her was her willingness to do physical comedy. Some actresses would rather play it straight or be sexy rather than silly. Jessica, however, was ready for anything physical and was fearless about trying something new. She was dedicated to the part and had an extremely strong work ethic. She confided in me one day that she always worried when a job came to an end that she would never act again. Yet her career continues to thrive. Jessica really clicked with Jennifer Garner. In one scene they did a funny routine while toasting champagne glasses, and Jamie Foxx said,

"I've seen that bit someplace before." He thought for a minute and then said, "I saw it in *Laverne & Shirley*! Garry, you're stealing from yourself. But, hey. That's okay. You're allowed to steal from yourself." Jamie even took the connection further and thought it would be great to pitch the idea of a *Laverne & Shirley* remake starring Jessica and Jennifer to a network. It might never happen, but it was fun to picture them skipping arm and arm to the *Schlemiel! Schlimazel!*

The irony in Hollywood is that if you stick around long enough, you get to work with people you missed the first time around. I took a lot of heat in *Frankie and Johnny* for passing over Kathy Bates and choosing Michelle Pfeiffer for the lead. In *Valentine's Day* I was finally able to work with Kathy when I cast her as Jamie Foxx's television executive boss. Kathy had only a small part, but she did a wonderful job and I wanted her to have fun with it. I told her, "Jamie is going to ad-lib, so just be flexible and go where he goes." Much like Anne Hathaway, Kathy loves to develop her character with a director. She said, "I never get to do a part where I chew gum." So I let her chew gum to add some quirkiness to her character.

I got to film *Valentine's Day* in Los Angeles, and some scenes were shot just a few blocks from my home, which made me comfortable. Filming in Los Angeles also meant that my six grandchildren all got to be in the movie, and I loved seeing them on the set. And the ensemble nature of the movie meant that no actor was on the set long enough to cause trouble. Even our biggest stars, like Julia Roberts, worked only three days, so the production pace left everyone in an upbeat, cheerful mood. It was like reunion day at camp every day, where everyone smiled big because they were spending time with old friends. The movie was the epitome of a love story, and that was why I'd been hired to direct it.

Like all of my other films, we took *Valentine's Day* out to test audiences before the nationwide release. I like to hear the laughter from real people to tell if a joke is working. When we asked what they liked best about the movie, the answer was overwhelmingly "the humor." I felt confident that this was the right response. It was a romantic movie, but more than that, it was a movie with big stars that could make audiences laugh. Some critics said we had too many stars. Audiences, however, loved it. During its first four days, *Valentine's Day* made $63 million, the highest-grossing film in the history of the Valentine's Day holiday.

I should have been on cloud nine, and I nearly was. Except again sometimes when you are enjoying success, real life intervenes and says "Ha!" I was getting ready to go to London on February 14 when my internist Dr. Paul Rudnick told me that I had a cancerous tumor behind my tongue. I had felt a small lump on the side of my neck earlier and thought it was just a swollen lymph node. We decided to go to London and then Rome to premiere *Valentine's Day* before returning home for a series of radiation treatments. My wife and I told only our three kids and close family about my illness.

I am a creature of habit. Every day I write a big *W* in the square on my calendar because I want it to be a "winning day." I wrote an *L* for "losing day" on the day I found out that I had cancer. *Valentine's Day* was breaking records at the box office, and I was wondering how painful radiation would be. I had spent most of my childhood sick in bed because of one thing or another, but radiation seemed like a whole new ball game. Plus, it was recommended that I do a combination of radiation and Erbitux chemotherapy, which sounded even scarier than radiation alone.

Barbara and I have a favorite bar, the Ritz-Carlton on Central Park South. After opening *Valentine's Day* in London and Rome, we stopped over in New York. One night we went to the bar at the Ritz. Barbara normally has a glass of champagne and I have either a cosmopolitan or a Harveys Bristol Cream on the rocks. But that night we were not in the mood for our usual drinks.

We had heard about a shot of brandy at the bar that cost two hundred dollars. We decided that night we were going to splurge. We toasted the new movie and the year ahead. We thought we should share such a fancy drink with other people, so we chose three in the bar with us: our favorite bartender, Norman; the piano player, Earl, who was on the keys that night; and the television producer Phil Rosenthal *(Everybody Loves Raymond),* because he just happened to be there and I knew him. We each took a sip and declared the brandy excellent. I remember saying a little prayer to myself that night, too:

"Thank you, God, for giving me the strength to do *Valentine's Day,* and please give me the strength to get through radiation and chemotherapy." The next day I appeared on Martha Stewart's television show and made soap with her. I'm just a glass-half-full kind of guy. You don't let cancer get you down. You go have fun with Martha on national television.

Many different types of cancer can be cured if you get them early enough. I caught mine early enough but relied on a village of people to survive the treatments. My doctors Barry Rosenbloom and Chris Rose were from the Bronx and Brooklyn. I felt secure having two guys from the neighborhood take care of me. Along with my friends Victoria Jackson and Susan Silver, my speech therapist Betty McMicken and extraordinary dentist Dan Copps were stars. I remain forever grateful to all of them.

25. NEW YEAR'S EVE

★

Celebrating the Splendor of
New York City

IT WAS JANUARY 2011, and our plane from Los Angeles to New York City was delayed, so my assistant Heather Hall and I were checking into the Park Lane Hotel near Central Park very late at night. As we approached the front desk, a sleepy clerk rose to attention and said the perfunctory "Welcome to the Park Lane. How long will you be staying with us?"

"Ninety days," said Heather without pausing.

"Ninety days?" said the clerk, alarmed.

"Yes," said Heather. "We are going to be here all winter."

That's how I began work on my seventeenth motion picture as a director. I was seventy-six years old and had just completed seven weeks of radiation and chemotherapy to combat the tumor behind my tongue. A challenge, and not something I would have planned, but I was excited to put the cancer behind me and get back to work behind the camera. I have never been a good patient. I play the part of a healthy person much better.

At the end of each day, just like I did on all my movies, I continued to open up my datebook and review the events of the day. When the day was done I would write a big *W* in the date square to signify a "winning day." However, when I got ready to direct *New Year's Eve,* I decided that simply getting through the day as a winner was not a strong enough statement. I needed to triumph each day. So at the end of each day on *New Year's Eve* I would go back to my hotel room, open my calendar, and write a *V* in the date square. *V* was for "victory" when I needed to feel like a victor most.

The script for *New Year's Eve* came quickly after the success of *Valentine's Day*. Katherine Fugate, who had written *Valentine's Day,* and I seem to be holiday people. The producers, Mike Karz, Josie Rosen, and Wayne Rice, sent me her script and were excited to work with me again. Working with so many actors from different generations on *Valentine's Day* had really appealed to me, so I decided to sign on for another ensemble cast movie. This picture followed the lives of several single people over the course of twenty-four hours on New Year's Eve. (Coincidentally, New Year's Eve was also important personally because it is when I asked my wife to marry me in 1962.)

I had never directed a movie after cancer treatment. And the fact was that very few people in my life even knew I was sick. I underwent treatment from February through April 2010. Even during my treatments I worked nearly every day and played softball once a week. I couldn't hit the ball out of the infield, but I could still play. When I started pre-production on *New Year's Eve* in the fall of 2010, many people thought I just looked thin. Before cancer I weighed 206 pounds. I started *New Year's Eve* weighing 164. Cast and crew members would ask me about my health, but I would just shrug it off as stress. Of course, I was a little afraid that my health might fail in the middle of the production. But I couldn't let that fear show to my cast and crew. My job as a director was to lead them.

The biggest problem we had right away was casting. We didn't have anyone. I was told if I didn't put together a cast quickly, the movie might not be made and our financing would go to another film. However, I never lost faith. I knew that once I attracted a few high-profile actors, I could attract more. I tried to think of an actor I could call personally and ask to be in the movie. I knew my sister had worked with Robert De Niro in *Awakenings,* which I considered Penny's best movie. De Niro is such a heavy hitter I thought he might be the perfect actor to start with. I got his phone number, and on a Sunday afternoon I called him and basically said, "Come shoot with me for five days in New York and we'll have some laughs." He was in the mood to laugh and said "Yes." Penny later told him the part was dramatic, but it took place in a bed, so he wouldn't have to move around a lot.

Before his first day on the set, I asked Penny if she had any advice on directing De Niro. She said, "He doesn't like shouting. So don't stand at the monitor and call out to him. Whispering is better for him." He also didn't like pranks. I found out that 2011, the year we started *New Year's Eve,* was the thirty-fifth anniversary of his movie *Taxi Driver.* The producers thought for the gag reel De Niro might be willing to look into the mirror of the hospital room we were shooting in and utter his famous line "You looking at me?" But he wouldn't do it even for the gag reel. He's a shy, introspective, serious, and dedicated actor. He is not a prankster. A few days later, however, he did two pranks for the gag reel just to show me he could.

Even with De Niro casting was coming together slowly. I heard that a deal was on the table to get the rock star Jon Bon Jovi. I was excited, but I needed to hear back from him so I could start looking for an actress to cast opposite him. Frustrated that I still hadn't heard anything, I called Penny again for help. "Penny, you know Bon Jovi. Will you call him up and see if he's going to say yes or no to my picture?" Penny called back in an hour to tell me she said, "Are you going to do my brother's movie or not?" Bon Jovi said "Yes," and then I knew how to proceed. Never underestimate the power of your sister.

With Bon Jovi in place we went after another A-list star: Halle Berry. She initially accepted the part of the ex-girlfriend chef to Bon Jovi's rock star character. However, the day before she was supposed to come to the set, Halle called and said she couldn't make it. She was involved in a custody case involving her daughter in California, and the judge wouldn't let her leave the state. As luck would have it, she was free a few weeks later, so we decided to cast her in another part: the nurse opposite De Niro. Ultimately, I think it was a better part for her life and her acting talents. So file that under the heading "Sometimes the casting gods are on your side and make things come out better than expected."

Working with Halle Berry was one of the highlights of the

movie for me. She was so happy to be working and not stuck inside a courtroom. She rarely went to her trailer to hide or to rest. Instead, she preferred to hang out on the set and chat with the cast and crew. Even with all of the drama going on in her personal life, she looked beautiful, and we did our best to help her cheer up. There is a scene at the end of the movie when she gets all dressed up for New Year's Eve and then walks through a hospital hallway. I noticed all the extras were acting pretty blasé about seeing her character walk by them, as if they saw this kind of thing every day. I said, "People! Are you crazy? A beautiful girl walks by in a great dress. You have to react!"

By the end of her time with us, Halle was so relaxed she was even up for a prank or two. We had balloons from another scene on the set, and she sucked some helium and did a funny scene with a Minnie Mouse voice. She was also a big hit in our gag reel, where we featured a few blooper scenes in which she broke down in giggles. The bottom line was that she rose to the challenge and gave 100 percent in her acting with De Niro. There is a scene in which she cries with her boyfriend, and when you watch that scene you just know that she was born to become a movie star. Also, having served in the army, I like to acknowledge our servicemen in our movies.

For years I have made it clear that I like shooting in Los Angeles. But on *New Year's Eve* we saved a ton of money by shooting in New York City because they offered us many location incentives. The budget for the film was originally $67 million, but if we shot it in New York, we'd save $10 million right off the top. We shot in two museums, and the funny thing about that was how we surprised the visiting patrons with our film crew. It is not every day you go to a museum and see a Cézanne, a Monet, and a Bon Jovi.

The schedule was for a forty-eight-day shoot, and we would have complete access to Times Square, which was unprecedented for a movie. The location and how we dressed the set were essential because the night of New Year's Eve and the gigantic ball were almost main characters in the film. I was lucky enough to get the unflappable and innovative production designer Mark Friedberg, who had last worked with me on *Runaway Bride* in Baltimore.

What I didn't know was that this would be one of my most challenging shoots, not because of the actors or the script but because of the weather. The winter of 2011 was one of New York City's worst. Each day I would show up to the set not knowing what we were going to shoot. I would just say, "What can we shoot?" My assistant Greg, who is religious, prayed each day for better weather, but we never got it. It rained and snowed, and it got to the point that it wasn't a matter of whether I was going to wear a hat and gloves to work but only which color I would choose. The weather made this physically the hardest movie of my career. We had to shoot on many streets and rooftops throughout New York. Even shooting the ball was difficult because we had to climb three flights of stairs—with no elevator—to get to it. I was feeling twenty-two years old inside, but when the wind cut right through me, I felt like a tired seventy-six-year-old man who just wanted to go back to my hotel, sip soup, and watch a sitcom. Recuperating from cancer didn't help.

However, the parade of A-list stars on the film made every day exciting. In addition to Oscar winners De Niro and Berry, we were able to cast Hilary Swank. I had never met her, and I have to say she was a delight to work with. She told me when she first moved to California she lived out of her car. She is a real person, who has worked hard to make her career what it is. Hilary was ready with some pranks of her own. One day I yelled, "Action!" and she led the cast in the theme song to *Laverne & Shirley*. I cracked up. She is a great actress, but on my movie she was ready not only to act but also to have a good time. She was hands down the star of our gag reel. She did gags to others and allowed them to be played on her. One of the funniest is when she was doing a serious scene and the crew threw confetti on her head.

An odd thing about Hilary is that she is one of the few movie stars who owns a pet bird and she can't talk highly enough about birds as pets. She told us she recently took her bird to Paris and he learned to speak French. In addition to pets we talked a lot about her character and her hair. She wanted her hair to move, so we agreed on hair extensions. When we weren't talking about her hair, we of course focused on how best to portray her character. As an actress she can switch from comedy to drama in a second. She has not only incredible magnetism but also concentration. We laughed over the fact that she is often mistaken for Jennifer Garner, a star of *Valentine's Day*. Hilary said it is because they have similar lips.

Sometimes as a director you have to recognize when to step back and let an actress do her own thing. Hilary and I worked well together mapping out the comedy scenes. But when it came to the serious speeches, I took a different approach. As she prepared to give her big speech, I said to her, "This serious stuff is what you do for a living. So I'm going to get out of your way and just let you do it." I gave her no direction because she didn't need it. You have to know your actors and then use different tactics with them to adjust to the tone and intent of each scene.

Hilary's character is the head of the Times Square Alliance, which oversees the dropping of the ball on New Year's Eve. Her character was afraid of heights, so we had a policeman, played by the wonderful Rob Nagle, carry her up and down the steps to the ball. When we were setting up the scene, I worried it would be difficult to see her face. Hilary said, "No matter how he carries me, I'll find the lens." She always knew where the camera was. New actors often don't know how to find the lens or the light, but Hilary is a veteran, and it was exciting to watch her work. She can even do improvisational comedy well. She was especially good in a scene that used improvisation with Matthew Broderick.

Saying goodbye on a movie set, however, is not easy. I found it touching that both Hilary and Halle didn't want to go home. Although the long hours and the work on a set can be hard, sometimes making a movie can be more fun than real living.

The forty-eight-day shoot on *New Year's Eve* felt too long. It was not the longest shoot I ever faced in my career, but the bad weather made it a true struggle for everybody. My wife and children visited often to help keep my spirits up. When I didn't have family in town, I used other methods to stay cheery. Years earlier Barbara and I had given money for a Central Park bench that now bears our names. When I had a day off, I would walk out of the hotel, cross the street, and sit on my park bench. It gave me some time to reflect on the movie and on my life, and how I was looking forward to wrapping and going back home, where it was warmer.

Sometimes I would sit on my bench and dream about returning to Los Angeles to be greeted by a heat wave, or going to Hawaii for a Christmas vacation, or playing softball in the broiling heat. My staff also did their best to keep me peppy. Heather would bring me good news from the outside world, especially about my grandchildren: Sam had won a baseball game, Siena had started preschool, Ethan was learning piano, and Emma had done great in her ballet recital. News of my family would lift my spirits as I stood in Times Square in the freezing cold. I vowed once and for all to become a warm-weather director. If Katherine Fugate wrote another ensemble script, I decided it would have to be about the Fourth of July or something I could shoot in Hawaii.

During a movie I don't have time to read books for pleasure, but I could reflect on books that had influenced my career. I did this sometimes while I was sitting on my park bench preparing my shot list, which is the outline I give to the crew each day to tell them what angles I want to shoot. I remembered J. D. Salinger's *Catcher in the Rye* and Thomas Mann's *Magic Mountain* always resonated with me: *Catcher in the Rye* because it reminded me of my own coming of age, and *The Magic Mountain* because it gave me hope that even a very sick kid, like I had been, could find love. Both inspired me to create my own stories and weave my own coming of age and love stories into the movies I directed.

I also reflected on jokes and comedians who changed my career. I mentioned it earlier, but it deserves repeating that I will never forget the Jack Benny episode in which someone tried to rob him. The thief said "Your money or your life?" Jack's character was set up as a notorious cheapskate, so he had to pause before answering. The question brought sheer silence from Benny and a roar of laughter from the audience. That joke made me want to write a character who was equally clever. Another line I liked was the opening of Albert Camus's *The Stranger*: "My mother died today, or was it yesterday?" I loved it because it established the narrator's character so well. My inspiration ranged from Jack Benny to Camus.

Paddy Chayefsky, Neil Simon, and Arthur Miller all went to my high school, DeWitt Clinton. All three men influenced my career, especially because I knew they walked through the same hallways that I had. When I first saw Chayefsky's movie *Marty,* I felt as if doors were opening before my eyes. I realized that if Chayefsky could write stories from his neighborhood, then so could I. I think *Marty* was one of the reasons I was able to create a series like *Happy Days.* Chayefsky's movie gave me the confidence to believe that my friends and my stories about them mattered.

From that point on I also never forgot a character with a quirk or flaw because I knew I could use it in my work. Many years earlier I'd worked for a team who were writing jokes for a trip by President Kennedy to Texas, well before his assassination in the same state. We wrote lots of jokes for him about putting on a big Stetson hat. But when he arrived in Texas he refused to put on any hats. He thought they made him look less dignified. So I wrote Kennedy's aversion to hats into Ashton Kutcher's character in *New Year's Eve.* When everyone in Times Square is putting on goofy hats, Ashton says, "I don't do hats."

Ashton is not only very talented but very practical. When I gave him the script there was more than one character I could see him playing, so I told him to choose. He decided that he wanted to be the cartoonist stuck in an elevator because it was a character who, unlike the rest of the cast, didn't like New Year's Eve. Ashton also knew that by choosing that character he would rarely shoot a scene outside and could thus avoid winter in New York. A good actor, and a wise man.

I thought a lot about being a sick kid while I was directing *New Year's Eve* because although I was now cancer-free, I didn't know how long I would be. The problem was that the radiation had burned the inside of my mouth, so it was still sore when I ate. I had directed so many movies in a healthy state that I found it difficult to direct with a sore mouth. But I learned that if I ate a big breakfast in the morning and then a big dinner at the end of the day, I could tread lightly at lunch and avoid hurting my mouth. No matter how I tried, however, I started to lose weight on the set. Barbara and my assistant Heather would give me soft food to ease the pain. Usually this kind of cancer requires a feeding tube, but my wife was determined to help me avoid one. She would puree Progresso soups and kept me alive on chicken noodle and corn chowder.

Despite my problems with eating, mentally I was sharp as a tack. Every morning I would wake up at 4:30 or 5:00 and go to the set. I would be greeted by a sea of hugs from my crew members. It sounds corny, but a hug is a great thing to get in the morning, especially at 5:00 A.M. when you aren't feeling well. The first assistant director Dave Venghaus would hug me. The script supervisor Carol DePasquale would hug me. The cinematographer Chuck Minsky would hug me. The costume designer Gary Jones would hug me. It was a hug fest. On days when I had to go to a cold sidewalk and direct and when I couldn't eat because of my sore mouth, a hug was a simple but great gift. The actors also inspired me. You're not going to complain about pain in front of Halle Berry and Robert De Niro.

On the weekends sometimes I wouldn't even get dressed. I would just hang out in my hotel room with my wife or kids and grandkids until it was time to go back to the set. My spirits were high until an odd thing happened: My friends started to die. I had five friends die during the filming of *New Year's Eve*. These were not just acquaintances but very close friends. My friend Mark Harris used to say that when the friends in your age group start to die it is like they are calling up your class. First was Joel Sterns from college; then Mark Smith and John Grahams from the army; my friend Bill Lowenberg, with whom we had spent countless Christmas holidays in Hawaii; and director Blake Edwards, who was married to my friend Julie Andrews. One of the things I admire most about Julie is that she always speaks so highly of her late husband. A negative word about Blake has never slipped from her lips in my presence. I try to behave the same way toward my wife.

My wife, the consummate intensive care nurse, accepts death as part of the universe. But I take it harder. In order to keep my spirits up during all the funerals, Barbara came to New York more than she would have on a movie location that was not in Los Angeles. One night we went out to dinner quite late at a favorite restaurant in midtown to celebrate our forty-eighth wedding anniversary. I was feeling tired but overall pretty well. I had a cream soup followed by some capellini, and then I didn't stop. I went for the osso buco. I had lost so much weight that I thought it might be a good night to have some excellent food that wouldn't hurt my mouth. This is where the night began to go very wrong. I started to feel clammy and anxious. I had had two Bailey's Irish Cream during the meal as well. By the end of the osso buco, I thought I was going to throw up. I put my head on the table. If you do this in other states it might go unnoticed, but in New York City if you put your head down on a restaurant table, people will call an ambulance because they think you might sue the restaurant. Before I knew it the restaurant manager had called the obligatory ambulance.

I think all along my wife knew that the dizziness and anxiety were just from my stress level and bad stomach. If I had been in Los Angeles we probably would have gone home and gone to bed. But when you're away you tend to err on the side of caution. The paramedics and policemen came and put me in an ambulance bound for New York–Presbyterian Hospital. Knowing that five of my close friends had recently died, I must admit there was a nagging little voice inside me saying "Maybe it's your time, too." But I told that little voice to be quiet because I was in the middle of directing a movie and I wasn't ready to go yet. After I arrived at the hospital the doctor worried there might be something wrong with my heart. Barbara and my assistant Heather, who had made a beeline to the hospital to meet us, both said to the doctor, "He can't stay overnight, he has to go to work tomorrow." Eventually things calmed down and I was fine. The doctors said it was just stress, exhaustion, and an upset stomach.

My trip to the hospital was the low point of the movie. But what kept me going on the set was seeing fresh faces each day. One of the peppiest was that of Sarah Jessica Parker, who played Abigail Breslin's mother. I had worked with her many years earlier in *Hocus Pocus* with Bette Midler and my sister Penny. It was great to see her, and after directing her for a few days I was struck by the fact that Sarah Jessica is truly one of the happier actresses working in Hollywood today. As the mother of a little boy and twins, she has a lot on her plate, but she seems genuinely at peace. I asked her what her secret was when so many actresses in Hollywood often seem unhappy. Her answer: "I've just been doing it so long." Harold Pinter directed her in a play when she was five years old, she starred on Broadway in *Annie,* and then she went on to a stunning run in *Sex and the City.* No matter how tricky a scene I set her up in, much like Hilary Swank, Sarah Jessica would look at me with pure confidence and say, "I'll get there." I like working with capable people, and two of the best were Tom Hines and Matt Walker, my on-set rewrite team. They are a major reason why *Valentine's Day* was a hit, and why the *New Year's Eve* script got completed.

Another familiar face I was happy to see again was Michelle Pfeiffer, with whom I hadn't worked since we made *Frankie and Johnny.* In *New Year's Eve* she plays a shy and unhappy Manhattan secretary until she meets up with a bike messenger who changes her life forever. Zac Efron and Michelle had worked together on *Hairspray.* She wanted to infuse her character with a touch of Asperger's syndrome, and Zac was brave in his comedy choices. Michelle is not an improviser. She likes to have every movement and line scripted. Zac also likes to make choices and plan out his character. Together we created an ultrahip bike messenger who was a wonderful foil for Michelle's secretary. One of the highlights of the film is at the end, when Michelle and Zac do a terrific dance together and we see her come out of her shell.

One of the problems we faced during our shoot was intense attention from the paparazzi, who had full access to us because we were in the streets of Manhattan, Brooklyn, and Queens. Michelle had to ride behind Zac on his Vespa, and the paparazzi had a field day taking what seemed like endless photographs. Michelle said the best direction I gave her was when I said, "Michelle, try not to give the paparazzi the bird because it will be in all the tabloids."

New Year's Eve was a time for me to work with old, familiar friends, too, such as Larry Miller and Jim Belushi. Another actor who stood out was Jake T. Austin, who played Max on the television series *Wizards of Waverly Place*. Every day hundreds of fans from ten to thirteen years old would fill the streets around our set to see him. At one point the mob grew so large that one of our producers went into a bar and hired patrons there to act as bodyguards for Jake because we didn't have enough security to protect him.

I liked meeting many new stars on the film, such as the sexy and strong Katherine Heigl and the Cary Grant-ish Josh Duhamel, who were both terrific. I also had two stars from *Valentine's Day*, Jessica Biel and Ashton Kutcher. Jessica played a pregnant woman, and Ashton, as I've said, was stuck in an elevator with Lea Michelle from *Glee* for most of the movie. It was Lea's first film, and she was a little nervous. When she came to audition for the part, she walked into my office and said, "Garry, you have to hire me. I'm from the Bronx. Arthur Avenue." Her family was part Italian and part Jewish, and I knew I liked her from the get-go. So did test audiences when we first screened the movie. When we asked them who their favorite actor was, the most votes went to Lea Michele.

At the end of the movie my daughter Lori came to visit.

"Are you having fun?" she asked as we sat in my room at the Park Lane.

"I had fun at the beginning," I said.

"The beginning of any movie is fun. You always like that part," she said optimistically.

"No," I said. "I mean the very beginning. *The Flamingo Kid* was fun."

Now I was ready to go home and sleep in my own bed. Also, I couldn't wait to start editing the picture. Editing is where my story comes together, and it is my favorite part of the moviemaking process. Would *New Year's Eve* be my last movie as a director? If you'd asked me the day I boarded the plane to fly home to Los Angeles from that winter in New York, I would have said yes.

I tried to rest, but I still wasn't feeling any better. Of course once you have had cancer you worry when you feel sick that the cancer has returned. But when I went to the doctor, I found out I had walking pneumonia instead. It was not the best thing for me, but it was certainly treatable. I had shot the last week of my movie (all nights) with walking pneumonia. I do not advise this.

Barbara nursed me through cancer and she nursed me through that pneumonia. When I felt better I wasn't sure if I should direct a movie, get back into television, or do something else at the theater. Whenever I don't have great clarity on a subject, Barbara seems to have it tenfold. I was seriously blue one day, and she came in with a stack of scripts.

"What are those?" I asked.

"Scripts," she said. "Pick one. A movie, a TV show, or a play. You can direct or produce one of these, or write a new one. Just pick something."

She knew I was not ready to retire and so did I.

Even though I was in my seventies, entertainment was my profession and it was not the right time to stop. If you can get out of bed each day and go to a job you love and return home to a family you love, that is the key to life, and the key to a successful career in Hollywood or anywhere.

What have I learned in my seventy-seven years? Not that much, but a lot about me. I have never been to a psychiatrist but instead have relied on my wife, family, and friends, particularly my basketball-playing psychiatrist pal Dr. Ira Glick to keep me sane. I always seemed to be confident about my own creativity and ability to work hard. Also, despite criticism, I learned how to win over difficult bosses like Jackie Gleason, Joey Bishop, Danny Thomas, and many studio heads. However, I was never completely secure about moving on to something new. I was more comfortable with the devil I knew. To combat this, I have always had ambitious partners.

The truth is that I always wanted a more stable life than my creative intellectual idols had. People like Arthur Miller, Roman Polanski, Woody Allen, Sylvia Plath, Anton Chekhov, and Albert Camus all had unconventional family lives. I dreamed of stability and a calm, low-profile family life. I was a product of the 1950s and was charmed eternally by *The Adventures of Ozzie and Harriet, Father Knows Best,* and the drawings of Norman Rockwell. Whether they were true or not didn't matter. I wanted to come home to a wife, children, and a sane family dinner hour. This is probably why I have been married for forty-nine years and have three children and six grandchildren.

What I haven't figured out is why some people face adversity and quit or stop trying, while others pick themselves up and go on time after time. Is it genetics, environment, encouragement? I have been whacked often by comedians, stars, censors, studio executives, and, of course, the critics. The critics have whacked me for so long that now sons and daughters of critics are whacking me. However, each time I feel like I can do better. So, it has been a life of ups and downs, but I will always keep going and try harder on the next project. When I figure out what really makes people go on or give up, I will let you know. But one thing I do know for certain is that I will tell you with three montages and a happy ending.

THE QUESTION I'm most often asked is "How does someone become a star?" I don't know. But having seen so many try
and so few succeed, I offer thirteen helpful hints on becoming an
actor or actress.

1. Go to school. Any school. Be in school plays. Study acting. At
   the very least it will help prepare you for the business you've
   chosen.

2. Whether you're in Hollywood or New York, try to do a play. In
   a play, a producer can see your skills better than in a ten-minute,
   two-page reading or audition.

3. It is just as hard to be a working actor as it is to be a star.

4. Spending most of your time getting an agent or manager is not
   as important as meeting people yourself at parties, charity affairs, church, or synagogue.

5. Getting a small part in a movie or TV show will not make you a
   star. It'll give you experience to do better on the next job. If there
   is one.

6. Give yourself a time limit to try to be a working actor. If after
   a certain number of years you have a few credits, take these
   credits home and teach. Even teach kids. It's sometimes more
   rewarding.

7. Relatives, romances, connections, or the like will not make you
   a star. Talent and showcasing will. Becoming an "extra" will not
   hurt when you're starting out.

8. Make your own video with help from friends and put it on the Internet. Someone might see it or send it to someone.

9. Spending large sums of money to keep getting new photos (head shots) is a waste of time. Spend your money going to film festivals. You might meet someone who will get you an audition.

10. Take all chances to be seen in small films or video (except nudity or material that grosses you out). Student films, festival films, music videos, short films, commercials, and documentaries all can help.

11. Don't rely on any one person to make your career. It takes a village, and the more different people who will give you a part or a chance, the better. And remember, luck can be a good part of success.

12. Stay healthy. Nobody wants a sick artist. And stay away from and avoid negative people who put down your dreams. That includes parents. Cultivate the positive.

13. Most important hint: Jealousy of others is a total waste of time and energy.

PROFESSIONAL CREDITS

FILM

★ DIRECTOR

New Year's Eve (2011)
Valentine's Day (2010)
Georgia Rule (2007)
The Princess Diaries 2: Royal Engagement (2004)
Raising Helen (2004)
The Princess Diaries (2001)
Runaway Bride (1999)
The Other Sister (1999)
Dear God (1996)
Exit to Eden (1994)
Frankie and Johnny (1991)
Pretty Woman (1990)
Beaches (1988)
Overboard (1987)
Nothing in Common (1986)
The Flamingo Kid (1984)
Young Doctors in Love (1982)

★ WRITER

The Other Sister (1999; screenplay, story with Bob Brunner)
The Flamingo Kid (1984, screenplay with Neal Marshall)
The Grasshopper (1969; screenplay, story with Jerry Belson)
How Sweet It Is! (1968, with Jerry Belson)

★ PRODUCER

New Year's Eve (2011)
The Twilight of the Golds (1996, executive producer)
Exit to Eden (1994)
Frankie and Johnny (1991)
Young Doctors in Love (1982, executive producer)
The Grasshopper (1970)
How Sweet It Is! (1968)

TELEVISION

★ WRITER

Happy Days (1974–1984, various with Bob Brunner)
Angie (1979)
Mork & Mindy (1978)
Blansky's Beauties (1977)
Laverne & Shirley (1976–1977)
Wives (1975, pilot)
Dominic's Dream (1974, pilot)
The Brian Keith Show (1972–1974)
The Odd Couple (1970–1973, with Jerry Belson and Bob Brunner)
Wednesday Night Out (1972, pilot)
Love, American Style (1969–1972)
Evil Roy Slade (1972, with Jerry Belson)
Me and the Chimp (1972, with Bob Brunner)

Barefoot in the Park (1970, with Jerry Belson)
The Murdocks and the McClays (1970, pilot with Jerry Belson)
Sheriff Who (1967, pilot with Jerry Belson)
The Danny Thomas Show: Road to Lebanon (1967, with Jerry Belson)
The Danny Thomas Hour: It's Greek to Me (1967, with Jerry Belson)
The Danny Thomas Anthology: My Friend Tony (1967, with Jerry Belson)
Hey, Landlord (1966, creator with Jerry Belson)
The Dick Van Dyke Show (1964–1966, with Jerry Belson)

TELEVISION *(continued)*

The Lucy Show (1964–1966, with Jerry Belson)

I Spy (1965, with Jerry Belson)

PILOTS
(writer, producer, and/or director)

Beach Brother, The Recruiters, Uncle Lefty, School for Scoundrels, Dreamsville, The Romans, Hank, Check Please, Tony Marko, Mean Mommy, Dominic's Dream, Wives, Ellie's House, Pinky Tuscadero (most with Jerry Belson, some with Bob Brunner)

The Danny Thomas Show (1961–1964, with Jerry Belson)

Gomer Pyle, U.S.M.C. (1964, with Jerry Belson)

Bob Hope Presents the Chrysler Theatre (1964, with Jerry Belson)

The Bill Dana Show (1964, with Jerry Belson)

The Joey Bishop Show (1962–1963, with Fred Freeman)

The Tonight Show with Jack Paar (1960–1961)

★ PRODUCER
(most with Jerry Belson)

Nothing in Common (1987)

Four Stars (1986)

Happy Days (1974–1984)

Herndon (1983, executive producer)

Laverne & Shirley (executive producer, 178 episodes, 1976–1983)

The New Odd Couple (executive producer, 1982–1983)

Joanie Loves Chachi (executive producer, 1982)

Mork & Mindy (executive producer, 94 episodes, 1978–1982)

Mean Jeans (1981, executive producer)

Beanes of Boston (1979, executive producer)

Angie (1979, TV series)

Who's Watching the Kids (executive producer)

Walkin' Walter (1977, executive producer)

Blansky's Beauties (1977)

The Odd Couple (1970–1975)

Dominic's Dream (1974)

Evil Roy Slade (1972)

Me and the Chimp (1972)

Barefoot in the Park (1970)

The Murdocks and the McClays (1970)

Sheriff Who (1968)

Hey, Landlord (1966–1967)

★ DIRECTOR

The Lottery (1989)

Herndon (1983, pilot)

Laverne & Shirley (1976–1983)

Mean Jeans (1981, pilot)

Mork & Mindy (1980)

Blansky's Beauties (1977)

Happy Days (1974–1982, mostly directed by Jerry Paris)

The Odd Couple (1971–1974)

Dominic's Dream (1974)

Me and the Chimp (1972)

THEATER

Elixir of Love (opera, director, 2008: San Antonio Opera)

Happy Days the Musical (book writer with Paul Williams, 2007, 2008: Goodspeed Opera House, East Haddam, Connecticut; 2007:

Paper Mill Playhouse, Milburn, New Jersey; 2008–09: La Mirada Theatre for the Performing Arts, La Mirada, CA. National tour and currently touring Italy)

The Grand Duchess (opera, director,
  2005: Dorothy Chandler Pavilion)
Everybody Say Cheese (writer, 2009:
  Falcon Theatre, Burbank)
Crimes of the Heart (director, 1999:
  Falcon Theatre, Burbank)
Wrong Turn at Lungfish (director/
  cowriter with Lowell Ganz, 1993:

Promenade Theatre, New York;
  1992: Coronet Theatre, Los Angeles;
  1990: Steppenwolf Theatre, Chicago)
The Roast (cowriter with Jerry Belson;
  1980: Broadway's Winter Garden
  Theatre, New York, New York)
Shelves (playwright; 1978: Pheasant Run
  Playhouse, St. Charles, Illinois)

ACTING

The Looney Tunes Show: Dr. Weisberg
  (2011)
The Simpsons: Larry Kidkill/Sheldon
  Leavitt (1999/2011)
Grande Drip: Larry Rosenberg (2009)
Race to Witch Mountain: Dr. Donald
  Harlan (2009)
ER: Harry Feingold (2009)
The Sarah Silverman Program: Sharkcorp
  President (2008)
Chronic Town: Psychiatrist (2008)
Hole in the Paper Sky: Warren (2008)
Brothers and Sisters: Major Jack Wiener
  (2007)
Keeping Up with the Steins: Irwin Fiedler
  (2006)
Chicken Little: Buck Cluck (voice, 2005)
Father of the Pride: Bernie (2004)
The Long Ride Home: Arthur (2003)
Sabrina, the Teenage Witch: Mickey
  Brentwood (2002)
Monk: Warren Beach (2002)
Mother Ghost: Arthur (2002)
Three Sisters: Vince (2001–2002)
Orange County: Arthur Gantner (2002)
The Majestic: (voice, 2001); Studio
  executive (voice-over)
Norm: Big Nick (1999)
Runaway Bride: First baseman in softball
  (1999, uncredited)

Never Been Kissed: Rigfort (1999)
CHiPs '99 (TV): Tour bus driver (1998)
With Friends Like These: Frank Minetti
  (1998)
City Guys: Mr. Giodano (1997)
Murphy Brown: Stan Lansing
  (1994–1997)
Pinky and the Brain: Mr. Itch—The Devil
  (1997)
The Twilight of the Golds: Walter Gold
  (1996)
Live Nude Girls: Mobster Don (1995,
  uncredited)
Hocus Pocus: The Master (1993)
A League of Their Own: Walter Harvey
  (1992)
Soapdish: Edmund Edwards (1991)
Jumpin' Jack Flash: Police detective
  (1986, uncredited)
Lost in America: Casino manager (1985)
Grand Theft Auto: Underworld boss
  (1977)
The Odd Couple: Drummer/Man/Werner
  Turner/Man #2 (1970–1974)
Psych-Out: Plainclothesman (1968)
Maryjane: Service station attendant
  (1968)
Hey, Landlord: Big Leonard (1967)
The Dick Van Dyke Show: Bartender/
  Referee (1965–1966)

ACKNOWLEDGMENTS

THERE ARE ALWAYS many people to thank when a book is published, and now is my time to do that. I would like to thank my book agent, Amy Rennert, for taking the first meeting with my daughter Lori in San Francisco. Amy has been our enthusiastic champion from the very beginning, and her loyalty has always encouraged us and never waivered. Amy found us the wonderful team at Random House's division of Crown Archetype where John Glusman started the book and then gave it to our new editor, Mary Choteborsky, who finished it. I am so grateful to everyone at Random House and Crown, including Campbell Wharton, for being so supportive of my book.

Closer to home, I want to thank my former assistants Diane Frazen and Barbara Nabozny, my current executive assistant Heather Hall and everyone at Henderson Productions, especially Kimberly Arnold, and the Falcon Theatre who helped with this book. My staff knows that I always have several projects going on at once, and they remain unflappable and dedicated to this book from beginning to end. I also want to thank the mysterious Yankee fan and the shnorrer, too. Many people often ask me why I never did just one profession, but instead chose to write, direct, produce, and act throughout my career. The answer is within the pages of this book. I never would have had so much to write about if I had just stuck with one career. The truth is I have never suffered from a moment's boredom since watching the movie *Gaslight* when I was ten years old.

Finally, I would like to thank my wife, Barbara Sue Wells, my three kids, their spouses, and my six grandchildren. My happy days in front of the camera have been equaled and surpassed by our laughs just sitting around the dinner table. Whenever we go out to a restaurant, other patrons often point and stare because we have so much fun together. It is priceless to see the little kids laugh when I put a white napkin over my head in a fancy bistro and become the invisible man. I never wanted to change the world but rather to entertain the world. To know that I could make my own family chuckle is all a dad and grandpa could ask for.

INDEX